THE SCHOOL ACHIEVEMENT
OF
MINORITY CHILDREN

NEW PERSPECTIVES

*With appreciative thanks to all the
Cornell "cognitive breakfasters" whose ideas and
arguments helped to make this book possible.*

THE SCHOOL ACHIEVEMENT
OF
MINORITY CHILDREN

NEW PERSPECTIVES

Edited by

ULRIC NEISSER

Robert W. Woodruff Professor of Psychology
Emory University

LAWRENCE ERLBAUM ASSOCIATES, PUBLISHERS
1986   Hillsdale, New Jersey   London

Lawrence Erlbaum Associates, Inc., Publishers
365 Broadway
Hillsdale, New Jersey 07642

Library of Congress Cataloging in Publication Data
Main entry under title:

The School achievement of minority children.

Bibliography: p.
Includes indexes.
1. Minorities — Education (Elementary) — United States —
Addresses, essays, lectures.   2. Academic achievement —
Addresses, essays, lectures.   3. Afro-American
children — Education — Addresses, essays, lectures.
I. Neisser, Ulric.
LC3725.S36   371.97   85-25339
ISBN 0-89859-685-8

Printed in the United States of America
10   9   8   7   6   5   4   3   2   1

CONTRIBUTORS

A. Wade Boykin is Professor of Psychology at Howard University in Washington D.C. He is editor (with A. J. Franklin & J. Yates) of *Research Directions of Black Psychologists* (Russell Sage, 1979).

Ann L. Brown is Professor of Psychology and of Educational Psychology as well as Research Professor in the Center for the Study of Reading at the University of Illinois in Champaign, Illinois. She is editor (with M. E. Lamb & B. Rogoff) of the first three volumes of *Advances in Developmental Psychology* (Erlbaum, 1981, 1982, 1984).

Richard B. Darlington is Professor of Psychology at Cornell University in Ithaca, N.Y. He is the author (with I. Lazar, H. Murray, J. Royce & A. S. Snipper) of *Lasting Effects of Early Education* (Society for Research in Child Development, 1982, *47*, Nos. 2–3).

Ronald R. Edmonds died on July 15, 1983. At the time of his death he was Professor in three departments at Michigan State University: Teacher Education, Administration & Curriculum, and Urban Affairs Programs. From 1978 to 1981 he was Principal Instructional Officer and Senior Assistant to the Chancellor for Instruction in the New York City School System.

Herbert P. Ginsburg is Professor of Psychology and Education as well as Chair of the Department of Human Development, Cognition, & Learning at Teachers College of Columbia University. He is the author of *The Myth of the Deprived Child: Poor Children's Intellect and Education* (Prentice-Hall, 1972) and editor of *The Development of Mathematical Thinking* (Academic Press, 1983).

Reginald A. Gougis is Assistant Professor of Psychology at Hampton University in Hampton, VA. He received his Ph.D. at Cornell University in 1983, and was a Post-doctoral Fellow in the Graduate Center of the City University of New York during 1983–84.

Ulric Neisser is Robert W. Woodruff Professor of Psychology at Emory University in Atlanta and Director of the Emory Cognition Project. He is the author of *Cognition and Reality* (Freeman, 1976) and editor of *Memory Observed: Remembering in Natural Contexts* (Freeman, 1982).

John U. Ogbu, a native of Nigeria, is Professor of Anthropology at the University of California in Berkeley. He is the author of *Minority Education and Caste: The American System in Cross-cultural Perspective* (Academic Press, 1978).

Annemarie S. Palincsar is Assistant Professor of Special Education at Michigan State University. From 1981 to 1983 she was affiliated with the Center for the Study of Reading in Champaign, IL; she has also been a public-school teacher and program supervisor.

Linda Purcell is Assistant Specialist in Education at the Center for the Study of Reading in Champaign, Illinois.

Contents

Preface

"Psychology advances by removing, one by one, the obstacles it has placed in its own path." William Stern's aphorism applies almost everywhere in psychology, but nowhere more painfully and poignantly than in our attempt to understand group differences in intellectual performance. A major obstacle to that understanding is the way that we usually formulate the problem itself — roughly as "What's the matter with those people?" Such a formulation leads inevitably to some form of deficit hypothesis, leaving only the question of whether the so-called deficit is produced by "cultural deprivation" in early childhood or by genetic factors. There is little real evidence for either of those interpretations; they persist because of an apparent lack of plausible alternatives. This book breaks with that pattern, by presenting a wide range of new ideas about group differences — at least, of ideas that were new to me. I believe that other readers will find them equally significant.

The conference that formed the basis for this volume was a remarkable intellectual experience for everyone who attended. It was sponsored by the Cornell Training Program in Comprehensive Cognitive Psychology, of which I was the Director. Plans for the conference were based on extensive prior discussions at breakfast meetings of the training program, and on an intensive effort to uncover sources of new and promising ideas about cognitive differences. In the end we invited eight speakers and all of them accepted: John Ogbu, Wade Boykin, Ronald Edmonds, Ann Brown, Carolyn Boyce, Richard Darlington, Herbert Ginsburg, and William Cross. As it happened, four of the speakers were black and four were white. Although they were all impressive, I found it especially rewarding to hear a substantial number of black intellectuals deal vigorously and imaginatively with this particular topic.

ix

Six of the eight chapters in this book are based on papers that were presented at the 1982 Cornell Conference. One of the remaining chapters is my own introduction; the other is a new contribution by Reginald Gougis, who attended the conference but did not present a paper there. I am grateful to Carolyn Boyce and William Cross for their stimulating presentations at the conference, and regret that it was not possible to include chapters based on those presentations here. I also want to acknowledge the organizational efforts of the graduate trainees in the Comprehensive Cognitive Psychology Training Program, who actually did most of the work that kept the conference running: Georgia Nigro, Sherri Matteo, Kathleen McNellis, Jack Carroll, Patrick Rooney, Reginald Gougis, and Carolyn Boyce. Funding for the conference was provided by the National Institute of Mental Health under Training Grant MH-15777.

Ulric Neisser
Emory Cognition Project

1 New Answers to an Old Question

Ulric Neisser

INTRODUCTION

Why is the school achievement of American minority children — especially black children — so often below that of their white counterparts? This is obviously a political question as well as an academic one, so political that few social scientists discuss it in public any more. Privately, many of them still assume that the only possible answers are those offered by the deficiency theories of the 1960s: either genetic inferiority or cultural deprivation. Although these notions seem more than a little old fashioned in the 1980s, they are still widely accepted at a tacit level. That acceptance can hardly be based on scientific grounds; there was never much direct evidence for either notion, and they have become even less plausible in light of recent developments.[1] Their persistence today does not reflect their own merits so much as the apparent lack of alternative explanations. Are there any other ways to understand the school performance of minority children?

Indeed there are. The subsequent chapters of this book offer a number of new and thoughtful explanations of the same facts. Although this introduction is written by a cognitive psychologist, these hypotheses are not just psychological; they are also anthropological, political, and educational. In a word, they are *cultural* hypotheses. That does not mean that they focus only on minority culture, however. Although several hypotheses are presented here by members of the black intellectual community, only one (Boykin's)

---

[1] For summaries of evidence relevant to the genetic theory, see Scarr (1981) or Mackenzie (1984). For a critique of the supposedly permanent effects of early experience, see Chapter 3 of Kagan et al. (1978).

1

deals at any length with black culture itself. Group differences in achievement are products of society as a whole — of American culture. In a sense, these differences are just examples of the effect of culture on cognition.

What are these new hypotheses? Although a separate section of this introduction and then an entire chapter of this book is devoted to each one, it is appropriate to begin with a preliminary list:

The effects of caste.   John Ogbu (Chapter 2) points out that the problem is not a specifically American one: lower-caste groups have poor school records everywhere in the world. Membership in a lower caste implies a limited set of possible adult careers. Black schoolchildren are preparing themselves for the roles that they expect to play later on.

Black culture and white hegemony.   Wade Boykin (Chapter 3) describes many aspects of Afro-American culture that are in more or less direct conflict with the social and cognitive structure of the school. He also argues that the schools, like American society as a whole, are structured in ways that maintain the hegemony of the white middle class.

Ineffective schools.   Ronald Edmonds (Chapter 4) demonstrates that public schools can be effective in teaching poor and minority children, but that most of them fail to do so. He goes on to document the principal differences between schools that are effective and schools that are not.

The Differential Treatment Effect.   Brown, Palincsar, and Purcell (Chapter 5) show that the instructional methods often used with poor readers may actually widen the gap between successful and unsuccessful students. They also report new participatory teaching techniques that may be able to reverse this trend.

The effects of prejudice and stress.   Reginald Gougis (Chapter 6) points out that emotional stress always has negative effects on learning. He argues that black students are subject to unique and persistent stresses because they are so often the targets of racial prejudice.

The fact that there are several cultural hypotheses does not mean that only one of them is right. It is likely that they are *all* right. Many factors contribute to the difficult situation in which minority children find themselves. Moreover, all of those factors are usually superimposed on the direct effect of poverty. Most minority children come from poor families; poor people experience a great many stresses from which the wealthier classes are sheltered, and poor people have fewer resources to spare for academic matters when something goes wrong.

Not all the contributors to this book present specific new hypotheses about group differences. The two final chapters are devoted primarily to reporting important observations.

Effects of Head Start Programs.   Richard Darlington (Chapter 7) presents the findings of the Consortium for Longitudinal Studies on the effectiveness of preschool programs. These data show that, contrary to what had been supposed, such programs have had substantial positive effects on subsequent school performance.

Cultural deprivation.   Herbert Ginsburg (Chapter 8), who attacked the deficiency theories ten years ago in a book called *The Myth of the Deprived Child*, reviews recent cross-cultural and subcultural research. The results of that research invalidate the myth still further: the basic abilities required for mathematics and other school subjects are equally present in every cultural group.

The contributors to this book are realists, and they do not propose easy remedies. The causes of the school achievement differential are so deeply embedded in the culture that it is difficult even to imagine them eliminated altogether. Nevertheless, the situation is by no means hopeless. American culture is far from homogeneous, and parts of it are changing with surprising speed. The "caste system" that Ogbu describes is changing: members of minority groups are now visible in social roles that were inconceivable a few years ago. The school system is changing too: Edmonds' concept of "effective schools" has already been widely influential, and achievement scores seem to be going up. Ideas about instruction are also changing, partly in response to ideas from cognitive psychology like those presented by Brown et al. Even the prevalence of overt prejudice is changing: racist attitudes may persist, but their open expression has become much less common. It is still too early to tell whether these changes are deep and lasting; the civil rights movement began only 20 years ago. Nevertheless, they have made a difference, and further movement in the same direction will make even more of a difference. If the situation gives no justification for complacency, there is also no reason to despair.

The arguments presented here focus on the actual school performance of minority children (most often, black children), i.e., on achievement test scores, mastery of academic material, promotion, and high school graduation. Most of the contributors to this volume are more interested in school performance than in test intelligence, even though the latter has attracted just as much public attention. So-called intelligence tests are merely predictors of academic achievement, and this book is concerned with that achievement itself. The IQ question cannot be ignored entirely, however, and several chapters consider it at least briefly. I return to it myself in the last section of this introduction. Nevertheless, IQ is not the central issue. The educational disadvantages of minority children in America would persist even if every standardized test were abolished tomorrow.

Much of this book is an outgrowth of the Conference on the Academic Performance of Minority Children at Cornell University in June of 1982. The Conference was sponsored by the Cornell Training Program in Comprehensive Cognitive Psychology, of which I was the Director. Although it was convened on the assumption that the study of school learning is within the scope of cognitive psychology, we soon learned that the critical variables in this area are also ecological and political. Like other cognitive processes, learning cannot be understood without a detailed knowledge of the environment in which it occurs (Neisser, 1985). Most of the arguments presented in this book can be interpreted as new analyses of that environment. They offer fresh perspectives on life and education in the United States as well as on the academic achievements of minority children. I turn now to more detailed consideration of those arguments.

AN INTERNATIONAL PERSPECTIVE

Most psychological and educational discussions of the discrepancy between black and white academic achievement assume that it is an "American dilemma," rooted in particular American circumstances. The genetic theory is especially dependent on that assumption; since it blames the discrepancy on specific weaknesses in the Afro-American gene pool. John Ogbu, a Nigerian anthropologist, points out that the assumption of a uniquely American dilemma is simply false. Similar caste-like distinctions exist in many countries and always produce similar educational results.

A caste society is one where different roles are assigned more or less rigidly to different subgroups and where everybody belongs by birth to one or another of the subgroups. Although the word "caste" is usually associated with India, India is not the only such society. In an earlier book, Ogbu (1978) described caste systems in Japan, Great Britain, Israel, and New Zealand, as well as in India and the United States. To be born into a lower caste or caste-like minority—a Buraku in Japan or a black in America, for example—is to grow up with the conviction that one's life will eventually be restricted to a small and poorly rewarded set of social roles.

Caste distinctions are not necessarily based on race. Caste-like minorities are racially distinct from the upper-caste groups in some countries (West Indians in Great Britain, Maoris in New Zealand, Afro-Americans in the United States), but this not the case elsewhere (Untouchables in India, Oriental Jews in Israel, Burakim in Japan). The educational consequences are the same everywhere. All over the world, lower-caste children do less well in school than upper-caste children, have lower test scores, and don't stay in school as long. The academic performance of black children in America has little to do with their race or their genes: it is a consequence of the structure of society as a whole.

Ogbu does not find that consequence difficult to explain. Individuals in caste-like minorities cannot realistically aspire to the kinds of social positions for which education is important. A "job ceiling" restricts their opportunities. Even if an occasional member of the caste has managed to break through that ceiling, the odds are overwhelmingly against their own chances. Lower-caste children understand this state of affairs and prepare themselves for the places they expect society to offer them.

This argument reverses the usual account of the relationship between school experience and adult career opportunity. It is generally supposed that blacks cannot get good jobs because they have done poorly in school. Often they are said to have the "wrong attitudes" as well. Ogbu suggests, to the contrary, that blacks do poorly in school (and acquire those attitudes) because they are sure they are not going to get good jobs anyway. Like members of other caste-like minorities, many Afro-Americans do not expect to lead the kinds of lives for which education will matter much. Recent developments may be changing those expectations, but they are still very strong.

Another of Ogbu's observations is also important. Because caste restrictions are based on birth, they do not apply to *immigrants*. The psychological situation of an immigrant is very different from that of an indigenous member of a lower caste. Immigrants are in a situation of their own choosing, whereas members of the lower caste are enduring a role they were born to play. Immigrants expect to better their lot; lower-caste children set sharp limits on their ambitions. From this perspective, it is not surprising that groups that came to America only recently (immigrant Asians and Cubans, for example) often have been more successful than native Afro-Americans. The immigrants do not see themselves as permanent members of a lower caste.

AFRO-AMERICAN CULTURE

Ogbu's argument applies to caste-like minorities everywhere and can be independently verified in many parts of the world. But Afro-Americans are not just any minority. They exist in a certain historical situation, to which they have responded by developing a certain set of cultural values and styles. Wade Boykin (Chapter 3) presents a thoughtful analysis of Afro-American culture and its relation to the culture of the dominant Euro-American majority. The relation is complex: not only do Afro-Americans suffer from oppression and white hegemony as other minorities do, but they have developed a set of styles and values almost dialectically opposed to those of the majority. As Boykin puts it, American blacks must negotiate their way through three separate realms of experience: They have to deal with the daily facts of poverty and oppression, they share many of the values of the majority group that is oppressing them, and they maintain a cultural identity that is particularly difficult to reconcile with those values.

Boykin is not the first to suggest that black cultural styles may be at odds with American educational practice, but he spells out the dimensions of the

conflict with particular care. Because schooling in America serves to maintain the hegemony of the white middle class, it puts Afro-American children
in a situation of political conflict; because it is based on Euro-American intellectual styles and values, it embroils them in a cultural conflict as well.
Boykin's argument overlaps Ogbu's in many ways—both show how poor performance in school can be a natural consequence of belonging to an oppressed minority in a caste society. Boykin goes further, however, to offer a
particular description of black culture. That culture is based partly on styles
and customs of African origin and partly on an implicitly defined role as the
negative reflection of the white middle class. These factors create a difficult
and conflict-ridden learning situation for black children, with consequences
for their behavior both in and out of school.

EFFECTIVE AND INEFFECTIVE SCHOOLS

Where our first two hypotheses treat group differences as products of society as a whole, the next two focus on a specific and critical social institution:
the school itself. What is often taken as minority children's failure to learn
can just as easily be seen as the schools' failure to teach them. Such an interpretation is hardly new, but it may not seem as obvious now as when the Su-
preme Court first struck down school segregation in 1954. Legally segregated
schools are "inherently unequal," but segregation is not the only source of educational inequality. Poor instruction and differential treatment within the
school itself may be just as important. What do we know about these factors?
How do they produce their effects? These questions can be answered at two
levels, one using whole schools as units of analysis and the other concerned
with details of classroom instruction. Edmonds takes the first approach in
Chapter 4; Brown, Palinscar, and Purcell review the effects of different
kinds of teaching in Chapter 5.

Although Ronald Edmonds died in 1983, his influence on American education is still growing. The idea of "effective schools" that Edmonds defined
has become a focus of contemporary educational reform. Edmonds insisted
that all children are educable. The fact that many poor and minority children
fail to master the school curriculum does not reflect deficiencies in the children but rather inadequacies in the schools themselves. He put it bluntly:
"Variability in the distribution of achievement among school-age children in
the United States derives from variability in the nature of the schools to
which they go. Achievement is therefore relatively independent of family
background, at least if achievement is defined as pupil acquisition of basic
school skills" (Chapter 4, pp. 94–95).

Edmonds did not merely propose this hypothesis; he tested it, proved it,
and implemented successful programs of school reform that were based on it.

The research was based on his definition of an "effective school" as one in which the proportion of children who reach minimum standards of academic competence is the same for the poor as it is for the rich. Such schools do exist, although they are, regrettably, rare. (One study identified only 55 "effective schools" in the entire Northeastern quadrant of the United States.) Often they are situated in the very same districts and serve essentially the same population of children as less successful schools. What makes the difference?

According to Edmonds' research findings, five factors are typically present in effective schools and absent in ineffective ones: (a) strong leadership by the principal; (b) an explicit commitment to educational goals; (c) a calm and cared-about school atmosphere; (d) teachers' acceptance of responsibility for each pupil's progress; and (e) frequent monitoring of that progress by means of objective achievement tests. In 1978 Edmonds became chief instructional officer of the New York City School System, where he instituted school reforms based on these principles. This work had born rich fruit by the time he left New York in 1981. Achievement test scores were rising in all parts of the city, and especially among minority children. Programs based on "Edmonds' five principles" are now in place in many American cities, and they seem to be working well.

Chapter 4 is a lightly edited transcript of a tape made of Edmonds' presentation at the 1982 Conference. The fact that Edmonds had no opportunity to edit the transcript himself means that some passages may not be worded as carefully as he would have wished, but his argument comes through eloquently nevertheless.

THE DIFFERENTIAL TREATMENT EFFECT

Because Edmonds' argument concerns the organization of the school as a whole, he says relatively little about the details of classroom instruction. His chapter includes only one substantive remark on teaching: the assertion that effective teachers demand adequate performance from every pupil, whereas ineffective teachers make fewer demands on children from certain groups. He offers no specific data in support of this claim, but it is plausible. Brown, Palincsar and Purcell document many similar effects in their chapter, "Poor readers: Teach, don't label." They deal with a wide range of controversial issues. Why do children from poor and minority families often seem to be at a disadvantage when they first get to school? Why don't the schools overcome this disadvantage, whatever it may be? Do teachers treat poor children differently from middle-class children, and, if so, how? Why does the gap between good and poor readers (and, by implication, between better and weaker pupils in every subject) get wider the longer they stay in school? Can this tendency be reversed? Are there methods of teaching poor readers that produce substantial and permanent improvements in skill?

To say that minority children often start school "at a disadvantage" might seem to echo the deficiency theories of the 1960s, but the tone of Chapter 5 is exploratory rather than critical. One difference between poor and middle-class families that may be important is the frequency of quasi-academic activities such as "known-answer questions." Middle-class parents often ask their children questions for purely instructional purposes, just as teachers do: "What's this called?" "What does doggy say?" This kind of dialogue is especially frequent when parents are reading to children, but it is by no means restricted to that context. Brown et al. cite Heath's (1981) report that almost a quarter of the utterances addressed to a middle-class 2-year-old in one 48-hour period were known-answer questions. Quasi-academic behavior is less common in poor and minority homes, where a question may more often be a genuine request for information or serve a different conversational purpose.

These findings suggest that many minority children may be initially unfamiliar with the sociolinguistic conventions of the classroom. In addition, they typically arrive with less reading experience than their middle-class peers. These may seem to be relatively minor disadvantages, easy for schools and teachers to overcome. Unfortunately, actual schooling and teaching tend to exacerbate them instead. The *differential treatment effect* documented by Brown et al. in Chapter 5 is a striking example. Where "good readers" are often asked comprehension questions and helped to find meanings, "poor readers" usually just get drill in phonics. As a result, the poor readers — often minority children — improve in phonics but not in understanding what they read. The net effect is to widen the initial gap between good and poor readers, accustoming one group to success and the other to failure.

This analysis suggests that the performance of poor readers might be substantially improved if they were helped to understand what reading is really about and given some practice that focused on comprehension. Brown et al. report a series of studies with just such results. Low IQ students (both black and white) from remedial reading classes participated in a 20-day program in which they summarized texts, made up test questions based on particular passages, and generally became familiar with the process of reading for meaning. The resulting gains in their comprehension-test scores were dramatic. Moreover, the improvement generalized to a wide range of school tasks. Both the children themselves and their teachers were impressed with their newly discovered intellectual abilities. If the success of these techniques can be confirmed, they will have a significant impact.

DIRECT EFFECTS OF RACE PREJUDICE

Probably no one would dispute the proposition that stress can have a negative effect on learning. A modest degree of stress is not necessarily harmful, but all of us have experienced occasions when we were just too anxious to pay attention in school or too upset to do our homework. Susceptibility to these effects is universal. Distress and anxiety impair the work of the rich as well as the poor, of whites as well as blacks. But although every group may be equally susceptible to stress, all groups are not equally exposed to it. The life of the poor is intrinsically more stressful: more things go wrong, and less can be done about them.

In Chapter 6, Reginald Gougis points out that blacks are subject to a special kind of stress because they are the targets of racial prejudice. To be black in America is to be often reminded of one's lower-caste status. The reminders need not take the form of personal insults and racial taunts, though these certainly occur. Objective news reports of racism and prejudice can have much the same effect. Such experiences are bound to create distress and resentment. Some of that distress, in turn, is bound to interfere with concentration on academic matters. It is difficult to follow a teacher's argument when one is still brooding on a racial slur. The effect may be small at first, but it is cumulative: a child who misses one argument has an additional reason to miss the next one, and the disadvantage grows from year to year.

To demonstrate that this type of stress can interfere with academic learning, Gougis conducted a controlled experiment. Black college students were asked to read over the script of a three-character play and then to study the lines of one of the characters for a subsequent test. There were actually two different plays, one read by subjects in the experimental group and the other by a control group. The lines to be studied in the second phase of the experiment were the same for everyone. They consisted of a dull lecture about weather systems. In the experimental group the lecture lines were embedded in a strongly-worded racial dialogue; this group was also shown pictures that depicted instances of race discrimination. The play read by the control group did not deal with race at all, and they were shown only pleasant pictures. The results were clear. The experimental subjects spent less time studying the weather material than did the controls, and they remembered less of it on a subsequent test. Gougis argues that the experience of the experimental group can be regarded as an encapsulated version of the day-to-day experience of black children in American schools. His hypothesis is that black children tend to study less and learn less than their white counterparts because they regularly encounter higher levels of stress.

THE POSITIVE EFFECTS OF PRESCHOOL PROGRAMS

All things considered, then, black schoolchildren are in a difficult situation. Not only do they belong to a caste-like minority traditionally restricted to jobs for which education is almost irrelevant, but the values of their own culture often seem to be at odds with those of the school they must attend. That school itself may be only half-heartedly committed to teaching them, and the methods used by their teachers often seem to make learning harder rather than easier. Finally, their experiences as targets of race prejudice seem to make academic work still more difficult. If these factors are strong today, they were surely even stronger in the mid-1960s, when the so-called "compensatory education" preschool programs were first undertaken. Nevertheless, the findings of the Consortium for Longitudinal Studies, reported by Richard Darlington in Chapter 7, indicate that those programs had substantial positive effects.

The theoretical basis of the preschool programs was the hypothesis of "cultural disadvantage." In other words, the school failure of black children was ascribed to the permanent imprint of inadequate early experiences. To compensate for that disadvantage, such children were offered a special preschool year. (Many white, middle-class children get a year of preschool as a matter of course.) The programs were often designed with an eye to subsequent evaluations. They included carefully matched control groups and provided for standardized testing of the children. Unfortunately, the early evaluations yielded almost uniformly negative results. There were initial gains in IQ, but those gains soon faded away. By the end of the second grade, the test scores of the Head Start children were essentially indistinguishable from those of the controls.

Jensen (1969) took this outcome to mean that the academic differences between blacks and whites are simply incorrigible: "Compensatory education has been tried and it apparently has failed" (p. 69). He interpreted that "failure" as evidence for a genetic interpretation of black/white academic differences. Such an interpretation is entirely irresponsible. The only thing that had "failed" was a brief intervention based on the simplest form of the cultural deprivation hypothesis. As has been seen, there are much more plausible ways to explain the differences in question. All of the hypotheses presented in this book are environmental rather than genetic, but none of them focuses on the years of early childhood. (Brown et al. do consider those years, as does Boykin, but both assign primary responsibility for group differences to children's experience in school and in society at large.) At first glance, these cultural hypotheses even seem to be at odds with the long-term positive effects reported by the Cornell Consortium. As will be seen, however, the contradiction is only apparent.

The effects themselves turned out to be substantial. By the time the children in the original samples were old enough to be in high school, those who had participated in the preschool programs were doing very much better than those who had not. In particular, they were only about half as likely to have been held back in grade or to have been assigned to so-called special education classes. According to Darlington, this effect cannot plausibly be attributed to bias in the school evaluations of the Head Start children. No difference appeared during the first few grades, when teachers might still have remembered which pupils had been in which program. (If anything, there is an opposite effect during this time.) It also seems unlikely that the effect stems from any specific feature of the preschool curriculum itself. There was a wide range of programs based on an equally wide range of learning theories and principles. It would be difficult to find any aspect of curriculum common to all of them. In any case, no traditional theory of learning can account for an effect that remains invisible for the first few years and has an impact only in the later grades of school.

Since Darlington does not propose any specific explanation of the preschool effect in Chapter 7, I suggest a tentative hypothesis here. The mere existence of the programs may have been more important than their specific contents. For one year at least, the schools took the children (and their parents) seriously: responded thoughtfully to their behavior, believed in their potential achievements, listened to what they had to say. The upshot may have been to give both children and parents an extra measure of confidence in subsequent dealings with the educational system. Those dealings are not easy for anyone, and they are particularly difficult for minority families. Children with Head Start experience may have been more likely than control children to keep at their schoolwork in the face of adversity; their families may have been more likely to encourage them and perhaps even to speak up on their behalf.

This interpretation of the positive effects of Head Start is entirely compatible with the other hypotheses presented here. Ogbu, for example, attributes the academic discrepancy between blacks and whites to the structure of society itself, as seen by members of the caste-like black minority. But the existence of Head Start programs committed to racial equality represented a real, if slight, change in that structure and may have been perceived as such by the children and their parents. Boykin attributes it to the alienated situation of blacks in American culture; again, the relation between the Head Start personnel and the children in their programs may have reduced that alienation a little. Edmonds notes that most American schools are not genuinely committed to educating the children of the poor, but these schools did affirm that commitment at least for a year. If I am right, the function of the preschool programs was not so much to remedy a cognitive deficit in the children as to signal a structural change in American society and its schools.

COGNITIVE PROCESSES IN EDUCATIONAL SETTINGS

Although the deficit hypothesis was widely accepted during the 1960s and 1970s, psychologists were by no means unanimous in its support. One of the strongest and most effective statements of a different point of view was

Herbert Ginsburg's book *The Myth of the Deprived Child* (1972). Ginsburg insisted that children of every group and social class have the same basic abilities and develop those abilities in ways that reflect their individual cultural situations. The fact that poor children get low scores on mental tests reflects inadequacies in the tests themselves. Minority children may be culturally different, but they are not culturally deprived.

A decade later, Ginsburg took the opportunity offered by the Cornell Conference to assess the current status of the deficit hypothesis and expand on his alternative interpretation. His contribution here (Chapter 8) reflects that assessment. The last decade has taught us a great deal about how to study (and how not to study) mental processes. In light of these insights, the old arguments for the intellectual inadequacy of poor and minority children seem even weaker than they did in 1972. Ginsburg also suggests that cognitive psychology is only now beginning to understand what really happens during school learning. The more we find out about such factors as developmental universals, cultural specifics, and cognitive strategies, the less plausible the deficit assumption becomes.

Methodologically, it is now clearer than ever that simple measures of overt performance (like mental test items) are poor ways to study or "measure" cognitive processes. On the one hand, such measures are often misleading: recent cross-cultural studies have shown that the same problem can mean very different things to different people. On the other hand, promising alternative methods exist; one example is the procedure of "thinking aloud" that has been used successfully in recent studies of problem solving. Taken together, these findings suggest that the study of cognition in school settings could benefit from the use of what Ginsburg (following Piaget) calls the "clinical method." In this method, children's answers to test questions are not taken at face value. Instead, the children are carefully questioned to discover exactly what they did on their way to reaching those answers. Ginsburg offers concrete examples of the clinical method in action. Wherever it is used, it reveals the same basic intellectual competencies in children from every social class and group.

That conclusion is reinforced by recent empirical findings. Ginsburg is especially interested in young children's knowledge of mathematics. Certain aspects of abstract mathematical competence are apparently universal. They require no schooling and appear at about the same age in all cultures. The young black children studied by Ginsburg and Russell (1981) had no more difficulty with these forms of mathematical reasoning than did any other group. It is *school* mathematics that is especially difficult for many children, and we are only now beginning to understand why. The difficulties are by no means all "cognitive," at least in the narrow sense of that word. Ginsburg is careful to remind us of the roles played by social, political, and motivational factors in the school performance of minority children.

INTELLIGENCE, INTELLIGENCE TESTS, AND GROUP DIFFERENCES

This volume is more concerned with what children do in school than with their test scores. Of the many good reasons to avoid entering the so-called intelligence controversy, perhaps the most compelling is the confusion surrounding the concept of intelligence itself. That confusion is profound. Some theorists think of intelligence as a central executive faculty of the mind; others are convinced that no such faculty even exists. On one side there are innatists who define intelligence as something genetically determined and neurally expressed; on the other are environmentalists, for whom a test score is just an outcome of the individual's educational history. Jensen (1980), like Spearman before him, insists that the most important aspect of intelligence is captured by the single factor *g*. For other theorists (Gould, 1981, for example), *g* is just the artifactual result of a particular statistical procedure. They have proposed various divisions of intelligence into different kinds: a half dozen or more primary factors (Thurstone, 1938); two or three higher-order factors (Cattell, 1971); 120 factors along three dimensions (Guilford, 1967). I myself have contrasted "academic" with "general" intelligence (Neisser, 1976); Sternberg et al. (1981) have gone further to show that the layman's concept of intelligence includes not only those two components but also a social factor. Gardner (1983) argued on the basis of developmental trends and neurological findings that one should think of distinct "intelligences" for distinct domains; special abilities in such areas as language, mathematics, music, spatial representation, bodily movement, and personal relationships.

Faced with such a plethora of definitions, I am convinced that progress in the study of intelligence (whatever it may be) must await a better understanding of the concept itself (Neisser, 1979). As things stand, that concept has nothing to contribute to the issues under consideration in this book. But, although *intelligence* may be bypassed for a while, it is more difficult to ignore intelligence *tests*. Everyone knows that there are consistent differences among the test scores of different social groups. Where do these differences come from? It is plausible to attribute them to environmental factors? Are the tests themselves biased? If so, what is the locus of that bias? A few words about these issues may not be out of place here.

Before I present my own views, it is appropriate to mention one other presentation that was made at the Cornell Conference. Carolyn Boyce did not prepare a chapter for this volume, but her talk at the conference was an important contribution to our understanding of bias in mental tests. She offered an incisive critique of Arthur Jensen's (1970) two-level theory of group differences, which asserts that black Americans have a specific deficiency in abstract reasoning. To test that theory, Boyce identified the particular subtests and individual items that were relatively most favorable to whites (largest black/white differences) and to blacks (smallest black/white differences) in several large data sets. The two-level theory must predict that these differences will be especially large on items that require abstract reasoning and inference. After making the appropriate corrections for overall item difficulty, Boyce found that this was nowhere the case. The relative difficulty of items for whites and blacks is affected by the way the items are worded, by their factual contents, by their reliance on visualization, and even by their length – but it does not depend on the amount of abstract thinking they require. These findings have since been published in Boyce's (1983) doctoral dissertation.

Whatever they actually measure, there is no doubt that intelligence tests predict school performance fairly well. The Binet scales were designed with that purpose in mind, and most of Binet's successors have had similar goals. Those goals have been achieved: there are substantial positive correlations between school grades and IQ scores. Such correlations do not prove that children's grades depend on their "intelligence," however; they show only that test performance depends on the same factors as school performance. It must be affected by those factors, at least to some extent, because many test items are related to school material. What one did not learn yesterday (for any reason at all) is not available to help one answer test questions today.

In general, the factors that have been proposed here as causes of group differences in academic achievement must predict similar differences in test scores. All of them – the low expectations created by membership in a caste-like minority, the special situation of Afro-Americans in a society characterized by hegemony of white values, the stresses of race prejudice, the systematic failures of educational commitment and teaching in the schools – exert their effects by interfering with learning in school settings. To the extent that the items on an intelligence test involve school-based skills or contents, these factors will produce lower scores on the test as well. (Some of them also directly interfere with test performance by undermining the motivation to work on intellectual tasks.) A certain degree of difference between the test scores of majority and minority children is simply a by-product of educational inequality itself.

This is not the whole story. Ineffective schooling cannot be entirely responsible for group differences in test scores, because similar discrepancies appear even before children enter school. These early differences are not difficult to explain in environmental terms: children who are experienced in the quasi-academic rituals of middle-class homes (Chapter 5) can be expected to score higher on academically-oriented tests than those who are not. In a society with an effective school system, such differences would be only transient. Perhaps the most unfortunate aspect of contemporary education in America is that the differences are anything but transient – schools usually exacerbate them instead.

Can we really believe that social and educational factors have produced group differences as large as those that exist today? The mean IQ of black Americans is about 15 points (one whole standard deviation) below the corresponding mean for whites. That may seem to be a large discrepancy, but a recent discovery helps to put it into perspective. Flynn (1984) has made a careful study of changes in the IQ of *white* Americans from 1932 to 1978, basing his analysis on comparisons between tests that were published at different times. By convention, every new intelligence test (and every revision of an old one) is scaled so that its normative sample has a mean of 100. Occasionally, however, two tests normed at different times have been presented to the same groups of subjects. According to Flynn (1984), such subjects tend to get higher scores on the older test. Put another way, a group that averaged 100 on the later-normed test usually has an average above 100 on the earlier one. This implies that test norms are effectively higher now than they used to be; the mean American IQ is going up. The rate of increase amounts to some 0.3 IQ points per year, and the total gain since 1932 has been more than 14 points.

It is not entirely clear how this large gain should be interpreted. Flynn himself suggests several possible causes: increasing sophistication about tests themselves, enhanced educational achievement, rising standards of living, etc.[2] In any case, the cause must be environmental; genetic changes would have to operate on a very different time scale. In short, unspecified differences between the American environments of 1932 and of 1978 have produced an IQ difference *just as large as that which now exists between blacks and whites.* We have already seen that there are major differences between the educational and cultural environments of blacks and whites today. Now we see that differences of exactly this kind can indeed produce a one-standard-deviation difference in IQ. In the face of these facts, only the sheerest racism could justify any further interest in genetic interpretations of group differences.

The substantial difference between the mean IQs of whites and blacks has often been interpreted as evidence that the tests are biased against the latter group. Are they indeed? Unfortunately, this question has no single answer. Everything depends on what is meant by "biased." Several possibilities can be considered.

1.   On its face, the question seems to mean something like, "Do the tests underestimate the true intelligence of the blacks who take them?" But this interpretation makes no sense unless one assumes that such a thing as "true intelligence" exists in the first place and that tests can measure it. I think that it doesn't, and they can't.

---

[2]Flynn notes, however, that some of these hypotheses are rendered less plausible by the fact that SAT scores have actually *decreased* during the same period.

2.   A more operational form of the question would be, "Do the tests predict the academic performance of black children less accurately than that of white children?" A "yes" answer here might mean (this is not the only possibility) that a black child with low test scores would be less likely to fail in school or college than a white child with low test scores. However, the correct answer is probably "no." There is little evidence for bias in this sense. Tests seem to predict school and college performance about equally well in every group.

3.   Another possible interpretation of the question about test bias might be, "Are the tests framed and worded in ways that put blacks at a special disadvantage?" A test could have such a bias even though it accurately predicted performance in school and college. In that case, one might conclude that the schools and colleges were biased in much the same way. One way of approaching this issue is to try to design a new test that produces smaller group differences than the old ones did. If this is possible, and if the new test is otherwise reasonable, then the old tests must have been biased in this third sense. Data on the recently developed K-ABC test (Kaufman, 1984) suggest that it *is* possible. Black/white IQ differences on the K-ABC are only about seven points (half a standard deviation) rather than the usual fifteen. This implies that the older tests do present special problems for black testees and that these problems are not inevitable aspects of the testing process. (The item analyses reported by Boyce, 1983, hint at the nature of some of the difficulties.) Of course, this does not imply that the K-ABC is necessarily a better measure of *intelligence*. All claims about intelligence are empty without a clearer definition of it than we have at present.

The hypotheses suggested in this book offer new perspectives on the school achievements of minority children. The difficulties encountered by those children as a group do not result from any intrinsic intellectual incompetence on their part, but from the conditions of their lives — from their membership in a caste and a culture, from the inadequacies of their schools and their teachers, from the stresses they encounter in the present and the barriers they expect to encounter in the future. Although changes in these conditions cannot occur without real shifts in American values, some of the data presented here show that those shifts may already be under way. Perhaps that is why the gap is beginning to narrow: Jones (1984) reports that black/white differences on achievement tests diminished appreciably during the 1970s. This is good news, but it must not distract us from the continuing responsibility to move toward a more open and less discriminatory society. We have a long way to go. If this book helps in some measure to replace familiar cliches about the education of minority children with a better understanding of their real situation in America, it will have served its purpose.

REFERENCES

Boyce, C. M. (1983) *Black proficiency in abstract reasoning: A test of Jensen's two-level theory.* Doctoral Dissertation, Cornell University.

Cattell, R. B. (1971) *Abilities: Their structure, growth, and action.* Boston: Houghton Mifflin.

Flynn, J. R. (1984) The mean IQ of Americans: Massive gains 1932 to 1978. *Psychological Bulletin, 95,* 29–51.

Gardener, H. (1983) *Frames of mind: The theory of multiple intelligences.* New York: Basic Books.

Ginsburg, H. (1972) *The myth of the deprived child: Poor children's intellect and education.* Englewood Cliffs, NJ: Prentice-Hall.

Ginsburg, H. P. & Russsell, R. L. (1981) Social class and racial influences on early mathematical thinking. *Monographs of the Society for Research in Child Development, 46,* Serial No. 193, #6.

Gould, S. J. (1981) *The mismeasure of man.* New York: Norton.

Guilford, J. P. (1967) *The nature of human intelligence.* New York: Mc-Graw Hill.

Heath, S. B. (1981) Questioning at home and at school: A comparative study. In G. Spindler (Ed.) *Doing ethnography: Educational anthropology in action.* New York: Holt, Rhinehart & Winston.

Jensen, A. R. (1969) How much can we boost IQ and scholastic achievement? *Harvard Educational Review, 39,* 1–123. Reprinted in A. R. Jensen, *Genetics and education;* New York: Harper & Row, 1972.

Jensen, A. R. (1970) Hierarchical theories of mental ability. In B. Dockrell (Ed.), *On intelligence.* Toronto: Ontario Institute for Studies in Education.

Jensen, A. R. (1980) *Bias in mental testing.* New York: Free Press.

Jones, L. V. (1984) White-black achievement differences: the narrowing gap. *American Psychologist, 39,* 1207–1213.

Kagan, J., Kearsley, R. B., & Zelazo, P. R. (1978) *Infancy: Its place in human development.* Cambridge, MA: Harvard University Press.

Kaufman, A. S. (1984) K-ABC and controversy. *Journal of Special Education, 18,* 409–444.

MacKenzie, B. (1984) Explaining race differences in IQ: The logic, the methodology, and the evidence. *American Psychologist, 39,* 1214–1233.

Neisser, U. (1976) General, academic, and artificial intelligence. In L. Resnick (Ed.), *The nature of intelligence,* Hillsdale, NJ: Lawrence Erlbaum Associates.

Neisser, U. (1979) The concept of intelligence. *Intelligence, 3* 217–227.

Neisser, U. (1985) Toward an ecologically oriented cognitive science. In T. M. Schlechter & M. P. Toglia (Eds.), *New directions in cognitive science.* Norwood, NJ: Ablex.

Ogbu, J. U. (1978) *Minority education and caste: The American system in cross-cultural perspective.* New York: Academic Press.

Scarr, S. (1981) *Race, social class, and individual differences in I.Q..* Hillsdale, NJ: Lawrence Erlbaum Associates.

Sternberg, R. J., Conway, B. E., Ketron, J. L., & Bernstein, M. (1981) People's conceptions of intelligence. *Journal of Personality and Social Psychology, 41,* 37–55.

Thurstone, L. L. (1938) *Primary mental abilities.* Chicago: University of Chicago Press.

2 The Consequences of the American Caste System

John U. Ogbu

Almost from the initial discovery of racial, ethnic, and class differences in IQ test scores, mental testers have generally offered three kinds of explanations: differences in genetic endowment; differences in home environment and parental childrearing practices; and differences in cultural backgrounds. Because it is assumed that IQ determines school performance, these explanations also have been offered as the ultimate causes of differences in school performance. The explanations have generally led also to different policy recommendations, which in some cases resulted in remedial programs. However, the latter cannot be said to have worked very well (S. White, Day, Freeman, Hantman & Messenger, 1973). In our view, none of these explanations incorporates the special problems of castelike minorities in a racially or castelike stratified society like the United States. These problems are the focus of this chapter, which is organized into five parts. The first is a critical review of the current explanations; the second deals with the specific structural context of the problem — castelike stratification in America and castelike status of black Americans. Parts three and four consider the consequences of the caste system for IQ and school performance. The final part concludes.

THREE CURRENT EXPLANATIONS OF RACIAL DIFFERENCES IN IQ AND SCHOOL PERFORMANCE

Genetic Endowment

Among those arguing that differences between blacks and whites in IQ test scores in the United States are due to genetic differences are Garrett (1971),

Ingle (1970), Jensen (1969), and Shuey (1966). Because Jensen provides the most elaborate view on the matter, his work is treated here as representative.

Jensen calculates that about 80% of the variance in IQs is due to genetic differences, and the remaining 20% is attributable to environmental differences. He suggests that both individual differences in IQ within a given population and mean differences between populations are largely due to genetic factors. That is, because the heritability of IQ is high within the white population (and almost as high within the black population), one can plausibly suppose that the difference between the two populations are also primarily genetic[1]. This is implied by his testimony before the U.S. Senate Select Committee on Equal Educational Opportunity (Jensen, 1972), where he stated that:

> A hypothesis that I believe comprehends more of the facts and is consistent with more of the converging lines of evidence than any other I know of, in its simplest terms, is the hypothesis that (a) the heritability of IQ is the same *within* the white and black populations as *between* the populations, and (b) the genetic variance involved in IQ is about one-fifth less in the black than in the white populations. (p. 10)

Jensen also proposes a related hypothesis. He distinguishes between two levels of intelligence or learning abilities (i.e., IQ). Level 1 is the ability for concrete rather than abstract learning. Level 2 is the ability for conceptual learning, abstract thinking and problem solving. The two types of abilities are functionally related but genetically distinct. He also suggests that level 1 intelligence is normally distributed in the lower class and the middle and upper classes alike, whereas level 2 intelligence is found mainly in the middle and upper classes only.

Predominantly middle and upper class children characterized by level 2 intelligence—the ability for conceptual learning, abstract thinking and problem-solving—do well in school because the traditional methods of classroom instruction emphasize cognitive and conceptual skills. Predominantly lower class children, characterized by level 1 intelligence—the ability to learn more concrete things—perform less well in school because the classroom methods of instruction do not utilize their inherited abilities or skills. To improve the school performance of the latter, Jensen suggests new techniques of classroom instruction that de-emphasize cognitive and conceptual learning. He believes that such techniques would enable these children to learn successfully the basic skills in which they are now behind (Jensen, 1969).

According to Jensen, there is consensus among psychologists that blacks average 15 points lower than whites in IQ. This difference may diminish but

---

[1] I am indebted to Professor Neisser for clarifying Jensen's statement here on heritability of IQ and its bearing on differences between black and white populations in the United States.

does not completely disappear when blacks and whites of the same education, occupation, and income backgrounds are compared. He concludes that the differences in IQ between the two races must be due to heredity. Jensen notes further that proportionately more blacks than whites are found in the lower class, which is characterized by level 1 intelligence. Blacks generally not only perform lower than whites on IQ tests, but also perform much lower than whites on those parts of IQ tests that require abstract reasoning.

There is some evidence that genetic factors may play a major role in differences in IQ *among individuals* (Hermstein, 1973; Jensen, 1969; Vandenberg, 1971; Vernon, 1969). This evidence comes from two types of studies: one is the study of similarity in IQ of (a) children and their parents, either biological or foster, (b) identical twins raised together or apart, and (c) identical and fraternal twins (Vandenberg, 1971). The other type of research is the study of gene-controlled differences in individual intelligence, such as the effects of inbreeding, of mutant genes, and of chromosomal abnormalities on intelligence (Vandenberg, 1971). It is doubtful, however, that these findings are sufficient to warrant the generalization that IQ has a very high heritability, because the macro environments in which the twins were raised, primarily in Britain and the United States, were more or less homogeneous. Vernon (1969) has suggested that "if the twins were raised in a much wider range of environments, say between Western middle-class families and African or Indian peasant or Australian aboriginal families, the proportion of heredity and environment influences would be about 50-50 percent or even reversed" (p. 13). Burt (1969), on whose twin studies Jensen relied for his calculation of heredity, suggested a few years before his death that, based on cross-cultural studies of his students, including Vernon, the heritability of IQ may be much less than he had previously supposed. Since then, the validity of Burt's twin studies has been called into question (Dorfman, 1978; Gillie, 1979; Hawkes, 1979; Hearnshaw, 1979; Phillips, 1976).

The assumption that the genetic factors that cause individual differences in cognitive skills or IQ within the black or within the white population are the same as those that cause differences in IQ between the black and white populations is questionable. This is not to say that whites and blacks may not differ in genetic equipment for cognitive development. Vandenberg (1971), reports, for instance, that one gene that causes the form of mental deficiency known as phenykketonuria (PKU) occurs more frequently in the white than in the black population. The point is that there exists no research showing that specific genes linked to lower IQ are found in higher proportion among blacks than among whites. Nor are there studies showing that specific genes that control conceptual skills, abstract thinking, or problem solving are found in higher proportion among whites than among blacks. There are, in short, no studies that have demonstrated empirically that gene-controlled deficiencies in mental abilities, such as those caused by inbreeding, mutant genes, and chromosomal abnormalities, are found in higher proportion among blacks than among whites.

A reasonable explanation of the black-white differences in level 2 "intelligence" lies more in the differences in the types of cognitive skills required by the different types of jobs and other adult positions that have been traditionally open to blacks and whites under the caste system than in differences in neural structures or heredity, as proposed by Jensen. It is also possible that blacks possess the same amount of level 2 intelligence as whites (see Boyce, 1983) but are not motivated to demonstrate that intelligence in test situations because of castelike barriers, such as a job ceiling. Both views are explored more fully later.

Home Environment and Childrearing Practices

Hereditists and environmentalists agree that the environment influencing cognitive development consists of prenatal influences as well as of certain traits that characterize individuals, families, and neighborhoods (see Denenberg, 1970; Hunt, 1969; Jensen, 1969; Kagan, 1973; Vernon, 1969). The environmentalists, however, assign greater weight to the postnatal environmental factors than to genes or prenatal factors. They usually consider the socioeconomic status of a child's parents as the most important environmental factor. They claim socioeconomic status determines the quality and quantity of the child's "interaction with other members of the family as well as the material resources available to him or her. Both of these can facilitate or impede the child's cognitive development" (Hunt, 1969, pp. 207–208). From this perspective, it is said that some people develop better or more intelligence or cognitive skills because they come from a rich environment and receive more and better stimulation in early childhood.

A fundamental assumption of the environmentalist is what has been termed the "critical period hypothesis." T. R. Williams (1972) summarizes the hypothesis as follows:

> There are critical periods, or stages, in the development of animals, including man, during which the individual is most receptive to learning from particular kinds of experiences. These periods are very limited in duration. If an experience is to become a regular part of an individual's later behavior it has to be acquired during the critical period when the individual is most ready to learn from that kind of experience. Earlier or later exposure to such experience will produce little or no effect on the individual's later actions. (p. 116)

Some environmentalists believe that there is a period in a child's life when he or she must receive a particular form of stimulation, or permanent damage will be done to his or her cognitive and social development. In one recent report, (White, Kaban, & Attanucci, 1979, pp. 181–183), the investigators concluded that such poor development during early years of life seems very difficult to overcome, and they are convinced after 20 years of research that "much that shapes the final human product takes place (in the home) during the first years of life."

The environmentalist explanation of the lower IQ test scores of castelike minorities like black Americans is that these children do not receive adequate stimulation from their parents (usually the mother) during the early years of life. They argue that black parents do not provide their children with the right stimulation because they do not have the child-rearing capabilities of white middle class parents. A good deal about what is thought to be missing in black childrearing can be learned from the emphasis of various remedial programs devised to resocialize minority children or to improve their parents' childrearing skills. For example, some programs are designed to increase, through lectures, counseling, and discussion groups, black parents' knowledge of white middle-class techniques of raising children; others train black mothers in specific techniques of cognitive stimulation and social training, such as how and how much to talk to and play with their children (Bloom, Davis & Hess, 1965; Ogbu, 1974; Rees, 1968; White, Day, Freeman, Hantman & Messenger, 1973).

It is now generally acknowledged that the remedial efforts have not been particularly successful in increasing significantly and permanently the IQ of blacks and similar minority children (see Darlington, Chapter 7). Explanations for the relative failure of these programs, however, only have encourage proponents to stress the need for earlier and earlier intervention, with more emphasis on parent education and training (Goldberg, 1971; Ogbu, 1978). However, as we have suggested elsewhere (Ogbu, 1979, 1981a, and 1982c), the real causal relationship between functional cognitive competencies and childrearing appears to be the reverse of conventional thinking. Cross-cultural studies suggest that, contrary to conventional assumption, it is probably the nature of instrumental competencies, including instrumental cognitive skills, that determines how parents and parent surrogates in a population raise their children and how children seek to acquire competencies as they get older (Aberle, 1961; Barry, Child & Bacon, 1959; Berry, 1971; Maquet, 1971; Mead, 1939; Miller & Swanson, 1958).

Moreover, the environmentalist view is ethnocentric; it sets up the white middle-class childrearing practices and competencies as standards and thus decontextualizes from realities of life cognitive skills and their acquisition. As a result, it confuses the process of acquiring adaptive or instrumental cognitive skills in a population with their causes or origins — the reasons for their presence or absence in the population.

Finally, the environmentalist conception of environment comes primarily from laboratory studies of animals (Denenberg, 1970; Hunt, 1969). Thus, it fails to include significant forces in human environment affecting development of cognitive and other abilities.

Cultural Differences

Other social scientists have long explained the lower test scores of minority group children as due to the fact that the tests are "culturally biased" (Eels, Davis, Havighurst, Herrick, & Tyler, 1951). Some have attempted to design tests that are "culture-fair," "culture-reduced," or even "culture-free." More recently some have even designed tests whose contents in terms of vocabulary, idioms, information and other items are drawn almost exclusively from the "culture" or experience of inner-city black Americans. Unfortunately, this approach, too, has not resolved the debate about IQ and race (Jensen, 1980; Williams, R. L. 1972).

Equalizing the test scores of blacks and whites through "culture fair" or "culture-reduced," or "culture-free" tests fails partly because of misapplication of the concept of culture. "Culture" in these tests is superficially defined to mean certain objects, vocabulary, idioms, and other "traits," assumed to be peculiar to blacks (Jensen, 1980). There is no reference to the "imperative of culture" (Cohen, 1971) — to the economic, political, and other institutional arrangements of American society and how the tasks within them are parcelled out to blacks and whites, tasks that require and stimulate cognitive skills. Nor is there a reference to the phenomenal world and the epistemology of blacks as a subordinate group in a castelike stratification. As a result of this narrow conception of culture, some mental testers quickly point to many other "traits" shared by blacks and whites suggesting that there are no fundamental cultural or language differences between the two races (Humphreys, 1973).

Another shortcoming of the cultural difference explanation is that it fails to distinguish between two kinds of cultural differences (Ogbu, 1982b). There is, on the one hand, a type of cultural difference that characterizes non-Western peoples who are being administered "intelligence" or cognitive tests or who are being introduced to Western-type schooling *in their homelands* in Africa, Asia, and elsewhere. To such peoples may be added *immigrant minorities within Western societies*. On the other hand, there is another type of cultural difference that is found mainly among *castelike minorities* like black Americans. It is true that cultural differences in both situations have been found to be associated with differences in test scores and perhaps in school performance (Cibrowski, 1976; Cole, Gay, Glick & Sharp, 1971; Cole & Scribner, 1974; Dasen, 1977; Ginsburg, this volume). However, the "cultural factors" responsible for lower test scores or lower school performance are not necessarily the same in both situations for at least two reasons: differences in content rather than style; and differences in responses to contact and change.

Content vs. Style

Among non-Western peoples, the cultural factors associated with schooling problems such as those pertaining to teaching, learning, language and communication, mathematical concepts and operations are often specific, due particularly to differences in specific content. For example, the Kpelle of Liberia do not have certain specific Western mathematical and related concepts that are aspects of Western middle-class school learning and test taking. The Kpelle do not, for instance, have the concepts of zero, and numbers. Their geometrical terms are few and imprecise, so that the Kpelle would use the term circle to stand for "the shape of a pot, a pan, a frog, a sledge hammer, a tortoise, a water turtle, and a rice fanner" (Gay & Cole, 1967, p. 53). Their term for triangle is equally imprecise. They measure length, time, volume, and money, but imprecisely; and they lack measurements for weight, area, speed and temperature. Yet, Kpelle children and adults acquire the "missing" concepts and their application, (although with the usual initial difficulties) when they begin to participate in Western-type schooling and technoeconomic activities.

In contrast, the "cultural factors" said to account for lower test scores and school failure of black Americans are not so specific. They are often described in terms of "style" — black "cultural style" as opposed to white "cultural style" (Boykin, 1980), black "communication style" as opposed to white "communication style" (Kochman, 1982), black "cognitive style" as opposed to white "cognitive style" (Jenkins, 1982; Jones, 1981; Shade, 1982). Differences in style may affect how blacks and similar minorities perform on standardized tests and in school, just as the cultural elements of peoples of non-Western nations affect their performance (see Ginsburg, Chapter 8; also Cole, Gay, Glick & Sharp, 1971; Cole & Scribner, 1974; Nyiti, 1982). But it appears that differences due to style do not allow for the kind of cognitive transition indicated for non-Western peoples, especially when linked to secondary cultural differences.

Response to Change

The two types of cultures differ in their responses to the influence of school culture. Among non-Western people, it appears that over time contact with school culture and the process of schooling usually modify the initial cultural and cognitive differences. Specifically, such people tend to acquire and demonstrate Western-type cognitive competence through going to school and participating in Western-type economic activities (Cole, Gay, Glick & Sharp, 1971; Cole & Scribner, 1974; Greenfield, 1966; LeVine, 1970; Wagner, 1982). For example, Hong Kong-born Chinese children differ from American-born Chinese (who are more like white Americans) in style of solving mathematical problems. However, the Hong Kong-born group tends to become like the American-born after immigrating and attending American public schools for some years (Tsang, 1983). Furthermore, non-Western people and non-castelike minorities often do not expect to be taught or tested in their own "cultures" or language but in those of the school or the dominant group. Consequently, they usually try to learn how to learn in the culture and language of the dominant group or the school.

Among castelike minorities, on the other hand, there appears to be some resistance or ambivalence toward acquiring and demonstrating the culture of and cognitive styles that are identified with those of the dominant group. For example, although blacks have long championed equal education with whites, many also identify school culture and language with white culture and language, which, they claim, are not appropriate for the teaching and learning of black children. Boykin (1980) comes close to articulating this position when he states that, although black children are eager to learn when they first come to school, they are soon turned off by the educational process "when confronted with articifical, contrived and arbitrary competence modalities (e.g., reading and spelling) that are presented in ways which undermine the children's cultural frame of reference" (p. 11). He suggests five ways in which black "cultural styles" differ from white "cultural styles." The limitation of this explanation is that it does not tell why other nonmainstream children with distinct cultural frames of reference are not turned off, as black children are by the same or similar educational process (Heyneman, 1979; Musgrove, 1953; Ogbu, 1982b).

The three perspectives discussed in this section — genetic endowment, environmental and cultural — ignore three things that more or less influence people's performance on intelligence tests and in school. These are: (1) ecological context of cognitive skills and schooling; (2) access to ecological resources and activities that affect cognitive skills and schooling; and (3) epistemology, which influence people's perceptions of and responses to test situations and to schooling. These factors are particularly important in any consideration of castelike minorities like black Americans. Therefore, to understand their effects on black performance on intelligence tests and in school, we first should specify what we mean by castelike minority status.

CASTELIKE MINORITY STATUS

Minority Types

In many contemporary societies and certainly in the United States, there co-exist several minority groups, some of whom do well in school and on intelligence tests and some of whom do not. What distinguishes those who are not successful from those who are? To answer this question, we have suggested elsewhere (Ogbu, 1978) a classification of minority groups into autonomous, immigrant, and castelike minorities. It is the last that frequently is associated with persistent disproportionate school failure and lower test scores.

Autonomous minorities such as the Amish, the Jews, and the Mormons in the United States are minorities primarily in a numerical sense. Although such minorities often possess distinctive ethnic, religious, linguistic, or cultural identity and may be victims of prejudice, they are not totally subordinated politically and economically by the dominant group. Nor are they forced to play specialized and denigrated roles. Autonomous minorities usually have cultural frames of reference that encourage and demonstrate success, and these minorities do not show disproportionate school failure.

Immigrant minorities, like the Chinese, Filipinos, Japanese, Koreans in the United States, are those who have come to America more or less voluntarily to improve their economic, political, or social status. These minorities may hold menial jobs, lack political power, and have little or no prestige initially. But this objective socioeconomic position does not reflect their true status in the social hierarchy, because it does not include how the immigrants themselves think of their position, which is not the same as the way dominant group members evaluate it. Contrary to the perception of dominant group members, the immigrants may consider their menial position better than what they had before they emigrated, or they may consider the menial job a temporary situation. Also, the immigrants tend to compare themselves, not with the elite members of the dominant group of their host society, but with their peers back home, the people they left behind. When they compare themselves with their peers back home — their reference group — they often find much evidence of self-improvement for themselves and good prospects for their children because of better opportunities (Shibutani & Kwan, 1965). Further, immigrants — unless they are political emigrés — have at least a symbolic option of returning to their homeland or re-imigrating elsewhere if they become too dissatisfied with living in America. Changes in diplomatic or economic relations between the immigrants' country of origin and the United States may also affect positively or negatively their reception and opportunities in America. These are some of the things that encourage immigrants to maintain instrumental attitudes and behaviors toward education and economic matters. It is probably for the same reason that the immigrants do relatively well in school and on various tests, even though they do not share the same culture as the white middle class.

The experience of *castelike minorities* are different and have different educational consequences. Castelike minorities are those who are incorporated into the country more or less involuntarily and permanently and then relegated to menial positions through legal and extralegal devices. Black Americans are a good example of castelike minorities, although American Indians, Mexican Americans, Native Hawaiians, and Puerto Ricans also share certain important features of the caste. Blacks were brought to America as slaves and after emancipation were relegated to menial status through legal and extralegal devices (Berreman, 1960, 1967; Myrdal, 1944). Indians, the original owners of the land, were conquered and then contained on reservations (Spicer, 1962). Mexican-Americans were conquered and displaced from power in the American Southwest. Those who immigrated later from Mexico were treated like the conquered group (Acuna, 1972; Schmidt, 1972).

Membership in a castelike minority group is often acquired at birth and retained permanently. Its members are regarded and treated by the dominant white group as inferior and are ranked lower than whites as desirable neighbors, employees, workmates, and schoolmates. Castelike minorities lack political power, and this powerlessness is reinforced by economic subordination. Castelike minorities face a job ceiling. That is, they are not usually hired for jobs on the basis of training as members of the dominant group are; rather, their low-status group membership keeps them from being hired and being paid wages commensurate with their training and ability. Moreover, the structural subordination of castelike minorities — economic, political and social — is reinforced by overarching ideology of the dominant group, which rationalizes the menial status of the minorities.

Blacks and similar castelike minorities do not accept their ascribed menial position. They reject the ideology and beliefs of the dominant group that rationalize their position. They believe that their economic, political, and social problems are due primarily to "the system," due to racism rather than to their own individual inadequacies. And they see these problems as more or less enduring. As a result, castelike minorities often develop what may be callled *a collective institutional discrimination perspective*. That is, they appear to believe that it is difficult for them to advance into the mainstream or achieve middle-class positions or self-betterment through individual efforts at school or by behaving like members of the dominant group. They believe that their chances are better through collective efforts and manipulating the system. This perspective leads the minorities to channel their time and efforts into collective struggle, i.e., to activities intended to change the system as a way of getting ahead or as a prerequisite for getting ahead.

Castelike Minorities versus Racial Minorities

Castelike minorities are not synonymous with racial minorities, as could be seen from the foregoing consideration of immigrant minorities. Not all racial minorities have the status of castelike minorities. In a number of cases (e.g., India, Japan, etc.) castelike minorities belong to the same race as the dominant caste. Here a castelike minority is designated as any racial, ethnic, or other population that has the characteristics previously described above for castelike minorities. The term *castelike* is used as an analytic tool or concept that implies a stratification more rigid than class (Ogbu, 1977).

Race, IQ, and School Performance

It is customary among mental testers and education researchers to treat race and racial-group membership as important variables. Alternatively, they treat black school and test problems as class-related problems. Both classifications are incorrect.

With regard to race differences, it is evident from cross-cultural studies that membership in different racial groups does not necessarily lead to differences in school performance or to lower test scores on IQ tests. One can see this by comparing Caucasians (whites) with some non-Caucasians (e.g., Chinese, Japanese-Americans) in the United States. Nor does membership in the same racial group necessarily result in similar test scores or similar school performance. This can be seen when the test scores of Oriental Jews are compared with those of Ashkenazi Jews in Israel (Ackerman, 1973; Lewis, 1979, 1981), and when the test scores of the Burakumin are compared with those of the non-Burakumin in Japan (DeVos, 1973; DeVos & Wagatsuma, 1967; Shimahara, 1971). Race becomes a significant variable in testing and in school performance only when the racial groups are stratified. "Specifically, it is when racial groups are organized hierarchically so that members of the group which is subordinate are restricted to low social, economic, political and other roles that racial differences result in persistent differences in IQ test scores and in school performance generally" (Ogbu, 1977, p. 2), that is, when racial minorities become castelike minorities.

Castelike Minority Status versus Lower-Class Status

Not only do blacks as a castelike minority group differ from other minorities, but blacks also differ significantly from whites in social class, so that blacks cannot easily fit into white class structure for an explanation of their performance in school and on IQ tests. This is particularly true of lower-class blacks (Ogbu, 1978), because black and white social classes are affected in different ways by the racial or castelike stratification described earlier. What must be emphasized are the coexistence of the two forms of stratification and the more powerful influence of castelike stratification in differentiating black and white social classes. That is, from our point of view, it is not enough to say that blacks and whites belong to the same social classes and so ought to behave alike because they are similar in certain objective criteria. Following Berreman's (1972) suggestion, we have tried elsewhere (Ogbu, 1977, 1981b) to show that the stratification between blacks and whites in America is different from class stratification with respect to closure and affiliation, social mobility, status summation, and cognitive orientation. Differences in status summation and cognitive orientation are probably the most pertinent to the problem of IQ and school performance of black children.

By status summation we mean that blacks, as members of a subordinate group in a stratified racial caste, have faced a job ceiling that is not experienced by lower class whites, who are involved only in class stratification. A *job ceiling* is the result of the consistent pressures and obstacles that selectively assign blacks and similar minorities to jobs at the low level of status, power, dignity, and income, while allowing whites to compete more easily and freely, on the basis of individual training and ability or educational credentials, for desirable jobs above that ceiling. Put differently, racial or castelike stratification gives class membership an added disadvantage for blacks; a white American who is lower class has impaired access to jobs and education but does not face a job ceiling. A black American who is lower class is also a member of a subordinate racial group that, in addition to impaired access to jobs and education due to lower-class status, also faces a job ceiling. Thus one can speak of a lower-class black as being subordinate in a double stratification, whereas a lower-class white is subordinate in a single stratification.

Because of the unique nature of black status mobility or opportunities for getting ahead (due to job ceiling and generally limited opportunity structure), the majority of blacks, especially lower-class blacks, have historically been menial workers, underemployed workers, or unemployed. They have also had very little access to desirable sociopolitical positions.

Membership in a double stratification generates a distinct type of cognitive orientation not found among whites, even among lower-class whites. This is the tendency to blame the system rather than oneself for personal and group failures. Unsuccessful whites often blame themseves and luck for their lack of success (Sennett & Cobb, 1967). Unsuccessful blacks, on the other hand, frequently blame the system. On the whole, blacks do not accept their low social, political, and economic status as legitimate outcomes of their individual failures or misfortunes. Blacks see racial barriers in employment, education, and politics as the primary causes of their poverty, menial jobs and unemployment. What distinguishes black Americans and similar castelike minorities from lower-class whites is not that their objective material conditions are different, but rather that the way the minorities perceive, interpret, and respond to their conditions is different.

The foregoing discussion of castelike minority status points to insufficiency of the explanation of the lower test scores and lower school performance of blacks in terms of genetic endowment, home environmental factors, and cultural differences. Given the castelike minority status of blacks, Jensen cannot reasonably argue that differences in the behavior of blacks and whites, such as test taking, are determined by a single element — genetic endowment; environmentalists can no longer ignore the effects of double stratification and minority cognitive orientation or epistemology. Nor can proponents of cultural difference explain the effects of stratification and cognitive orientation on cultural "traits" and "styles." The following brief cross-cultural comparison further underscores the importance of the structural subordination of the minorities in generating their educability problems.

Castelike Minority Status And Educability In Cross-Cultural Perspective

Most people know about the existence of castes in India, Pakistan, and Sri Lanka, but many may not know that castes and castelike groups also exist in other societies, both nonindustrial and modern industrial societies. Most people probably do not know either that, wherever such groups exist and tests have been given, the lower caste groups usually have lower IQ test scores and lower academic achievement than the dominant groups. In this section we look at a few examples.

The existence of castes and castelike groups outside India and neighboring countries has been documented by anthropologists and other researchers. Castes have been found to exist, for example, in precolonial, preindustrial societies of the Ibos of Nigeria (Ogbu, 1981b), the Nupe of Nigeria, the Beni Amer of East Africa, and the Tira of Sudan (Nadel, 1954), in Rwanda and Urundi (Maquet, 1961, 1971), among the Senufo of West Africa (Richter, 1980; Todd, 1977), and the Konso of Ethiopia (Hallpike, 1972).

Contemporary Japan is a good example of a modern industrial society with castes. Within our definition of *castelike status* as a subordinate minority group is a stratification system more rigid than classification stratification, the following minorities can be described, for comparative purposes, as *castelike* in their respective countries; blacks in the United States, West Indians in Britain, the Maoris in New Zealand, Buraku outcastes in Japan, Harijans (formerly Untouchables) in India, and Oriental Jews in Israel. The Harijans of India and the Buraku outcastes of Japan are castelike minorities par excellence. In 1947, the Indian constitution abolished the pariah status of the Harijans, and their rights as ordinary citizens were reaffirmed by a legislative act in 1955 (Beteille, 1969). In Japan, a royal edict in 1871 emancipated the Burakumin from their pariah status (Price, 1967). However, the formal abolition of the pariah status of these two minority groups has not significantly changed the way their members are perceived and treated by members of the dominant groups of their societies — the Brahmin and other high-caste groups in India, and the Ippan dominant group in Japan. In general, the Harijans and the Burakumi are still relegated to menial social and economic roles on the basis of traditional conceptions of their caste status.

In Britain, West Indians are technically an immigrant group. However, unlike other "colored" immigrants, they were forced by economic, political, and social circumstances to emigrate permanently to Britain, which they regard as their mother country. Here they occupy the most inferior position in a system of color-caste (Krausz, 1971; Rose, 1969). The Maoris, the indigenous people of New Zealand, were conquered in the 19th century by European colonists, or Pakeha, and then relegated to an inferior position in a system of color-castes (Ausubel, 1961; Metge, 1967). Oriental Jews in Israel are probably the least castelike of the minority groups discussed here. This is partly because, in spite of their inferior position and poor treatment, they share with the dominant Ashkenazi, or Jews of European ancestry, the Zionist utopian vision that all Jewish citizens will eventually have full and equal rewards in the new society, provided they become Westernized (Lewis, 1979; Matras, 1970).

What is significant for our purpose is that these castelike minorities are characterized by educability problems similar to those of black Americans. That is, where IQ or intelligent tests have been given, the children of these castelike minorities score about 10 to 15 points, on the average, lower than dominant group children of their society. Members of the castelike minority groups are often 1 or 2 years behind members of the dominant groups in basic subjects as reading and mathematics and are overrepresented in remedial programs (where these exist) and among school dropouts. The castelike minorities are also underrepresented in higher educational attainment and in higher education institutions. These differences remain when minority and dominant group members are of similar socioeconomic background. What is even more significant is that the gaps in IQ test scores and in academic achievement exist when castelike minorities and dominant groups belong to the same race (e.g., in India, Israel, and Japan) as they do when the minorities and the dominant groups belong to different races (e.g., in Britain, New Zealand, and the United States).

Although IQ tests are not widely given in India, where they are, the Harijans have lower scores (Chopra, 1966). The Harijans also have lower school enrollment, literacy rates, classroom performance, and graduation rates from various levels of schooling (Chauhan, 1967). Oriental Jews are behind the dominant Ashkenazi in IQ test scores (Ortar, 1967; Rosenfeld, 1973; Similansky & Similansky, 1967), in scholastic achievement, and admission to and graduation from academic secondary schools and universities (Ackerman, 1973; Adler, 1970; Avineri, 1973). In Japan, the Buraku outcastes do no better, with their lower literacy rate, higher school dropout rate, and lower performance on scholastic achievement tests and IQ tests (DeVos, 1973; DeVos & Wagatsuma, 1967). Table 2.1 illustrates the type of gap that exists between the Buraku minority and the dominant Ippan on the Tanaka-Binet Intelligence Tests used in Japan.

The Harijans in India, Oriental Jews in Israel, and the Buraku outcastes in Japan, despite their membership in the same racial group as the dominant group members of their societies, have lower test scores. The situation is the same for West Indians in Britain, whose racial affinities are different from

TABLE 2.1
A Comparison of the Scores of Buraku and
Non-Buraku Students on the Tanaka-Binet
Intelligence Test, Takatsuki City
(percentage groupings)

IQ	Buraku children (N = 77)	Non-Buraku children (N = 274)
125 or higher	2.6	23.3
109–124	19.5	31.8
93–108	22.1	23.3
77–92	18.2	11.7
76 or lower	37.6	9.9

Note: From George A. De Vos and Hiroshi Wagatsuma,
(Eds.) (1967) *Japan's invisible race.* Berkeley: University of
California Press, p. 261.

those of the dominant group. Members of this group perform substantially lower on IQ tests than do the Anglo-British and lower than other "colored" immigrants. As a result, West Indian students are overrepresented in classes and schools for the mentally retarded (Haynes, 1971; Houghton, 1966; Parliamentary Select Committee, 1973; Tomlinson, 1982.) West Indians gain few places in the top tracks of regular classes and are overrepresented in the bottom tracks. Because they are underrepresented in grammar school and academic secondary schools, very few qualify for higher education or university education (Parliamentary Select Committee, 1973).

The Maoris in New Zealand perform lower than the whites, or pakeha, on IQ tests and on standardized achievement tests (Ausubel, 1961; Harker, 1977; Ritchie, 1957). Many Maoris drop out of school before reaching the compusory school age of fifteen, and very few go further (Hunn, 1960).[2]

To reiterate, these cross-cultural cases teach that regardless of their racial affinity with the dominant group members of their society, castelike minority-group children generally have lower test scores. When members of a castelike minority group emigrate to another society, the twin problem of low IQ test scores and low academic achievement appears to disappear. This is well illustrated by the case of the Japanese Buraku immigrants to the United States. In Japan, as was indicated previously, low caste Buraku children continue to underperform in comparison with the children of the domi-

---

[2]Personal communication with officials of New Zealand Department of Education in the office of Maori and Island Education: Ms. Winifrid M. Perman, Sept. 1979; Mr. B. V. Penfold, March 1981; Ms. M. Middleton, May 1983.

nant Ippan group. But in the United States, where American society and Americans treat the Buraku exactly as they treat other Japanese immigrants, the Buraku do at least as well at school and the work place as do their Japanese counterparts (Ito, 1967; G. A. DeVos, personal communication, June, 1983). Let us examine cultural-ecological factors for some of the reasons why castelike minorities do not do so well in their homelands.

CASTELIKE MINORITY STATUS AND IQ

Cultural-Ecological Context of "Intelligence"

IQ as Cognitive Skills, not Cognitive Capacities or Processes.   Some psychologists (e.g., Jensen, 1969) claim that intelligence is a technical term used to designate whatever it is that intelligence tests test. However, we need to make the kind of distinctions suggested by Cole and Scribner (1973) and Vernon (1969). Cole and Scribner distinguish between intelligence as cognitive capacities or cognitive processes, which are universal, and intelligence as cognitive skills, which vary from culture to culture. All human populations or cultural groups share the same basic cognitive capacities or processes. That is, they can remember, generalize, form concepts, operate with abstractions, and reason logically. Inner-city blacks and suburban whites share these capacities, as do the Ibos of Nigeria and the Australian Aborigins. If these capacities are genetically based, then all human groups share the underlying genes.

According to Cole and Scribner, cognitive skills are not universal. Cognitive skills are the different ways in which the universal cognitive capacities are utilized to solve various problems in different situations. The repertoire and pattern of cognitive skills tend to become culture specific because the problems that face members of different populations are different (Scribner & Cole, 1973; Ogbu, 1981b).

The repertoire of cognitive skills typical of a given population is not simply a product of childrearing practices of its present members. It consists rather of the cognitive skills that the population as a whole has developed over time to deal with past, continuing, and new social, political, economic, technological, and other problems facing its members in their specific environment. In one population, some of these problems may require and encourage a high degree of verbal skill; in another, the problems may require and encourage emphasis on numerical or mathematical skills (see Ginsburg, Chapter 8); in still another, it may be spatial-perceptual skills or memorization skills that are important and prevalent. And there may be cultures where some combination of these emphases is the key to survival. Thus, if two populations differ in repertoire of cognitive skills, a clue to the reason for the difference may lie in the nature of their macroenvironment or the realities of their economic, social, and political lives that may pose different cognitive problems for the two populations.

Intelligence (IQ) Testing in Cross-Cultural Perspective. We must further distinguish cognitive capacities and cognitive skills from IQ or what intelligence tests test. The latter is the observed cognitive behavior or responses to selected cognitive-skills questions. IQ is not the total cognitive repertoire of the members of any culture; nor is it the same for all cultures or populations. Vernon (1969) has suggested a useful distinction that appears to clarify the differences between the three meanings of intelligence, i.e., differences between cognitive processes or capacities, the culture-specific cognitive skills, and the sampled cognitive skills that make up IQ.

Vernon (1969) distinguishes between what he calls Intelligence A, B, and C. Intelligence A and B correspond to the geneticist's distinction between the genotype and the phenotype respectively. (In our framework these correspond roughly to Cole and Scribner's (1973) cognitive capacities and cognitive skills.) Intelligence A, the genotype, is the innate capacity that the child inherits from his or her ancestors through the genes and that determine the limits of the child's intellectual or cognitive growth. Similarly, for members of a given culture, Intelligence A represents their genetic potential for cognitive development. But there is no way anyone can directly observe or measure Intelligence A.

Intelligence B, the phenotype, refers to observed behavior that is considered intelligent or unintelligent by members of a culture. It is a product of both nature (genetic equipment) and nurture (environmental factors). Intelligence B varies from one population to another because different cultures require and stimulate the development and use of different types of cognitive skills to cope with their specific environmental problems. Intelligence B is not fixed; it may rise or fall with changes in formal education of individuals or a whole population. Vernon suggests that in Western societies Intelligence B has probably increased as a result of industrialization and urbanization. He also notes that the repertoire of cognitive skills of the contemporary Western middle class may have developed in response to the cognitive requirements of industrial, bureaucratic, and urban culture. The solution of many problems posed by this culture stresses the need for symbolic thinking and grasping relations. These skills have, in the course of time, come to permeate almost all other cultural activities of Western middle class, including those of daily life, school, and workplace. Vernon further tells us that Intelligence of B of the people in the Soviet Union may have also increased in the last 80 years because of industrialization, bureaucratization, and urbanization in that nation. Under the impact of Western formal education, technology, economy, and urbanization, some African and Asian peoples are known to be acquiring cognitive skills characteristic of Western middle class Intelligence B (Cole, Gay, Calick & Sharp, 1971; LeVine, 1970; Vernon, 1969).

Intelligence C refers to those cognitive skills usually sampled by IQ tests from Intelligence B. Intelligence C differs from Intelligence B because: (a) the skills sampled by the IQ tests may be selected deliberately to serve a particular function, such as to predict scholastic performance; (b) Intelligence C is more "scientific" and more objective than Intelligence B (everday observation) because IQ test items are carefully selected and standardized; and (c) Intelligence C is more circumscribed, in that it excludes some important cognitive skills that do not predict scholastic performance or other specific tasks and yet are important for survival within the culture. Thus, IQ, or Intelligence C, may not correspond to what members of the culture consider intelligent or unintelligent behavior or thinking.

In contemporary Western cultures, IQ tests are constructed to measure certain aspects of Intelligence B that are vital to solving problems associated with industrialization, bureaucracy, and urbanism. As a number of people have pointed out, the same cognitive skills sampled in IQ tests are emphasized in Western middle-class formal schooling; that is why the test scores correlate with school performance (Alland, 1973; Brookover & Erickson, 1965; Gartner & Riesman, 1974; Jensen, 1969; Kagan, 1973). IQ tests, then, are constructed to show how well children in Western cultures learn cognitive skills that will be required for their successful participation as adults in the technoeconomic and bureaucratic organization of their societies. If hunter-gatherers of the arctic or tropical forest environment, with their different sociocultural and technoeconomic adaptation, were to construct an intelligence test, they would probably include psychological tasks that would measure those cognitive skills and strategies required for effective adaptation to their own environment, rather than tasks that tap the cognitive skills functional in contemporay Western corporate economy, bureaucratic, and urban culture. According to LeVine (1970), in a non-Western culture, Western IQ tests tend to measure mainly those cognitive skills that enable members of the culture to participate effectively in Western schools and technology; they do not measure the cognitive skills and strategies that people have developed in order to cope effectively with their own traditional environment.

To what extent is Intelligence C (i.e., IQ) an index of Intelligence A (i.e., genetic equipment)? That is, to what extent is IQ determined by heredity? There seems to be no empirical evidence for any precise answer to this question. What is observed in everyday life (Intelligence B) and in IQ test scores (Intelligence C) is the phenotype, not the genotype (Vernon 1969). And no one has been able to show that particular genes determine particular cognitive skills. For, as Alland (1973) points out, "Divergent behavioral phenotypes could emerge from the same basic genotype through environmental shaping just as similar phenotypes could arise from different genotypes conditioned in different ways" (p. 176).

The distinction here is different from that of Jensen in his latest book (Jensen 1980). He follows both Hebb (1949) and Vernon (1969) in his definition of Intelligence A as the genetic potential — the genotype that cannot be measured; but he rejects Vernon's definition of Intelligence B as a cultural phenomenon shared by members of a given population, a definition that we adopted in this chapter. Jensen, on the contrary, defines Intelligence B psychometrically, as an attribute of the individual:

> Intelligence B is best regarded as an average of many measures over a limited period of time, so as to average out momentary and idiosyncratic features of specific tests and situations. Intelligence B is the individual's general intelligence, not his performance in any specific situation of his score on any particular test (p. 184).

In other words, Intelligence B is "the general factor common to all test scores" of an individual; Intelligence C (i.e, IQ), on the other hand, "is the individual's score on a specific test" (p. 185). In Jensen's distinction, neither technoeconomic activities nor formal education affects people's cognitive skills. His view is certainly contradicted by cross-cultural research that repeatedly shows the influences of both on cognitive skills (Cole & Scribner, 1974; Greenfield, 1966).

These activities certainly are important in shaping the cognitive skills of members of a given cullture or society. The question is, however, how do they affect the cognitive skills of two populations co-existing in the same society in a kind of castelike stratification? Specifically, what is the nature of the technoeconomic and other adult tasks open to castelike minorities, and what is their impact on the latter's cognitive repertoire? What is the nature of the formal education of the minorities, and what is its impact on their cognitive skills? Are the cognitive skills sampled by IQ tests the same as those required and enhanced by the caste-determined activities (e.g., jobs and education) of the castelike minorities?

The Consequences of Caste Stratification

Status Summation, Job Ceiling, and Jensen's Level 2 Intelligence.   The restricted opportunity structure that confined blacks to menial jobs and comparable sociopolitical positions obviously ensured that generations of blacks developed certain instrumental competencies, including the cognitive skills required for such menial positions. At the same time their exclusion from high-status, more desirable, white middle-class jobs and positions meant that they did not participate in activities that require and stimulate the cognitive competencies associated with such activities. A close examination reveals that Jensen's level 2 intelligence is made up of cognitive skills typically required by high-status, white middle-class jobs and sociopolitical positions, especially jobs above the job ceiling. Jensen's level 1 intelligence appears to consist of cognitive skills associated primarily with menial jobs below the job ceiling, to which most blacks have historically been relegated. This interpretation is supported by Vernon's (1969) suggestion that the contemporary Western middle class developed its distinctive cognitive skills (i.e., conceptual skills, abstract thinking, problem-solving skills) through its involvement in activities above the job ceiling, such as scientific analysis, scientific control and exploitation of the physical environment, and large-scale and long-range planning and implementation of economic and other programs. It is also supported by Baumrind's (1977) suggestion that the white middle class developed its analytical intelligence in the course of its involvement in the capitalist mode of production, which requires and promotes such analytic intelligence. If it is true, as Jensen has said, that black children do less well than white children mainly in that portion of the IQ tests requiring level 2 intelligence, then the reason is probably that blacks were for centuries not given equal opportunity with whites to participate in activities that required and promoted level 2 intelligence. From this standpoint, Jensen and like-minded psychologists cannot argue that the lower test scores are due to genetic differences.

The environmentalists also seem to err in suggesting that blacks, particularly inner-city blacks, do less well in these tests involving operative intelligence (which corresponds roughly to Jensen's level 2) because of the failure of black parents to use the childrearing practices of the white middle class parents (Connolly & Bruner, 1974). The white middle class did not become managers of modern technology and corporate economy *after* white middle-class parents had learned the correct methods of childrearing that inculcated operative intelligence in their children. Rather, white people probably developed this operative intelligence after they had gained the opportunity to work at managerial and other positions above the job ceiling in modern techno-economic system. As we have suggested elsewhere (Ogbu, 1981), the development of appropriate cognitive competencies for managing modern economy and technology must have gone hand in hand with the development of appropriate techniques of childrearing to inculcate the functional cognitive skills. Given the same opportunity as whites, blacks probably would have developed the same operative intelligence and similar techniques of childrearing as whites.

But operative intelligence or level 2 intelligence can also be found in activities other than conventional jobs above the job ceiling in modern corporate economy. For example, pimps and hustlers in the inner-city, among others, appear to possess white middle-class types of operative intelligence, which they apply to the management of an underground or street economy. Yet hustlers, pimps, and other "smart" people in the inner-city may not have done well in school and were probably dropouts. They are probably the people who, Jensen says, behave outside the test situations more intelligently than their test scores would suggest. In other words, black children who are as smart as white children may not necessarily do as well as their white peers on the standardized tests or in school. Why? We cannot adequately explain this apparent discrepancy until we have studied black epistemology, an area in which there is currently a dearth of knowledge.

Inferior Education and the Lower Test Scores.   We suggest that generations of inferior education also affect the black cognitive repertoire. As is shown in the next section, "black schools" in the South and in the inner-cities of the North have not usually emphasized academic curriculum as "white schools" did. Specifically, the schools have not encouraged blacks to develop white middle-class cognitive skills, problem-solving skills, and the like (Leacock, 1969; Moore, 1967).

The Consequences of Caste: Black Epistemology

How blacks perceive and respond to intelligence testing may also play a significant role in lowering their test scores. Elsewhere we have suggested that the job ceiling and education-related discriminatory treatment tend to disillusion blacks about the real worth of schooling (Ogbu, 1978). This disillusionment, in turn, prevents them from developing "effort optimism," or perseverance to maximize their performance at school and on IQ tests as a cultural norm. This is treated more fully in the next section. Furthermore, blacks have a cultural interpretation of the intelligence testing phenomenon that is not fully understood but which may play an important role in their response to these tests.

In summary, the lower test scores of black children on intelligence tests, especially with respect to level 2 intelligence, appear to be due partly to three related factors: (1) the castelike system's long denial to blacks of adequate access to desirable jobs and other societal positions and activities that require and promote white middle-class types of cognitive skills; (2) black disillusionment because of the job ceiling and related factors, which has not encouraged them to develop a cultural norm of maximizing their test scores; and (3) the symbolic meaning of intelligence tests, which may have a negative influence on blacks' approach to these tests.

CASTELIKE MINORITY STATUS AND SCHOOL PERFORMANCE

Cultural-Ecological Context of Schooling

In contemporary United States and other societies, formal education is usually structured on the common sense idea of training in marketable skills. The labor market largely determines the training that children receive in school.

In addition, schools teach children the beliefs, values, and attitudes that support the economic and sociopolitical systems (Spindler, 1974). At the end of training, schools certify or credential the children for entry into and renumeration in the labor force (Jencks, 1972). However, what makes children succeed in learning and demonstrating what schools teach them is not merely the type of genes they bring to school, the type of homes or environment they come from, or their cultural, language, interactional or cognitive styles. It is, instead, a combination of two factors: the diligence with which schools teach the children (see Edmonds, Chapter 4); and how the students perceive and respond to schooling. To understand the school behavior of a given population, it is necessary to study what schools do or do not do, as well as how the client population perceives and respond to schooling and on what epistemological basis.

Focusing on the client population, our comparative studies (Ogbu, 1974, 1978) suggest that children respond positively to schooling IF they observe that older people in their community usually obtain jobs, wages, and other societal benefits commensurate with their level of schooling. Children are also likely to respond positively to schooling if their community develops a shared knowledge and folklore that support such observations or perceptions. Where available options (i.e., the mainstream type of labor market elsewhere) require educational credentials, children also are likely to respond positively to schooling. Positive response means that children accept and internalize the beliefs, values, and attitudes supporting the economic and sociopolitical systems or institutions taught by schools; that they make serious efforts to learn the basic and practical skills schools teach; and that they strive consciously or unconsciously to develop the qualities they need to be successful in the labor force.

Some economists have used these ideas to formulate what they call a theory of education as an investment in human capital. The investors are both society and the individual. Focusing on the individual component, the theory states that what a person invests in education are the actual expenses incurred as school fees, supplies, transportation and the like, plus the wages that would have been earned had the person been in the labor force instead of attending school. This investment is made because a reasonable profit or "return" is expected later, in postschool adult life. The benefits or profits one expects are one's total earnings, due to education or due to additional years of schooling, minus the costs of the education or investment. It is said that, in the United States, a high school graduate can expect to earn 20% more than a person with only an elementary school education. A college graduate can expect earnings about 15% higher than those of a high school graduate. Proponents of the human capital theory say that people use these calculationns to decide whether "it pays" to get additional schooling (Blair, 1971; Blaug, 1970; Doire, 1976; Harrison, 1972; Schultz, 1961; Weisbrod, 1975).

We suggest that high rates of return for individual members of a society or its segment translate eventually to a high rate of return for the society or for its segment. And such a favorable group experience leads to favorable group perceptions of schooling and to the development of culturally sanctioned instrumental attitudes and behaviors that enhance academic efforts and group success. In such a population, parents and other childrearing agents would tend to transmit these attitudes and behaviors to children and also see to it that the children behave as expected (LeVine, et al., 1967; Ogbu, 1981a). Moreover, children in such a community would learn from both direct and indirect teaching in the home, community and school to form appropriate ideas or cognitive maps about how their society works, especially about its status mobility system or how to get ahead, and the place of schooling within it. Where schooling facilitates getting ahead, children learn and believe that school success, which leads to success in adult life, requires some conformity to school requirements and expectations. That is, their expectations and behaviors tend to complement those of the schools. In the terminology of cultural ecology, schooling is a part of the effective environment of the population.

The Consequences of Caste: Inferior Education

Under structured inequality, particularly castelike stratification, a number of new elements emerge that affect both what schools do to the minority clients and how the latter respond to schooling. For example, the educational pattern is no longer determined chiefly by the requirements of the economic system, such as competencies required by work roles and credential systems. Instead, the kind of education offered to minorities depends on the epistemology of the dominant group. That is, how the dominant group interprets the working of the system or social reality and the place of the minorities within it determines the education offered to minorities. Dominant group epistemology depends on the degree of job ceiling and other forms of subordination of the minorities.

Prevailing levels of job ceiling and other forms of domination, including unequal power relations or share in decision making, shape the dominant group's view of the minority's place in society, including the minority's economic role and how its members get ahead or should get ahead. This dominant group's epistemology determines how minority education is designed, how much and what kind of access the minorities have to formal education, whether the minorities should attend the same schools as the dominant group (integrated/desegregated schools) or whether they should attend separate (segregated) schools, and how the minorities should be treated in school.

It is well known that blacks have been given inferior education throughout the history of the public schools all over the nation. For example, for many decades black children in the South were provided mainly with an "industrial" education, whereas white children were given an academic education. The former was chiefly training in manual skills to prepare the children for manual labor (Bond, 1966; Bullock, 1970; Harlan, 1968). A study for the U.S. Commission on Civil Rights (Sexton, 1968) found that in the 1961–1962 academic year the Chicago school system spent almost 25% more money per pupil in white schools than in black schools, that teacher salaries were almost 18% higher in the white schools, and that "nonteaching operating expenses — clerical and maintenance, salaries, supplies, and textbooks — were 50% higher in the white schools" (p. 228). White schools had an average of 30.95 pupils per classroom; black schools had an average of 46.8 pupils per classroom. The education committee of NAACP in San Francisco found similar differences between white and minority schools in the city in the second half of the 1960s, findings that contributed to the court order that the city should desegregate its schools. The same kind of differences have been found in other major cities across the nation, including Washington, DC (Hughes & Hughes, 1973). One common subtle technique now used by school systems that results in inferior education for blacks is the channelling of black children into special education classes for the mentally retarded and channelling of white children into special education classes for the gifted (Kirp, 1976; U.S. District Court for Northern California, *Opinion*, 1979).

Inferior education contributes to lower school performance. For example, children whose school does not stress academic curriculum do not do as well on academic tests as children whose school focuses on an academic curriculum. Furthermore, it is unlikely that children who are not taught diligently will have the competitive advantage of others where teaching is taken more seriously (see Edmonds, this volume). Finally, where the caste system has a tradition of providing blacks with inferior education, inferior performance may develop as a norm.

Consequences of Caste Stratification: Lower Economic Benefits for Black Education

Not only does American society provide blacks with inferior education, which contributes to inferior performance, but blacks also receive fewer economic and other rewards in the form of employment status, level and type of employment, and wages. This experience also contributes to lower school performance.

Education and Employment.   A number of investigators have reported that, with any level of education, blacks have more difficulty getting jobs than do their white peers. Furthermore, until recently, the black unemployment rate relative to the white unemployment rate tended to increase as the

level of education increased. That is, the gap in unemployment between blacks and whites was widest at the highest level of education, as the following table shows for 1964 (see Broom & Glenn, 1967; Killingsworth, 1967, 1969; Ross, 1967).
A more recent study for the U.S. Commission on Civil Rights shows that this problem still persists (U.S. Commission on Civil Rights, 1978).

Overqualification for Accessible Jobs.   Another way to measure the rewards that American society accords to blacks for their educational accomplishments, or the rate of return for the investment blacks make in their education, is to examine the extent to which the jobs blacks hold are commensurate with their eduational qualifications. Research (U.S. Commission on Civil Rights, 1978; see also Newman et al., 1978) suggests that, although Americans in general tend to be overqualified for their jobs, overqualification is most acute among blacks, particularly black males. Black male high school graduates are the most overqualified for their jobs, and black male college graduates are second only to Filippinos as holders of jobs for which they are overqualified. Black female high school graduates are also highly overqualified for their jobs. The problem of overqualification was visibly demonstrated in 1960, when 75% more black than white high school

TABLE 2.2
Reported Unemployment Rates of the Male Civilian Labor Force, 18 Years and Over, by Years of School Completed and Color, March, 1964

Years of School Completed	Unemployment Rates		Ratio Nonwhite/White
	White	Nonwhite	
TOTAL	4.7	9.4	200
Elementary School			
0–4 years	10.4	7.7	74
5–7 years	7.1	10.5	148
8 years	6.5	10.6	163
High School			
1–3 years	5.9	11.3	192
4 years	3.8	8.7	229
College			
1–3 years	3.6	7.3	203
4 years	1.3	4.3	331

Note: From Killingsworth, 1967, p. 214.

graduate males were overqualified for their jobs. In 1970 and 1976, the rate of overqualification for black males was 76% and 52% respectively. Among college graduates, the black overqualification rate was 38%, 26% and 23% higher than for white males in 1960, 1970 and 1976 respectively.

Education and Unequal Earnings.   Blacks also earn lower wages than their white peers with comparable education. This is illustrated by the U.S. Commission on Civil Rights Study (1978) of the nationwide situation in 1959, 1969 and 1975. For those years, blacks with four or more years of college education earned 66%, 73% and 81% respectively of the average earned by their white peers with the same educational attainment. Published studies of earning differentials in specific localities are rare. However, a study of the experience of Mexican Americans in Santa Clara County, California, another castelike minority group, illustrates the problem. Blair (1971, 1972) compared Mexican Americans with Anglo Americans living in the barrios as well as Mexican Americans with Anglo Americans living outside the barrios. He found that among those living in the barrios, on the average, the annual earnings of Mexican Americans were $880 less than those of their Anglo-American peers with the same level of education. Among those living outside the barrios Mexican Americans, on the average, earned $1713 annually less than their Anglo-American peers with the same level of education. Perhaps more significant is that the earning gap between Mexican-American and Anglo-American school dropouts was less than among high school graduates.

In our own study in Stockton, CA (Ogbu, 1977), we also found differences in the financial return on educational investment for blacks and whites. For 10 of 13 census tracts in the city for which data were available by race in 1969, the median years of schooling was higher for blacks than for whites; but in 7 of these 10 tracts, blacks had substantially lower median family income. In the other 3 of the 10 census tracts, where they had more schooling, blacks had only slightly higher income. In only 1 of the 13 census tracts was income slightly higher for blacks although they had less education. This was because many black business people, such as morticians, beauticians, and builders who served other blacks, lived here. These occupations do not necessarily require much education.

Change in Opportunity Structure

Wilson (1978) reports that this situation just described has been changing since the 1960s. As a result of Civil Rights Act of 1964 and an affirmative action policy encouraged by the federal government, college-educated young blacks are increasingly finding jobs and earning wages both comparable to their white peers and commensurate with their schooling. So dramatic is the change in opportunity structure for young blacks that, according to Brimmer (1974), between 1960 and 1970 the number of blacks in the top-level occupational category rose by 128%, although the increase for the general population was only 49%. In the second highest occupational category, the increase for blacks was 100% but only 23% for the general population. Wilson (1979) further reports that college-educated young blacks have not only achieved employment opportunities equal with college-educated young whites, they have also achieved income parity. In fact, he reports that collge-educated black females earn nearly $1000 more annually than their white peers.

There are two items of note about these reported changes. One is that the dominant group controls the rates of return for black investment in education. In 1964, when the greatest difference between blacks and whites in unemployment rate was among college graduates. Killingsworth (1967, 1969) could rationalize the discrepancy on the grounds that black college graduates were younger than white college graduates, that blacks did not come from family backgrounds that equipped them with appropriate manner of speech, mode of dress, deportment, etc.) and that they had inferior education. It is significant that after the passage of the Civil Rights Act of 1964 and the introduction of affirmative action policies, suddenly youthfulness and family background were no longer a hindrance to the employability of college-educated blacks. On the contrary, college-educated young blacks became a highly-priced commodity in the labor market. For example, Freeman (1976, cited in Wilson, 1979) reports that the average number of representatives of American corporations on recruitment visits to predominantly black colleges rose from 4 in 1960, to 50 in 1965, to 297 in 1970. Significantly, black colleges that had not been visited at all in 1960, such as Clark College, Atlanta University, and Southern University, received 350, 510, and 600 corporation representatives respectively in 1970.

The second item of note—the more important—is that these positive and dramatic changes in black opportunity structures have affected mainly middle-class blacks, especially college-educated young blacks. The situation of lower-class blacks, especially inner-city blacks, remains relatively unchanged and in some cases has gotten worse. This segment of the black population has not been the target of corporate or other recruitment drives, nore has there been a strong affirmative action policy directed toward their employment. Of course, during the Vietnam War and under the social programs in the 1960s, when there was an overall increase in the pool of jobs, there was an increase in black employment at all levels of the job ladder. In the early 1970s, the pool of jobs decreased as a result of economic recession. This not only slowed down the employment of noncollege-educated blacks, but it also caused many already employed blacks to lose their jobs partly because they were the last hired and hence the first to be fired. This loss of jobs by the noncollege educated, inner-city blacks, has continued into the 1980s. For this segment of the black population, investment in education continues to bring marginal returns (Newman et al. 1978; Ogbu 1978; Willie, 1979; Wilson, 1979).

Consequences of Caste: Black Epistemology and Responses

The phenomena of inferior education and inadequate opportunity for self-advancement — status summation and job ceiling — very much shape the way blacks see American society and its institutions, i.e., their view of social realities. Black epistemology as it developed under this circumstance was described in our earlier discussion of the cognitive orientation that emphasizes the collective institutional discrimination perspective. In this section, we focus more closely on black responses to the inferior education and the limited postschool opportunities generated by this perspective and show how such responses may contribute to poorer school performance and lower test scores. It is probably partly because these responses arise from black experiences under the caste system that black children, unlike other nonmainstream children whose cultures differ from the culture of the white middle class, appear to be turned off by the educational process. It is also probably because of these responses that black children who are as "smart" or as "intelligent" as white children do not do as well as the latter in IQ test scores and in academic work generally. While the responses do not affect blacks uniformly, they are collective, historical, and structural and thus may be said to be cultural. They are not simply manifestations of individual maladaptation. The way they affect test performance and academic pursuit is often indirect, subtle, and unconscious but nonetheless significant. What are these responses and how do they affect black performance?

Disillusionment and Lack of Effort Optimism.   One response to the job ceiling is disillusionment about the real value of schooling, tests, and related matters. This disillusionment appears to have discouraged blacks from developing a tradition of serious attitudes toward and persevering efforts in academic tasks and test taking. Our own ethnographic studies in Stockton, CA, (Ogbu, 1974) suggest that one reason black children, especially older inner-city children, do poorly in various tests is that they do not bring to the test situation serious attitudes and do not persevere to maximize their scores, because they are disillusioned about the job ceiling.

It should be stressed that, although blacks desire education as much as whites do, blacks feel they have to work twice as hard as whites for the same rewards. Perhaps partly for this reason they have reduced their academic efforts, even though they still believe in the overall value of education. This apparent reduction in academic efforts is not necessarily conscious, but rather may be an adaptive response to a history of unequal and inadequate rewards for their educational efforts.

Both Blair (1971) and Shack (1970) have pointed out that the caste system sends different messages about the relationship between schooling efforts and postschool rewards to white and castelike minority children by rewarding adult members of the two communities differently for their educational achievements. These different messages cause the two groups of children to adjust differently to school and to respond differently to the beliefs, values, and attitudes that schools teach them. In regard to the wage gap between Mexican-Americans and Anglos being smaller for school dropouts and larger for school graduates, Blair says that the message to the Anglo student is consistent with the American ideology that hard work in school and more education lead to greater self-improvement. To the castelike minority student, the message is that remaining in school long enough and working hard enough to obtain a high school or college credential can only increase the wage gap between him and his Anglo peer, to the minority student's disadvantage.

Shack's analysis is particulaly germane to our discussion because he deals with the problem historically. He aptly captures the evolution of the disillusionment and lack of persevering academic efforts among black children. He does this by comparing the factors that underlie the differential attitudes of blacks and whites. He notes that the absence of a job ceiling for whites has enabled them to receive adequate payoffs for their educational efforts and suggests that this experience has probably helped them to develop "effort optimism" toward work and education. That is, because white people have traditionally received social and economic rewards proportionate to their educational efforts, they have tended to develop the maxim: "If at first you don't succeed, try, try, again." The contrary experience of blacks, Shack points out, has taught them that social and economic rewards are not proportionate to their educational efforts; consequently, they have tended to develop a different maxim: "What's the use of trying?" (See also Dollard, 1957; Frazier, 1940; Ogbu, 1974; Ransom & Sutch, 1977; Schulz, 1969).

It is in this context that one begins to understand why the children studied in Stockton were not particularly worried by their poor performance. Many of them appeared to have learned to blame the system for their low test scores and school failures, just as local adult blacks blamed the system for their social and economic problems. However, we emphasize that the children did not learn this discouraging message from explicit or deliberate teachings of their parents. Rather, it is the actual texture of parents' lives that comes through strongly, producing a message powerful enough to undercut parents' own exhortations that their children should work hard to succeed in school.

Survival Strategies and Incongruent Competencies.   Test scores are affected also by the response to the job ceiling that results in the development of survival strategies, or alternative means of achieving subsistence and self-advancement. Among these are *collective struggle* or "civil rights" struggle, *clientship* or "Uncle Tomming," and *hustling*. The attitudes, knowledge, skills, and rules of behavior for achievement fostered by these survival strategies often are not compatible with those required to do well in school or to do well on IQ tests. For example, collective struggle teaches black children not to accept personal responsibility for failure but to "blame the system." Clientship teaches them that societal rewards (including getting good jobs, wages, and promotions) do not depend on personal efforts advocated by the dominant group or on following the rules of behavior for achievement that work for whites, such as obtaining school credentials; rather, access to good jobs, wages, and promotion depends on white patronage, which can be won by being dependent, compliant, and manipulative. Hustling teaches that one can and should succeed, or "make it," without working, without following the conventional work ethic, and without being employed by white people; instead, one should be smart enough to invest one's efforts and know-how in exploiting and manipulating others for the desired goods and position. These survival strategies are a part of "black culture" learned by children in varying degrees from preschool years on. Children who enter school with some degree of competence in the survival strategies are likely to perform poorly in school and on IQ tests; and as the children get older and become more competent in the survival strategies, their academic and other difficulties increase.

Conflict and Distrust.   A third response to the job ceiling is hostility and distrust toward the public schools, which has grown out of a long history of unpleasant experiences with the school and with white society in general. Throughout the history of public education in America, blacks have learned to perceive their frequent exclusion and discrimination as designed to prevent them from qualifying for the more desirable jobs open to whites. Consequently, the thrust of the black collective struggle has been to force whites and the schools to provide them with equal education; the thrust has not been to work cooperatively with the schools to maximize the academic accomplishments of black students.

Initially the struggle of the blacks was against total exclusion from the public schools. For over a century they have fought against inferior education in both segregated and integrated schools. The segregated schools blacks attend are theoretically black schools, so that one might expect blacks to identify and work with such schools. However, such identification and cooperation of blacks have often been undermined by simultaneous perceptions of segregated schools as being inferior to white schools. Consequently, attention and efforts have been diverted toward integration and equalization of education.

There is a widespread feeling that the public schools cannot be trusted to educate black children because of their gross and subtle mechanisms of discrimination. These conflicts also force the schools to treat blacks defensively, to resort to various forms of control, paternalism, or contest. The schools' responses, too, divert efforts from educating black children. These observations, which can be documented in many American cities, suggest that black-school relations, riddled with conflicts and suspicion, make it difficult for blacks to accept and internalize the schools' goals, standards, and teaching and learning approaches, and that this situation contributes to test and school performance lag of black children. Specifically, this situation makes it difficult for black children to persevere and maximize their performance in test and academic situations.

Cultural Inversion.   A fourth response is what Holt (1972) calls *cultural inversion* and what we have elsewhere (Ogbu, in press), called a *secondary cultural difference*. Briefly, cultural inversion may be defined as a tendency to regard a cultural behavior, event, entity of meaning as *not* black because it is characteristic of whites or vice-versa. For example, a style of walking, talking, dressing, interacting, or religious workship among blacks is defined largely *in opposition* to the white style of walking, talking, dressing, interacting, and workship. In her discussion of the inversion phenomenon in black communication and language, Holt (1972) notes that the inversion consists of speech devices that permit blacks verbally to repudiate white stereotypes of blacks, to turn the tables against whites, or to manipulate whites.

Cultural inversion is manifested in education in the tendency of some black children to regard as "white" academic tasks and certain extracurricular activities that are therefore not for blacks. Thus, in school blacks tend to regard athletics as a legitimate and appropriate extracurricular activity for themselves, and they praise black students who excel in these activities. On the other hand, black students who excel in academic work or are involved in conventional political and cultural activities are condemned as acting white, as being "Uncle Toms."

A study reported by Petroni (1970) illustrates how this phenomenon may affect the test scores and school performance of black children. Petroni found that black high school students complained that their exclusion from certain activities was due to white prejudice; at the same time, blacks who successfully entered collge-prepatory classes, student government, madrigals, the senior play, and similar activities were generally condemned as "Uncle Toms" and thus were unacceptable. Here is one of many cases of individual experiences he described in the report: One young man, with As in all his courses, as well as active in speech and debating activities, told the researcher:

Well, I participate in speech. I'm the only Negro in the whole group. I find it kind of interesting that I'm the only Negro. I'm always contrasted in pictures of the group. The Negroes accuse me of thinking I'm white. In the bathroom one day, some Negroes wrote in big letters "B.B. is an Uncle Tom." It's this kind of pressure from other Negro kids which bothers me most. (p. 262)

Petroni aptly suggests from the cases he studied that the fear of being called an "Uncle Tom" or of being accused of "acting white" may prevent black children from making the efforts necessary to do well in school. Our own data from Stockton support this idea; some black and Chicano students in Stockton told us that doing well in school was "doing the whiteman thing" or "acting white."

In summary, these responses — disillusionment, survival strategies, distrust, and cultural inversion — are logical within the context of the caste system. But they work independently and cojointly to inhibit the development of a strong tradition or orientation toward academic or intellectual pursuits, especially among inner-city blacks.

CONCLUSION

The performance of Black-Americans on IQ and other tests is not a true reflection of their intellectual ability or knowledge. It also is not evidence that black parents have failed to raise their children as white middle-class parents raise their children. Nor is it due merely to differences between blacks and whites in selected cultural traits. Rather, as we have tried to suggest in this chapter, it is the product of black subordination in the caste system; it is partly the result of generations of lack of opportunity for blacks to participate in activities that require and promote certain cognitive and other attributes that, in turn, facilitate higher test performance and school success; it is also the result of certain responses blacks have made to their treatment under the caste system treatment that makes it difficult for blacks "as smart" or "as intelligent" as whites to perform as well as their white peers.

ACKNOWLEDGMENT

Research for this paper was supported by faculty research fund, University of California, Berkeley, and by NIE grant, G-80-0045. The writing of the paper was supported by the Wisconsin Center for Education Research (University of Wisconsin, Madison) which is supported in part by a grant from the National Institute of Education (Grant No. NIE-G-81-009). I am grateful for the support of these institutions. However, opinions expressed in the paper are solely mine.

REFERENCES

Aberle, D. F. (1962). Culture and socialization. In F. L. K. Hsu (Ed.), *Psychological anthropology*. Evanston, IL: Dorsey Press.

Ackerman, W. (1973). "Reforming Israeli education." In M. Curtis & M. Chertoff (Eds.), *Israel: Social structure and change*. New Brunswick, NJ: Dutton.

Acuna, R. (1972). *Occupied America*. San Francisco: Canfield Press.

Adler, C. (1970). The Israeli school as a selective institution. In S. N. Eisenstadt, R. B. Yosef, & C. Adler (Eds.), *Integration and development in Israel*. New York: Praeger.

Alland, A. (1973). *Human diversity*. Garden City, NY: Doubleday.

Ausubel, D. (1961). *Maori youth: A psychoethnological study of cultural deprivation*. New York: Holt, Rinehart & Winston.

Avineri, S. (1973). Israel: Two nations? In M. Curtis & M. Chertoff (Eds.), *Israel: Social structure and change*. New Brunswick, NJ: Dutton.

Barry, H. 11, Child, I. L. & Bacon, M. I. (1959). Relation of childtraining to subsistence economy. *American Anthropologist, 61*, 51–63.

Baumrind, Diana (1977). "Subcultural Variations in Values Defining Social Competence: An Outsider's Perspective on the Black Subculture." *Journal of Social Issues*, Vol.

Berreman G. D. (1972). Race, caste, and other invidious distinctions in social stratification. *Race, 13*(4), 385–414.

Berreman, G. D. (1967). Caste in cross-cultural perspective: Organizational components. In G. A. DeVos & H. Wagatsuma (Eds.), *Japan's invisible race*. Berkeley: University of California Press.

Berreman, G. D. (1960). Caste in India and the United States. *The American Journal of Sociology, 66*, 120–127.

Berry, J. W. (1971). Ecological and cultural factors in spatial perceptual development. *Canadian Journal of Behavioral Science Review, 3*(4), 324–337.

Beteille, A. (Ed.) (1969). *Castes: old and new*. New York: Asian Publishing House.

Blair, P. M. (1972). Job discrimination and education: Rates of return to education of Mexican-Americans and Euro-Americans in Santa Clara County, California. In M. Carnoy (Ed.), *Schooling in a corporate society: The political economy of education in America* New York: David McKay.

Blair, P. H. (1971). *Job discrimination and education: An investment analysis*. New York: Praeger.

Blaug, M. (1970). *An Introduction to the Economics of Education*. Baltimore, Md: Penguin Books.

Bloom, B. S., Davis, A., & Hess, R. (1965). *Compensatory education for cultural deprivation*. New York: Holt, Rinehart & Winston.

Bond, H. M. (1966). *The education of the negro in the American social order*. New York: Octagon.

Boyce, C. M. (1983). *Black proficiency in abstract reasoning: A test of Jensen's two-level theory*. Doctoral Dissertation: Cornell University.

Boykin, A. W. (1980). *Reading achievement and the social cultural frame of reference of Afro American Children*. Paper presented at NIE Roundtable Discussion on Issues in Urban Reading, Washington, DC.

Brimmer, A. F. (1974). Economic development in the black community. In E. Ginzberg, & R. M. Solow (Eds.), *The great society: Lessons for the future*. New York: Basic Books.

Brookover, W. B. & Erickson, E. L. (1965). *Society, schools and learning*. Boston: Allyn & Bacon.

Broom, L. & Glen, N. (1967). *Transformation of the negro American*. New York: Harper & Row.

Bullock, H. A. (1970). *A history of negro education in the south: From 1619 to the present.* New York: Praeger.

Burt, C. (1969). Intelligence and heredity. *New Scientist, 1,* 226–228.

Chauhan, B. R. (1967). Special problems of the education of the scheduled castes. In S. M. Gore & I. P. Desai (Eds.), *Papers in the sociology of education in India.* New Delhi: National Council of Educational Research and Training.

Chopra, S. L. (1966). Relationship of caste system with measured intelligence and academic achievement of students in India. *Social Forces 44,* 573–576.

Ciborowski, T. (1976). Culture and cognitive discontinuities of school and home: Remedialism revisited. In G. E. Kearney & D. W. McElwain (Eds.), *Aboriginal cognition: Retrospect and prospect.* Jersey City, NJ: The Humanities Press.

Cohen, Y. A. (1971). The shaping of men's minds: Adaptations to the imperatives of culture. In M. L. Wax, S. Diamond, & F. O. Gearing (Eds.), *Anthropological perspectives on education.* New York: Basic Books.

Cole, M., Gay, J., Glick, J. A., & Sharp, D. W. (1971). *The cultural context of learning and thinking: An exploration in experimental anthropology.* New York: Basic Books.

Cole, M., & Scribner, S. (1973). Cognitive consequences of formal and informal education. *Science, 182,* 553–9.

Cole, M., & Scribner, S. (1974). *Culture and Thought: A Psychological Introduction.* New York: Wiley.

Connolly, K. J. & Bruner, J. S. (1974). Introduction. In K. J. Connolly & J. S. Bruner (Eds.). *The growth of competence.* London: Academic Press.

Dasen, P. (Ed.) (1977). *Piagetian psychology: Cross-cultural contributions.* New York: Gardner Press.

Denenberg, V. H. (1970). *Education of the infant and young child.* New York: Academic Press.

DeVos, George A. (1973). Japan's outcastes: The problem of the Burakumin. In B. Whitaker (Ed.), *The Fourth World: Victims of Group Oppression.* New York: Schocken Books.

DeVos, G. A., & Wagatsuma, H. (Eds.) (1967). *Japan's invisible race.* Berkeley: University of California Press.

Dollard, J. (1957). *Caste and class in a southern town,* 3rd ed. Garden City, NY: Doubleday.

Dore, R. P. (1976). *The diploma disease.* Berkeley: University of California Press.

Dorfman, D. D. (1978). The Cyril Burt question: New findings. *Science, 201,* 1177–1186.

Eells, K., Davis, A., Havighurst, R. J., Herrick, V. E., & Tyler, R. W. (1952). *Intelligence and cultural differences: A study of cultural learning and problem-solving.* Chicago: University of Chicago Press.

Frazier, E. (1940). *Negro youth at the crossways: Their personality development in the middle states.* Washington, D.C.: American Council on Education.

Freeman, R. B. (1976). *Black elite: The new market for highly educated black americans.* New York: McGraw-Hill.

Gartner, A., & Riessman, F. (1973). The lingering infatuation with I.Q.: A review of Arthur Jensen' *"Educability and group differences."* Unpublished manuscript.

Garrett, H. E. (1971). *Heredity: The cause of racial differences in intelligence.* Kilmarnock, VA: Patrick Henry Press.

Gay, J., & Cole, M. (1967). *The new mathematics and an old culture: A study of learning among the Kpelle of Liberia.* New York: Holt, Rinehart & Winston.

Gillie, Oliver (1979). "Burt's Missing Ladies." *Science* 204:1035–37.

Goldberg, M. L. (1971). Socio-psychological issues in the education of the disadvantaged. In A. H. Passow (Ed.), *Urban education in the 1970s.* New York: Teachers College Press.

Greenfield, P. M. (1966). On culture and conservation. In J. S. Bruner, Oliver, R. R., & Greenfield, P. M. (Eds.), *Studies in cognitive growth.* New York: Wiley.

Hallpike, C. (1972). *The Konso of Ethiopia.* Oxford: Clarendon Press.

Harker, R. K. (1977). *Cognitive style, environment and school achievement.* Palmerston North, New Zealand: Massey University.

Harlan, L. R. (1968). *Separate and unequal.* New York: Atheneum.

Harrison, Bennett (1972). *Education, training and the urban ghetto.* Baltimore, MD: Johns Hopkins University Press.

Haskins, Ron (1980). *Race, family, income, and school achievement.* Unp. Ms.

Hawkes, N. (1979). Tracing Burt's descent to scientific fraud. *Science, 205* 673–75.

Haynes, J. (1971). *Educational assessment of immigrant pupils.* London: The National Foundation for Educational Research in England & Wales.

Hearnshaw, L. S. (1979). *Cyril Burt, psychologist.* Ithaca, NY: Cornell University Press.

Hebb, D. O. (1949). *The organization of behavior: A neuropsychological theory.* New York: Wiley.

Herrnstein, R. J. (1973). *I.Q. in the meritocracy.* Boston: Little, Brown.

Holt, G. S. (1972). "Stylin' outta the black pulpit." In T. Kochman (Ed.), *Rappin' and stylin' out: Communicating in urban black America.* Chicago: University of Illinois Press.

Houghton, V. P. (1966). Intelligence testing of West Indian and English children. *Race 8*(2), 147–156.

Hughes, J. F. & Hughes, A. O. (1973). *Equal education: A new national strategy.* Bloomington: Indiana University Press.

Humphreys, L. G. (1973). Statistical definition of test validity for minority groups. *Journal of Applied Psychology, 58*(1), 1–4.

Hunn, J. K. (1960). *Report on department of Maori Affairs.* Wellington, NZ: Department of Maori Affairs.

Hunt, J. McV. (1969). *The challenge of incompetence and poverty: Papers on the role of early education.* Urbana, IL: University of Illinois Press.

Ingle, D. J. (1970). Possible genetic bases of social problems: A reply to Ashley Montagu. *Midway, 10*, 105–121.

Ito, H. (1967). Japan's outcastes in the United States. In G. A. DeVos & H. Wagatsuma (Eds.), *Japan's invisible race.* Berkeley: University of California Press.

Jencks, C. (1972). *Inequality.* New York: Basic Books.

Jenkins, Y. L. (1982). *The relationship of playfulness and play style contexts to divergent thinking in pre-schoool, low-income Afro-American children.* Unpublished doctoral dissertation, University of California/Berkeley.

Jensen, A. R. (1969). How much can we boost IQ and scholastic achievement? *Harvard Educational Review, 39,* 1–123.

Jensen, A. R. (1972). *Senate Select Committee on Education, Statement of Dr. Arthur R. Jensen.* (February 24, 1972). Unpublished manuscript.

Jensen, A. R. (1980). *Bias in mental testing.* New York: Free Press.

Jones, V. C. (1981). *Cognitive style and the problem of low school achievement among urban black low SES students, grades, 2, 4, & 6.* Unpublished doctoral dissertation, University of California/Berkeley.

Kagan, J. (1973). What is intelligence? *Social Policy,* 88–94.

Killingsworth, C. C. (1967). Negroes in a changing labor market. In A. M. Ross & H. Hill (Eds.), *Employment, race, and poverty: A critical study of the disadvantaged status of Negro workers from 1865 to 1965.* New York: Harcourt, Brace & World.

Killingsworth, C. C. (1969). Jobs and income for negroes. In I. Katz & P. Gurin (Eds.), *Race and the social sciences: A survey from the perspectives of social psychology, education, political science, economics, and sociology.* New York: Basic Books.

Kirp, D. L. (1976). Race, politics, and the courts: School desegregation in San Francisco. *Harvard Educational Review, 46*(4), 572–611.

Kochman, T. (1982). *Black and white styles in conflict.* Chicago: University of Chicago Press.

Krausz, E. (1971). *Ethnic minorities in Britain*. London: MacGibson & Kee.

Leacock, E. B. (1969). *Teaching and learning in city schools*. New York: Basic Books.

LeVine, R. A. (1970). Cross-cultural study in child psychology. In P. Mussen (Ed.), *Carmichael's manual of child psychology*. (3rd ed., Vol. 2) (pp. 559–612). New York: Wiley.

LeVine, R. A., Klein, N. A., & Owens, C. R. (1967). Father-child relationship and changing lifestyles in Ibadan, Nigeria. In H. Miner (Ed.), *The city in modern Africa*. New York: Praeger.

Lewis, A. (1979). *Power, poverty and education: An ethnography of schooling in an Israeli town*. Forest Grove, OR: Turtledove Publishing Co.

Lewis, A. (1981). Minority education in Sharonia, Israel and Stockton, California: A comparative analysis. *Anthropology and Education Quarterly, 12*(1), 30–50.

Maquet, J. (1961). *The premise of inequality in Ruanda*. London: Oxford University Press.

Maquet, J. (1971). *Power and society in Africa*. New York: World University Library.

Matras, J. (1970). Some data on intergenerational occupational mobility in Israel. In S. N. Eisenstadt (Eds.), *Integration and development in Israel*. New York: Praeger.

Mead, M. (1939). *From the South Seas: Studies of adolescence and sex in primitive societies*. New York: William Morrow.

Metge, J. (1967). *The Maoris of New Zealand*. New York: The Humanities Press.

Miller, D. & Swanson, G. (1958). *The changing American parent*. New York: Wiley.

Moore, A. (1967). *Realities of urban classroom*. Garden City, NY: Doubleday.

Myrdal, G. (1944). *An American dilemma: The Negro problem and modern democracy*. New York: Harper.

Nadel, S. F. (1954). Caste and government in primitive society. *Journal of Anthropological Society of Bombay, 8*, 9–22.

Newman, D. K., Amidei, B. K. Carter, D. D., Kruvant, W. J., & Russell, J. S. (1978). *Protest, politics and prosperity: Black Americans and white institutions, 1940–1975*. New York: Pantheon Books.

Nyiti, R. M. (1982). The validity of "Cultural difference explanations" for cross-cultural variation in the rate of Piagetian cognitive development. In D. A. Wagner & H. W. Stevenson (Eds.), *Cultural perspectives on child development*. San Francisco, CA: W. H. Freeman.

Ogbu, J. U. (1974). *The next generation: An ethnography of education in an urban neighborhood*. New York: Academic Press.

Ogbu, J. U. (1977). Racial stratification and education: The case of Stockton, California. *ICRD Bulletin, 12*(3), 1–26.

Ogbu, J. U. (1978). *Minority education and caste: The American system in cross-cultural perspective*. New York: Academic Press.

Ogbu, J. U. (1979). Social stratification and socialization of competence. *Anthropology and Education Quarterly, 10*(1), 3–20.

Ogbu, J. U. (1981b). Education, clientage, and social mobility: Caste and social change in the United States and Nigeria. In G. D. Berreman (Ed.), *Social inequality: Comparative and developmental approaches*. New York: Academic Press.

Ogbdu, J. U. (1981a). Origins of human competence: A cultural-ecological perspective. *Child Development, 52*, 413–429.

Ogbu, J. U. (1982a). Equalization of educational opportunity and racial/ethnic inequality. In P. G. Altbach, R. F. Arnnove & G. P. Kelley (Eds.), *Comparative education*. New York: Macmillan.

Ogbu, J. U. (1982b). Cultural discontinuities and schooling. *Anthropology and Education Quarterly, 13*(4), 290–307.

Ogbu, J. U. (1982c). Socialization: A cultural ecological perspective. In K. Borman (Ed.), *The socialization of children in a changing society*. Hillsdale, NJ: Lawrence Erlbaum Publishers, pp. 251–265.

Oliver, D. (1976). *Education and community*. Berkeley, CA: MaCutchen.

Ortar, G. R. (1967). Educational achievements of primary school graduates in Israel as related to their socio-cultural background. *Comparative Education, 4,* 23–34.

Parliamentary Select Committee on Immigration and Race Relations, Sessions 1972–73. (1973). *Education, vol. 1: Report*. London: H.M.S.O.

Petroni, F. A. (1970). "Uncle Tom:" White stereotypes in the black movement." *Human Organization, 29*(4), 260–266.

Phillips, I. (1976). The Case of Sir Cyril Burt. *Science, 204*, 1377.

Price, J. (1967). A history of the outcaste: Untouchability in Japan. In G. A. DeVos & H. Wagatsuma (Eds.), *Japan's invisible race*. Berkeley: University of California Press.

Ransom, R. L. & Sutch, R. (1977). *One kind of freedom: The economic consequences of emancipation*. New York: Cambridge University Press.

Rees, H. E. (1968). *Deprivation and compensatory education: A consideration*. Boston: Houghton Mifflin.

Richter, D. (1980). Further consideration of caste in West Africa: The Senufo. *Africa, 50,* 37–54.

Ritchie, J. E. (1957). Some observations on Maori and Pakeha intelligence test performance. *Journal of the Polynesian Society, 66*(1) 351–356.

Rose, E. J. B. (1969). *Color and citizenship*. London: Oxford University Press.

Rosenfeld, E. (1973). *A strategy for prevention of developmental retardation among disadvantaged Israeli preschoolers*. (Research Report No. 175). Jerusalem: The Henrietta Szold Institute.

Ross, A. M. (1967). The Negro in the American economy. In A. M. Ross & H. Hill (Eds.), *Employment, race and poverty*. New York: Harcourt.

Schmidt, F. H. (1972). *Spanish surnamed employment in the southwest*. Washington, DC: U.S. Government Printing Office.

Schultz, T. W. (1961). Investment in human capital. *American Economic Review, 51*, 1–17.

Schulz, D. A. (1969). *Coming up black: Patterns of ghetto socialization*. Englewood Cliffs, NJ: Prentice-Hall.

Sennett, R. & Cobb, J. (1972). *The hidden injuries of class*. New York: Random House.

Sexton, P. C. (1968). Schools: Broken ladder to success. In L. A. Ferman, et al. (Eds.), *Negroes and jobs*. Ann Arbor, MI: University of Michigan Press.

Shack, W. A. (1970). *On black American values in white America: Some perspectives on the cultural aspects of learning behavior and compensatory education*. Paper prepared for the Social Science Research Council: Sub-Committee on Values and Compensatory Education, 1970–71.

Shade, B. J. (1982). *Afro-American patterns of cognition*. Madison, WI: Wisconsin Center for Education Research, University of Wisconsin.

Shibutani, T. & Kwan, K. M. (1965). *Ethnic stratification: A comparative approach*. New York: Macmillan.

Shimahara, N. (1971). *Burakumin: A Japanese minority and education*. The Hague: N. Martinus Nijhoff.

Shuey, A. M. (1966). *The testing of negro intelligence*. New York: Social Science Press.

Similansky, M. & Similansky, S. (1967). Intellectual advancement of culturally disadvantaged children: An Israeli approach for research and action. *International Review of Education, 13*, 410–429.

Spicer, E. H. (1962). *Cycles of conquest*. Tucson, AZ: University of Arizona Press.

Spindler, G. D. (1974). The transmission of culture. In G. D. Spindler (Ed.), *Education and culture: Toward an anthropology of education*. New York: Holt.

Todd, D. M. (1977). Caste in Africa? *Africa*, vol. 47 (4), pp. 398–412.

Tomlinson, S. (1982). *A Sociology of Special Education*. London: Routledge & Kegan Paul.

Tsang, S. L. (1983). "Mathematics Learning Styles of Chinese Immigrant Students: A Summary of Research Findings." Paper presented at the 61st annual meeting of the National Council of Teachers of Mathematics, Detroit, Michigan, April 12.

U.S. Commission on Civil Rights (1978). *Social indicators of equality for minorities and women.* Washington, DC: U.S. Government Printing Office.

U.S. District Court for Northern California (1979). *Opinion: Larry P. vs. Riles, W.* San Francisco, CA: Mimeo.

Vandenberg, S. G. (1971). What do we know today about inheritance and how do we know it? In R. Cancro (Ed.), *Intelligence: Genetic and environmental influences.* New York: Grune & Stratton.

Vernon, P. E. (1969). *Intelligence and cultural environment.* London: Methuen.

Wagner, D. A. (1982). Ontogeny in the study of culture and cognition. In D. A. Wagner & H. W. Stevenson (Eds.), *Cultural perspectives on child development.* San Francisco, CA: W. H. Freeman.

Weisbrod, B. A. (1975). Education and investment in human capital. In D. M. Levine & M J. Bane (Eds.), *The "inequality" controversy: Schooling and distributive justice.* New York: Basic Books.

White, B. L., Kaban, B. T. & Attanucci, J. (1979). *The origins of human competence: The final report of the Harvard Preschool Project.* Lexington, MA: D. C. Heath.

White, S. H., Day, M. G., Freeman, D. K., Hartman, S. & Messenger, K. P. (1973). *Federal programs for young children: Review and recommendations. Vol. 1: Goals and standards of public programs for children.* Washington, DC: U.S. Government Printing Office.

Williams, R. L. (1972). *The BITCH Test (Black Intelligence Tests of Cultural Homogeneity).* St. Louis, MO: Black Studies Program, Washington University.

Williams, T. R. (1972). *Inroduction to socialization: Human culture transmitted.* St. Louis: C. V. Mosby.

Willie, C. V. (1979). Relative effect of race and social class on family income. In C. V. Willie (Ed.), *Caste and class controversy.* Bayside, NY: General Hall.

Wilson, W. J. (1979). The declining significance of race: revisited but not revised. In C. V. Willie (Ed.), *Caste and class controversy.* Bayside, NY: General Hall.

Wilson, W. J. (1978). *The declining significance of race: Blacks and changing American institutions.* Chicago: University of Chicago Press.

3 The Triple Quandary and the Schooling of Afro-American Children

A. Wade Boykin

There is serious concern about the educational plight of those children who do not enjoy mainstream status in the American social system. The academic performance of minority children remains a persistent, troubling, and seemingly intractable national problem. Although recently released reports (Center for the Study of Social Policy, 1982) give some cause for guarded optimism, significant alleviation of the problem continues to elude us (Boykin, 1983; Ogbu, 1978). Poor performance relative to mainstream children and a high incidence of school dropout are still the rule rather than the exception for these children, despite two decades of national concern. We must ask why there has been so little progress toward solving this problem, in spite of the apparent best of intentions and the commitment of very considerable resources. The question is particularly crucial today, at a time of declining political interest in minority affairs. Minority children no longer enjoy national attention, but their educational problems persist.

I believe that the problem continues because we have not adequately analyzed its causes. In particular, it is we as *psychologists* who have failed to ask the right kinds of questions. Although my own disciplinary training is in psychology, I have concluded that the situation of minority children in the schools cannot be understood in terms of the scholarly traditions of our field alone. Psychology may offer important insights, but only after we have overcome the arbitrary boundaries that divide it from other disciplines. In particular, we must consider issues of social structure and culture that have usually been defined as beyond the scope of psychology itself. Incorporation of such factors into our explanatory frameworks can take us a long way toward a proper understanding of the dilemmas faced by these children.

Consider the title of the present volume: "The School Achievement of Minority Children." Such a title, as well-intentioned as it may be, is crucially limited in scope. First, the problems that face "minority children" in American schools are not limited to the domain of academic achievement. Low "achievement" is not the only cause for concern; indeed, it may be just a symptom of more profound difficulties. Even if we could miraculously eliminate the performance gap between Euro-American and Afro-American children, other dilemmas would remain. The real issue is the process of schooling itself, as it is embedded within the postindustrial capitalist society of the United States. The individualistic, self-actional (as opposed to interactional), and noncontextual explanations typically offered by psychologists are simply inadequate to the task at hand. Schooling in America represents a form of social domination, or *hegemony*. The structure of society itself plays an overarching role in determining the nature of the schooling process. That process supports the existing social order in many ways: for example, it performs the critical function of socialization throughout most of the years of childhood (Carnoy, 1974; Parsons, 1959; Silverstein & Krate, 1975).

There is a second reason to question the title of this book. The apparently innocuous term "minority" tends to suggest that all the targeted groups are in essentially the same situation, that all of them are disenfranchised from the larger society in much the same way. It takes no account of the cultural integrity of different groups in American society. The separate identities of those groups must inform the way we think about the problems of childhood and schooling. Psychology has not adequately met its responsibility to deal with questions of culture (Cole & Scribner, 1974; Jones, 1983; Sampson, 1978). This chapter considers those questions in some detail, but its focus is restricted to Afro-American issues; limitations of space make it impractical to describe the distinct character of more than one cultural group. The Afro-American frame of reference is chosen because it has proven difficult to specify in the past, and some observers do not even even acknowledge that it exists. Moreover, the school problems of Afro-American children have historically been the most visible and the most intractable of those of any minority group. Nevertheless, I hope that it may be possible to extend the form of the present analysis to other groups at a later time.

The first half of this chapter attempts to describe the psychological situation of Afro-Americans. After a brief discussion of the now-discredited "cultural deficit" approach, an analysis of the concept of *Black culture* is presented. That concept is important, but taken alone it does not give an adequate account of the psychological experience of Black Americans. It is supplemented here by the notions of *biculturality* and *cultural patterning*, and by the special hypothesis that black culture is in almost dialectical opposition to the culture of mainstream America. It further is suggested here that Black Americans must negotiate simultaneously in three realms of experience: the mainstream, the African-rooted Black culture, and the status of an oppressed minority. That is, they face a triple quandary. Their position is further complicated by the prevailing hegemony of the Euro-American ethos, which makes it difficult even to consider alternative ways of structuring experience.

The second part of the chapter deals with the socialization and education of Black children. We consider the inevitable conflicts faced by children who must learn to negotiate in the three realms of experience, and the strategies that they adopt to deal with those conflicts. We examine the children's school experience, the ways in which coping strategies are expressed in school settings, and their effects on the learning process. The ideological functions of schooling in the prevailing hegemony of Euro-American values are also considered. Finally we suggest some alternative modes of education that may be more compatible with the realities of a pluralistic America, and some directions for research that might contribute to a better understanding of the issues involved.

THE AFRO-AMERICAN SITUATION

The Deficiency Approach

From the beginning of social science to about 1930, the dominant doctrine in matters of race and culture was social Darwinism (Hofstadter, 1955; Loye, 1971). Among other things, that doctrine placed Black people on a lower point on the evolutionary scale and thus implied that their culture was biologically inferior to that of White people. Against such a backdrop, the view that there are no inherent racial differences — that the deficiencies of Black people are environmentally based — appeared very progressive. This position, identified with the liberal tradition, has been dominant since the 1930s (Ginsburg, 1972; Valentine, 1968). It reached its zenith in the 1960s, when the idea that blacks were at a cultural disadvantage became the intellectual basis for the social intervention programs of the "Great Society" era (Zigler & Valentine, 1979). The academic difficulties of Afro-American children were attributed to an environmental deficiency of some kind: if that deficiency could somehow be counteracted, Blacks and Whites would function in fundamentally the same ways and the Afro-American academic problem would disappear.

From this perspective, Black children were seen as growing up in a web of social pathology and inadequate life experiences. The attitudes and behaviors produced by those experiences might enable the children to cope with their immediate environment, but left them unprepared to handle even the minimum requirements of the larger world around them (Deutsch, 1963;

Hunt, 1973; Marans & Lourie, 1967; Proshansky & Newton, 1973; Rainwater, 1966). Afro-American academic difficulties were typically explained in terms of the student's own inadequacies and problems. If Black children do badly in school, we must discover what is the matter with them: they may have maladaptive reactions to adversity or inadequate socialization experiences, especially in the home. This position is well expressed by Rollins, McCandless, Thompson, and Brassell (1974): "For inner city children, school failures often occur early, since they typically enter school poorly prepared to handle both the standard public school curriculum and the middle-class format of the classroom" (p. 167). Because these children are poorly equipped, they fail. That early failure becomes a continuing pattern; such children are said to be ". . . forever behind, confused, and as a consequence probably lose all interest in undertaking new academic tasks. As a result, inner city classrooms are filled with unhappy restless children who are relatively uninvolved in academic work and often are highly disruptive" (p. 167).

The modal intervention strategy in response to these problems was some form of remediation. "Culturally disadvantaged" and "learning disordered" are functionally similar labels (Feshbach & Adelman,, 1974). Hence, the prevailing tendency was to devise ways of altering the cognitive, personality, and motivational dispositions of Afro-American children in order to exact from them competent task/test performance.

In recent years, this line of explanation has been sharply criticized. Critics argue that it does not really define the problem and that its concepts do not hold up under scrutiny; that it does not account for enough of the variance; and that it has not substantially altered academic performance (Allen, 1978; Bradley & Bradley, 1977; Caplan & Nelson, 1973; Labov, 1970; Ogbu, 1978; Ryan, 1971). Most important for our present purposes, the "deficiency" approach really does little except to find fault with Afro-Americans and their life experiences; it does not illuminate the real cultural basis of their orientation to academic settings and tasks (Gay, 1975; Hale, 1980, 1982). Despite these indictments, the model of "deficiency" and remediation still has many adherents. It cannot be expected to wither away under the heat of criticism, because – as we see in a later section – it is consistent with the underlying ideology of mainstream American society.

On Black Culture

The "deficiency" approach assumes that so-called deprived children come from a group with no cultural integrity of its own. That assumption must be rejected. Because the Afro-American experience is not widely understood, and because failure to recognize the integrity of Afro-American culture is a basic weakness of currently dominant views (Jones, 1983), it is useful to mention some aspects of that experience here. Many of these aspects have been described before, especially by scholars who emphasize its roots in traditional West-African culture (Akbar, 1976; Banks, 1976; Dixon, 1976; Gutman, 1976; Jones, 1979; Levine, 1977; Smitherman, 1977; Wilson, 1972; Young, 1970). Analysis of their descriptions suggests the existence of at least nine interrelated dimensions of Black culture (Boykin, 1983): (a) *spirituality,* an approach to life as being essentially vitalistic rather than mechanistic, with the conviction that non-material forces influence people's everyday lives; (b) *harmony,* the notion that one's fate is interrelated with other elements in the scheme of things, so that humankind and nature are harmonically conjoined; (c) *movement,* an emphasis on the interweaving of movement, rhythm, percussiveness, music, and dance, which are taken as central to psychological health; (d) *verve,* a propensity for relatively high levels of stimulation, to action that is energetic and lively; (e) *affect,* an emphasis on emotions and feelings, together with a special sensitivity to emotional cues and a tendency to be emotionally expressive; (f) *communalism,* a commitment to social connectedness which includes an awareness that social bonds and responsibilities transcend individual privileges; (g) *expressive individualism,* the cultivation of a distinctive personality and a proclivity for spontaneous, genuine personal expression; (h) *oral tradition,* a preference for oral/aural modes of communication in which both speaking and listening are treated as performances and in which oral virtuosity — the ability to use alliterative, metaphorically colorful, graphic forms of spoken language — is emphasized and cultivated; and (i) *social time perspective,* an orientation in which time is treated as passing through a social space rather than a material one, in which time can be recurring, personal, and phenomenological.

There should be little doubt about the existence of these cultural manifestations in the lives of Afro-Americans. Some have argued that they reflect the existence of an entirely autonomous and intact Black culture that effectively insulates Afro-Americans from the mainstream of American society (Baratz & Baratz, 1970; Hannertz, 1969; Henderson & Washington, 1975; Miller, 1973; Stewart, 1970; Williams, 1974). This "cultural difference" view has been valuable in restoring a balance, correcting the notion that the fabric of Afro-American experience is weakly or incoherently organized. However, the cultural difference view may lack wisdom in certain respects. It underestimates the diversity and heterogeneity of Afro-Americans (Blackwell, 1975; Valentine, 1971), presenting instead a stereotypical portrait based primarily on the Black northern urban male experience (Akbar, 1982; G. Jackson, 1979). In fact, important regional differences in personality expression among Afro-Americans have been identified (Shade, 1978). In addition, statements of the cultural difference view often overemphasize the putative strengths of black people and ignore the possibility that the culture may have maladaptive features. Such exercises in psychological glorification are unrealistic (Allen, 1978; West, 1978).

Most important, the cultural difference position fails to acknowledge the commitments that Afro-Americans have made to mainstream American society. In Nobles' (1976) phrase, they may be of African root but they are of American fruit. The goals and values of child-rearing in Black families are much like those of the American middle-class ideal (Billingsley, 1969; Gottlieb, 1967; Kamii & Radin, 1967; Lewis, 1970), with a strong occupational and educational orientation (Hill, 1972; Moos & Moos, 1976). Black students have educational and vocational aspirations as high or higher as their white counterparts (Massey, Scott, & Dornbush, 1975; Milgram, Shore, Riedel, & Malasky, 1970; Picou, 1973; Simmons, 1979), and black teenagers hope to have life styles like those of the middle class (Gottlieb, 1967). Black parents have similar goals for their children. Those parents may approve of children using Black English at home and in the community, but they prefer the use of standard American English in school and at work (Hoover, 1978).

These facts imply that a wider conceptual framework is needed if we are to capture the richness and coherence of the Afro-American experience, and especially if we are to understand the schooling of Afro-American children. My own view is also based on the premise that there is a social-cultural integrity — not a disadvantage or a deficit — that informs the psychological lives of Black people. Yet this framework (Boykin, 1983) must also contrast with the cultural difference view in some respects, even while incorporating many insights from that position. For example, it must acknowledge that Black parents typically want their children to function successfully in mainstream America, even while they retain many traditional African propensities in their psychological transactions. The Afro-American experience is fundamentally bicultural.

Biculturality

Biculturality is a way of life for all distinct social groups in America, but it is manifest for Afro-Americans in a special way. We have the burden of trying to fuse two cultural traditions that are sharply at odds: non-commensurable, if you will. Prager (1982) puts it this way:

> It is not the mere fact that blacks hold a dual identity which has constrained achievement; to one degree or another, every ethnic and racial group has faced a similar challenge. The black experience in America is distinguished by the fact that the qualities attributed to blackness are in opposition to the qualities rewarded by society. The specific features of blackness, as cultural imagery, are almost by definition those qualities which the dominant society has attempted to deny in itself, and it is the difference between blackness and whiteness that defines, in many respects, American cultural self-understanding. For blacks, then, the effort to reconcile into one personality images which are diametrically opposed poses an extraordinarily difficult challenge. To succeed in America

raises the risk of being told — either by whites or by blacks — that one is not 'really black.' No other group in America has been so acutely confronted with this
dilemma, for no other group has been simultaneously so systematically ostra-
cized while remaining so culturally significant (p. 111).

Prager's remarks provide a new vantage point for understanding one of the
most important and often-quoted passages ever penned: "One ever feels his
two-ness — an American, a Negro; two souls, two thoughts, two unreconciled
strivings; two warring ideals in one dark body, whose dogged strength alone
keeps it from being torn asunder" (Dubois, 1903, p. 17).

Given the prevailing doctrine that all groups in our society should ultimately become like Euro-Americans, it has been easy to see Afro-Americans
as deficient deviations from the social ideal. Psychoculturally speaking,
Black people in their "deficient" state are needed to provide living testimony
of the cultural sanctity of being Euro-American: "Things may be tough for
me, but thank God at least I'm not black."

To characterize Afro-Americans as culturally different from Euro-
Americans is not graphic enough. To the extent that the Black experience reflects a traditional West African cultural ethos, the two frames of reference
are *noncommensurable*. There are fundamental incompatibilities between
them; they are not quite polar opposites, but they are almost dialectically related. The African perspective emphasizes spritualism, whereas the Euro-
American one emphasizes materialism. The former stresses harmony with
nature; the latter stresses mastery over nature. The first relies on organic metaphors, the second on mechanistic ones. An orientation toward expressive
movement contrasts with a compressive orientation toward impulse control.
One culture emphasizes interconnectedness, whereas the other puts a premium on separateness; one values affect, and the other places reason above
all else. An event orientation toward time contrasts with a clock orientation;
and an orally-based culture, with one based on print. In African culture there
is an interplay between expressive individualism and communalism, so that
possessions belong to the community at large, and uniqueness is valued.
Euro-American culture juxtaposes possessive individualism and an egalitarian conformity: private property is an inalienable right, and sameness is
valued. The former has a person-to-person emphasis, with a personal orientation toward objects; the second has a person-to-object emphasis, with an
impersonal (objective) orientation toward people (Boykin, 1983; Dixon,
1976; Dubois, 1972; Furby, 1979; Israel, 1979; Silverstein & Krate, 1975).

This incommensurability makes it difficult to put black cultural reality in
the service of attainment in Euro-American cultural institutions, such as
schools. The ideology that informs those institutions is a profound negation
of the most central attributes of African culture. Other American social
groups do not experience the same degree of conflict. The Asian frame of ref-

erence is distinct from both the European and the African, but the integration of the Asian cultural ethos into the Euro-American can be accomplished more readily (Caudill, 1952; Devos, 1982; Kitano, 1969). For example, the Japanese emphasize a self-cultivation that enables them to "more perfectly discharge obligations" toward family and society; that emphasis is distinct from, yet fairly compatible with, the effort-optimism of the Puritan work ethic (Dubois, 1972).

Cultural Patterning

The cultural distinctiveness of Euro- and Afro-Americans is not a question of who has what and who doesn't. It is overly simplistic to say that White people are "this" way and Black people are "that" way. People perform behaviors for many reasons, and any given activity may have several "causes." Similar behaviors may be informed by divergent values, or divergent behaviors by converging reasons. (We must also remember that there are wide differences among individual Euro-Americans, as there are among Afro-Americans.) It is a mistake to consider only the surface characteristics of behavior and/or to seek singular causes. We must venture to understand cultural deep structure: it is the ordering, patterning, and meaning of a given complex of behaviors that undergird cultural distinctiveness, and not just the presence or absence of various traits (Gay & Abrahams, 1973). As Dixon (1976) has stated, instead of taking an either/or approach to distinctiveness, we should understand cultural expression as a function of weightings across the "expanse of potential cultural attributes."

In essence, culture implies that which is cultivated. It is not a matter of what is absolutely present or absolutely absent: certain behaviors may be found among all groupings of people. We may even find that a given behavioral style appears in several different cultural groups and takes almost equivalent forms. In order to apprehend a given group's cultural ethos, it is essential to look at the total pattern of behavioral attributes, the contexts of their expression, and the underlying matrix of factors that inform them. Water (H_2O) and hydrogen peroxide (H_2O_2) contain identical elements, but their physical properties are very different because the elements are present in different proportions. Table salt and and hydrochloric acid are utterly unlike each other, although both have the same proportion of chlorine, because the chlorine is combined with a different element in each case.

By analogy, consider the role that "affect" may play in various cultures. The question is not whether the "affective element" is present or absent; no cultural group is devoid of affective expression. But groups differ in the emphasis placed on affect or in how it should (ideally) be integrated with reason, or in how it is expressed stylistically. Affect may be salient in cultures other than the African, but it is unlikely to combine in the same way with orality or social time perspective or the rhythmic and percussive qualities of movement. Thus the integration of affect into the total cultural complexes will be different, and the reasons for its emphasis will diverge as well. The affective styles of two cultures can differ fundamentally even if they exhibit comparable amounts of laughter or "strong emotional expression"; they thus deceive the superficial observer into thinking that they are equivalent.

This principle is the basis of Nobles' (1976) "transubstantive error." If we give to, say, Chicanos and Afro-Americans a undimensional assessment scale that was generated out of a Euro-American framework, we may find that they are equally displaced from the "ideal" end of the continuum. We then run the risk of treating them as culturally identical, when in fact they are fundamentally divergent. Our assessment device is not sensitive enough to discern the difference. The groups are just equally non-Euro-American on the construct that is measured by the device. Suppose, for example, that Afro-Americans and Chicanos both score further from the "reflective" end of a reflectivity/impulsivity scale than do Euro-Americans. It would be highly misleading to assert that Afro-Americans and Chicanos are impulsive, for their behaviors may be affirmations of quite different cultural ideals. Indeed, it is a fundamental mistake to suppose that "impulsive" (or "field-dependent," or "external in locus of control," etc.) are culturally relevant labels for Afro-Americans or Chicanos at all.

We have only begun to describe the biculturality of Afro-Americans. In particular, it is inappropriate to suppose that Afro-Americans possess two fully intact cultural systems. Given the ravages of racism and the historical discontinuities with the African past, it is obvious that American Blacks do not have an intact and untransformed African ethos. (Indeed, owing to the intrusion of colonialism, many present-day African systems are discontinuous with that ethos as well.) Yet, given the outgroup status of Afro-Americans, it is just as obvious that we have not wholly embraced or mastered Euro-American ideals either. In addition, racial and economic oppression have had their own impacts on the behavioral "grammar" of Afro-Americans. A more cogent way of capturing the richness and integrity of the Afro-American experience is needed.

The Triple Quandary

One way to capture the richness and integrity of the Afro-American experience is to cast it in terms of the interplay among three realms of experiential negotiation: the mainstream experience, the minority experience, and the Black cultural experience (Cole, 1970; Jones, 1979). Mainstream forces are the most pervasive, and all members of the society have contact with the mainstream realm of negotiation. Young (1974) has observed:

> Participation in standard American culture is characteristic of [Blacks] of all social classes, rural and urban. [Blacks] participate in work systems, judicial systems, consumption systems, bureaucratic systems both as clients and employees. They share values transmitted by general American institutions and by the mass media. (p. 406)

That participation, however, is tempered by concomitant negotiation through the minority and Black cultural realms. As we see shortly, it is also tempered by the hegemony of Euro-American values in every aspect of mainstream culture, a hegemony that defines all other values as essentially illegitimate.

The minority experience is based on exposure to social, economic, and political oppression. For Black people, this oppression is linked to race, but other groups as well have minority status, and not necessarily for racial reasons. That status produces adaptive and compensatory reactions, social perspectives, and defensive postures that help one to cope with the predicament created by the oppressive forces. This creates a minority experience that is shared, to some extent, by all oppressed people in this society. Nevertheless, each group also develops a unique set of adaptive reactions, based on the unique attributes that have made them a target of oppression. In particular, the dialectical cultural relationship between Euro- and Afro-Americans leads to a distinct Afro-American response.

Finally, Afro-Americans participate in a Black cultural experience that is rooted in a traditional African ethos. Some aspects of that culture have already been mentioned, and others are described below. The Afro-American's psychological repertoire is not merely expedient or defensive (see Blauner, 1970), and it does not just represent an inadequate imitation of White people. It is a culturally indigenous basis from which Afro-Americans interpret and negotiate social reality.

The conflicts created by these three realms of negotiation create a triple quandary for Afro-Americans. They are incompletely socialized to the Euro-American cultural system; they are victimized by racial and economic oppression; they participate in a culture that is sharply at odds with mainstream ideology. A similar position has been stated by the anthropologist/sociologist DeVos (1982):

> True, the individual within a minority group is interacting basically with his own group, but such minority ethnic enclaves are seldom independent cultures that are totally free from alternative considerations. What one has to assess, therefore, is the relative degree and in what manner values originating in the dominant society penetrate a given subgroup. Second, adaptation is influenced by how the socialization pattern of any given group coincides or comes in conflict with that of the dominant society. Third, one must consider how this conflict is resolved both adjustively in certain defense mechanisms and adaptively in manifest behavior. (p. 103)

Hegemony

The mainstream and the minority do not simply exist side by side: one of them has hegemony over the other. According to Apple (1979), hegemony "leads to and comes from unequal economic and cultural control". The term refers to "an organized assemblage of meanings and practices, the central effective and dominant system of meaning, values and actions which are *lived,*" which constitute one's "ordinary understanding of man and his world," and are tantamount to one's "sense of reality" (p. 5). It embodies the expectations of the way people do things, the way people behave, the significant moments, traditions, and practices. It has to do with what is taken for granted. Hegemony is a difficult concept to pin down because it is essentially inseparable from the air around us. To understand hegemony, one must challenge the very aspects of society that generally go unchallenged (Wirth, 1936).

The principal vehicle of hegemony is ideology. An ideology consists of the creeds, opinions, and ways of thinking of a particular class or group. It is necessarily biased by the interests of that class or group (Persell, 1977; Schwebel, 1975). Those interests can be either *structural*—concerned with the distribution of power, wealth, and status—or *cultural*—concerned with the patterning of values, life styles, behavioral reactions, and beliefs. The ideology of the prevailing group in a given society necessarily serves to perpetuate the status quo. In America, it necessarily supports the existing unequal distribution of wealth and power in the society and the prevailing cultural ethos.

The intellectuals produced in a hegemonic system typically fail to understand that the status bestowed upon them is linked in a zero-sum relationship to the oppression of other groups. They uncritically accept certain "ideological categories" (Apple, 1979), such as value-free, dispassionate science or the abstraction and absoluteness of the individual; they rarely realize that their status depends on that acceptance. They do not comprehend that they are being rewarded for embracing those categories, for legitimizing the way the system operates. The approach they take to their responsibilities shields them from questioning the social system from which they themselves have profited. Thus educators, and for that matter educational researchers, can all too easily become personal agents of hegemony in spite of the best of intentions.

In American society, the prevailing ideology is based on the Euro-American frame of reference described earlier. It stresses acquisitive individualism—one's identity is based on what one acquires and possesses—and egalitarian conformity. It defines truth as objective empirical facts, neutrally derived through the elimination of the knower's standpoint from the knowledge gained (Boykin, 1983; Dubois, 1972; Israel, 1979). The system of things is mechanistically conceived and is to be understood on a materialistic basis. Humankind's mastery over nature is emphasized and is consistent with mastery over putatively less endowed peoples. Effort is valued for effort's sake (effort optimism), and the cognitive takes precedence over the affective. The confluence of these considerations leads further to a brand of egalitarianism that sees equality, sameness, and uniformity as virtually synonymous; to a penchant for seeking universal laws and principles that are applicable to all individuals or groups; and to a premium's being placed on human perfectability (DuBois, 1972; Sampson, 1978).

The upshot is an approach to human diversity construed in terms of differing levels of competence. If individuals or groups are different, they are seen as less or greater than some reference group or reference point (Valentine, 1971). Those who differ from Euro-American cultural ideals are easily seen as inferior along a single linear dimension of human perfectibility. Either they are unable to (conservative doctrine) or haven't had the opportunity to (liberal doctrine) achieve the desired similarity—to embrace White middle-class beliefs, values, and patterns of behavior. The achievement of that similarity (melting into the pot) is understood to be the responsibility of the "deviant" individuals themselves (Sampson, 1977); they must acquire some "commodity" that they do not yet possess.

The prevailing cultural ideology sees social homogenization as a natural goal because it treats deviations from the cultural ideal as deficiencies and imperfections. In turn, the existence of those deviations provides support for the ideology itself: it becomes a convenient rationalization for the unequal distribution of wealth and status. It has been suggested that the maintenance of this structural sorting function is one of the major responsibilities of the American school system (Bowles & Gintis, 1976; Carnoy, 1974; Persell, 1977). By sorting people according to their acquisition of skills and their behavioral repertoires, the educational system processes youth for the eventual assignment of status in the adult society. Such a sorting process might be considered just and fair if it were being conducted in a racially and culturally homogeneous society. America, however, is fundamentally pluralistic, so that the sorting out of "deviants" usually occurs along racial and cultural lines. Afro-Americans are often the most prominent examples of the problems and persecutions thus created.

The hegemony of mainstream American culture is strengthened by an insensitivity to the culturally bounded nature of the rules and measures themselves. The emphasis on universalism and mastery has resulted not only in a posture of cultural imperialism, but in a paradoxical denial of the importance of culture itself. As Khan (1982) put it:

> . . . characteristic of . . . Western cultures of dominance are the twin notions that culture is dispensable and that it is detachable. First, culture is not seen to have any power in its own right. For many, it is an esoteric misguided system of beliefs and/or quaint behaviour held by others. This is the notion that "They have culture; we have civilization," or "We base our action on rational behavior; they have irrational beliefs." Following from this, "If they become

Westernized/English-assimilated, they will become civilized/rational beings."
Therefore culture is dispensable, serving no useful functions. It only serves to
mystify or to maintain conservative tradition. Second, there is the notion that
culture is detachable from the social and economic system in which it has its reality. In these perspectives culture is taken out of context and three important
relationships are ignored: between meaning and action, between the social system and its economic base, and between the individual and collective represen-
tations transmitted through cultural institutions and practices across generations. (p. 205)

This view is surely what Jones (1972) had in mind when he introduced the
concept of *cultural racism,* defined as "the attitude characterized by ethnocentrism, coupled with the power to make normative one's ethnocentric
values" (p. 173). For Jones this form of racism is more pervasive, more fundamental, and less well understood than either of the more "established"
forms of racism, i.e. individual and institutional. When these attitudes get
played out in actual behavioral transactions or have consequences for certain
victimized groups, cultural racism becomes transformed into oppression.
Freire (1973) calls it *cultural invasion*:

> . . . the invaders penetrate the cultural context of another group, in disrespect
> of the latter's potentialities; they impose their view of the world upon those
> whom they invade, and inhibit the creativity of the invaded by curbing their ex-
> pression . . . it is essential that those who are invaded come to see their reality
> with the outlook of the invaders rather than their own; for the more they mimic
> the position of the invaders, the more stable the position of the latter becomes.
> (pp. 150–151)

As we come to understand the workings of hegemony, we should recognize
that racist individuals are not needed to maintain the system. It doesn't require malevolent people or malevolent intentions. Indeed, agents of hegemony can just as easily carry out their roles with the very best and sincerest of
intentions. They need not even be Euro-Americans: surely many of the hegemonic agents that affect the lives of Black children are themselves Afro-
Americans who may be taken as role models by the children. (See Rist, 1970,
for an illuminating example.) Some of those agents may embrace hegemonic
ideologies very tenaciously, trying to out-do White people in an attempt to diminish their own perceived marginality or to gain the perceived fruits of
American society. At the very least, their reward for embracing those ideals
will be to be told occasionally that they are not like the others of their race:
they are "special" and act "better."

The all-encompassing, saturating character of hegemony makes it difficult
to detect its presence, let alone struggle to diminish its influence or provide viable alternatives. A prevailing cultural ideology that espouses the acontex-
tualization of the individual, promotes value neutrality, and denies that it is

either cultural or ideological makes it very difficult to formulate alternatives. A perspective that emphasizes the democratization of equality, human perfectibility, and the human being's right to mastery can pride itself on being morally correct while simultaneously imposing its will on others in the name of amelioration. If other systems are consciously considered at all, they can readily be dismissed as morally inferior. Hegemony is a self-reinforcing phenomenon that aids and abets the continuation of things as they are. In spite of the recent attention given to the amelioration of inequitable conditions in society at large (and especially in educational settings), the general direction of change in America has not been in the direction of those avowed goals. The gap between the rich and the poor, between the powerful and the powerless, is increasing rather than decreasing (Apple, 1979; Carnoy & Shearer, 1980). The gains made by Afro-Americans, women, and other disenfranchised groups have atrophied, if they have not been reversed. The distributions of health, nutrition, and education remain sharply unequal, and attempts to make such goods more widely available are becoming very unpopular politically. Hegemony is surely at the root of this "ameliorative stagnation": the social order naturally generates and reproduces inequality.

THE SOCIALIZATION AND EDUCATION OF AFRO-AMERICAN CHILDREN

Socialization and Black Cultural Styles

The triple quandary has a far-reaching impact on the socialization of Afro-American children. Socialization into the American mainstream is culturally at odds with the imperatives of coping with a racially hostile society and also with negotiating in the proximal Black cultural context (which, as we have seen, is dialectically related to the mainstream itself). For this reason, inculcation of the values of the dominant order cannot be pervasive: other social-cultural influences will interfere. Rewards for being "properly" socialized into the wider society may not really be expected, and there will be a competing commitment to prepare individuals to be cynical, skeptical, and on guard. Even if Afro-American parents try to socialize their children primarily in terms of the ideals and values of mainstream American society, they are bound to encounter difficulties. Their facility with that socialization process, their commitment to it, and the resources they can devote to it are usually limited. Despite wide variation across households and neighborhoods, mainstream cultural ideals will be less pervasive and the corresponding behavioral repertoire less entrenched in Afro-American children than in their Euro-American counterparts. (See Staples, 1976, for a similar argument.)

The socialization of Black children is also affected by the aspects of their culture that arise out of the traditional African ethos. However, given the discontinuities with the African past as well as the long-standing influence of Euro-American values, it would be a mistake to suppose that they acquire a wholly intact African cultural scheme. I suggest that the African influence is effective in a more tacit way, by the conditioning of Black *cultural styles*. By cultural style, I mean a habitual, nonreflective pattern of behavior — an enduring and cross-situational motif rather than a conscious set of values. The relation between such a style and more explicit cultural values may take several forms.

Every cultural system has a broad set of beliefs that address universal concerns about the nature of the cosmos and humankind's relation to it, as well as about people's relations to one another (Dubois, 1972). Those beliefs become manifest in core cultural values that specify preferences, interests, and goals (Dixon, 1976; Kluckhohn & Strodbeck, 1961), and these in turn may lead to the cultural styles I have described. In an intact monocultural framework like that of extant Euro-Americans, there is typically a hierarchical relationship among beliefs, values and styles (Young, 1974). Although no precise one-to-one relation may exist, there is likely to be a consistent correspondence between basic beliefs, articulated values, and stylistic manifestations. However, there is another possibility. Styles do not have to grow out of belief systems and values directly. They can also be conditioned within a child's familial rearing experience, without articulation of any corresponding worldview or values. Such is likely to be the case for Afro-Americans.

The African-based motifs of Afro-Americans are manifested in spite of the fact that Blacks are embedded in a Euro-American social reality. I contend that they largely reflect a tacit understanding of the beliefs and values that inform them, rather than an active articulation of those beliefs and values. There may be some instances where an explicit statement of the underlying values and beliefs is made, but even then their African origin will seldom be understood, and it is unlikely that they would represent a fully elaborated, coherently interwoven traditional ethos. Thus many Afro-Americans experience a kind of bifurcation: their explicit beliefs and values are shaped primarily by the dominant society; their habitual patterns of action and feeling come more from proxemic participation in family and community settings. This can happen because stylistic patterns are molded earlier in the socialization process than beliefs and values. The latter require greater awareness on the part of the developing child and are put systematically in place only when the child begins to interact with the socialization agents of the larger society (e.g., schools and school personnel). Those agents soon complement or supersede any earlier family-based attempts to teach mainstream values; they also counter whatever efforts may have been made to teach alternative values based (ultimately) on an African ethos.

It is crucial to distinguish between *tacit* and *elaborated* cultural styles. Tacit styles are forged implicitly out of the fabric of one's proxemic socialization experiences. Elaborated styles are inculcated under the explicit guidance of social beliefs and values, and typically result from the top-to-bottom elaboration of a homogeneous cultural ethos. (Tacit styles may eventually be linked to explicit expression, but that expression will not be fully articulated within a systematic cultural framework.) Black cultural motifs can exist alongside espoused Euro-American values because they were formed by a largely tacit cultural conditioning process. They flow out of the sights, sounds, rhythms, and life styles that are present in the proxemic environment of Black children. It can be persuasively argued that such styles are rooted in Africanity.

These culturally conditioned sylistic tendencies are difficult to put in the service of the goals of the dominant society. The attempt to do so is often maladaptive, because of the noncommensurate relationship between Black and Euro-American cultural ideals. The two stances are essentially incompatible. This may explain why low-income black parents who hold middle-class-like goals for their children so often fail to persuade the children to adhere to middle-class patterns of behavior (Kamii & Radin, 1967; Lewis, 1970). These parents may be providing their children with mixed socialization messages. One message is overt, verbal, and yet inconsistent; the other is tacit, behaviorally based, and more consistently reinforced in the child's immediate ecological environment. It is not difficult to conceive that the Black cultural conditioning process may take precedence during a child's formative years (Lewis, 1975). A more detailed elaboration of that process and of how it provides for the preservation of Black cultural motifs has been presented elsewhere (Boykin, 1983).

Coping Strategies

These socialization conditions must also be understood in terms of the oppressive conditions under which Afro-Americans must live. It is difficult enough to negotiate between two dialectically opposed cultural systems. That difficulty is compounded by the effects of racial discrimination: the truncated opportunity structure open to Black Americans, which Ogbu (this volume) describes as a "job ceiling"; the low expectations for success via conventional and institutional routes. Indeed, those who bring up children in Black communities are in a perplexing situation. They may understand and even accept the goals of the Euro-American socialization process and value the benefits that accompany success in the existing social order, but they are fully aware that really accomplishing those ends is more apparent than real. The resulting ambivalence is part of the socialization message picked up by the next generation.

At the same time, parents and siblings and others in the immediate environment are modeling various strategies for coping with the oppression the children will surely face. Most coping styles conform to one or the other of two patterns, two alternative adaptive reactions to oppression. One of these is essentially a form of mental colonization, in which hegemony has become fully effective. In this pattern Black people do not seriously entertain any possibilities other than the existing situation, and essentially come to accept their lot. This leads to the adoption of one or more passive coping strategies. For example, Blacks may strive to out-white White people and get what Harrell (1979) calls "a piece of the action"; in trying to get their "fair share" of the American pie, they forego consideration of the inherent oppressiveness of the system itself. Another possibility is to assume subservient or "Uncle Tomming" postures in order to withstand at least the harshest manifestations of racial oppression (Ogbu, 1978). In this mode, Black people may come to identify with the oppressor and promote the "rightness of whiteness," even at the expense of the integrity of the Afro-American experience (Friere, 1973; Memmi, 1965). These postures of black self-hatred may not be widely prevalent (Baldwin, 1979; Banks, 1976), but Black communities have not escaped them entirely.

Passive coping strategies may take other forms as well. In the "survivalist" strategy, for example, one turns on one's own community without regard for others, adopting a "dog eat dog" philosophy simply in order to survive. Another possible attitude is passive resignation and acceptance of life as it is, trying not to get involved. Such apathy often leads to what is commonly known as a "welfare mentality," but it may have adaptive cardio-vascular consequences (Harrell, 1981).

Not all Black people who are victimized by oppression adopt passive coping styles. More active strategies arise out of resistance to oppression. One of these is dissembling (Williams, 1980), in which individuals conceal their true feelings and provide a pretense to the outside world of oppression. This is often done to camouflage small-scale subversive acts against the victimizers. Similarly, individuals may go along with the status quo while developing a cynical and hypercritical posture toward society and their own place in it. In the "get-over" strategy, they recognize that Black success in American society requires playing a kind of game; they strive to outfox the power brokers and credentialling agents, typically through cunning, expedience, and trickery, in order to gain the stamps of approval that signify success. A very different strategy is to resist oppression by defying the system, to be consistently against anything that "whiteness" stands for. One can adopt a survivalist strategy from this perspective as well, turning aggressive techniques outward toward the dominant society. Finally, some believe that oppression is best resisted by embracing a distinct system of values, such as the black nationalist movement (Harrell, 1979), that can serve an essentially insulating function.

This list is not exhaustive, and the strategies delineated here could be elaborated much further. Moreover, any one individual may use a mixture of several coping styles. The important point is that some such set of psychobehavioral reactions and attitudes is required of everyone who occupies a minority status in this society. These forms of adaptation may help one to negotiate through harsh and oppressive realities, but they do not necessarily promote adaptiveness within the "proper" channels of mainstream America.

The triple quandary presents Afro-Americans with three realms that must be socially negotiated: mainstream American, Black cultural, and oppressed minority. These three domains require three distinct, largely nonoverlapping psychological and behavioral repertoires. Given the inherent limitations of time and space, it is apparent that being truly effective in any one realm will diminish effectiveness in the others. The three realms operate at cross-purposes in quite possibly a zero-sum game.

Negotiating in the Three Realms of Experience

Afro-Americans must try to integrate three divergent psychological realities at once: mainstream, minority, and Black cultural. Given this triple burden, it is small wonder that traditional conceptual models conceived with the Euro-American in mind are ill equipped to describe the Afro-American psychological experience. The negotiational demands placed on Euro-Americans are much simpler. The three realms of mainstream, majority, and Euro-American cultural are essentially isomorphic, so their psychological/behavioral repertoires are more convergent and their demands can be more easily integrated. Thus, they provide for a more focused or concentrated codification of reality.

The contrasting negotiational schemes are illustrated in Figs. 3.1 and 3.2. The diagram of the triple quandary in Fig. 3.1 depicts the three realms as functioning almost independently of each other. Their only contact is through certain coping strategies: some passive strategies that derive from mental colonization are connected to the mainstream (e.g., "a piece of the action"), and some active strategies are related to Black culture (e.g., identification with Black nationalist movements). Figure 3.2 shows, on the other hand, that mainstream experience in America is tantamount to the Euro-American cultural experience; both are equivalent to the majority mentality itself.

The single arrow impinging on the individual in Fig. 3.2 is an attempt to depict the convergence of the three realms of Euro-American social negotiation. It shows why Euro-Americans have a highly focused codification of reality, to th point where they become oblivious to other honorable negotiational possibilities. Note that although, technically, the cultural system is organized from top to bottom (broad world views result in particular values

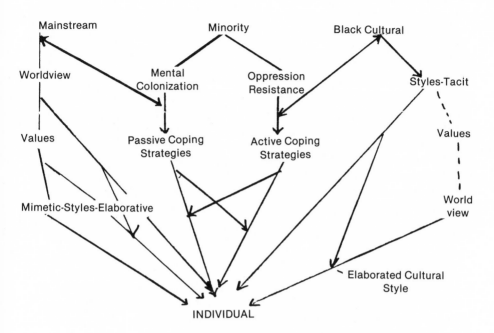

FIG. 3.1   Afro-American Negotiational Scheme.

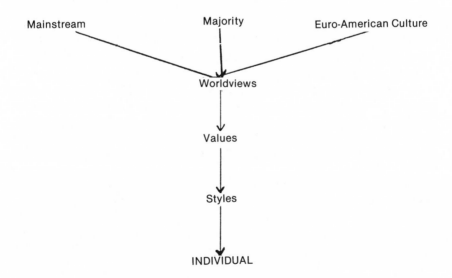

FIG. 3.2   Euro-American Negotiational Scheme.

that give rise to specific styles), it is acquired in the opposite direction. The Euro-American child learns the cultural styles first, as all children do. But, in the Euro-American case, these styles easily hook up later on with the corresponding values and beliefs, especially as the child begins to encounter formal schooling. The schools make the coupling process easy, because they espouse those beliefs and values themselves.

The situation of the Afro-American child is very different. The multiple arrows impinging on the individual in Fig. 3.1 show the complex combinations of experience that can characterize the socialization of any given Afro-American. These make themselves felt in particular ways during the educational process. Let us consider the implications of the triple quandary for the Afro-American school experience, with due consideration of hegemony and the social function of schooling itself.

The Afro-American School Experience

As children mature, their behavioral styles, values, and belief systems become more stable. During the period when the young child's initial repertoire of styles is becoming stabilized, the sphere of primary socialization influence is the home and the immediate community. When that sphere enlarges to include social institutions such as the school, the child becomes increasingly attuned to the values that are promoted by those institutions. As mentioned previously, this process is relatively straightforward for Euro-American children because the institution just extrapolates from styles previously learned. The situation is very different for Afro-American children because the school requires them to acquire values and beliefs that are incongruent with the cultural styles they have learned at home. Thus it has often been suggested that a kind of mismatch or clash of cultures occurs when Black children enter school.

Such a conclusion has some merit, but it is too simplistic. It does not do justice to the interactional dynamics of the process of schooling or to the complexity of the Afro-American experience as depicted in this chapter. It implies that, because Black children are culturally Black, they cannot do well in Euro-American cultural settings. As we shall see, this would be a serious misrepresentation.

To understand the situation better, we must take into account four distinct planes of interaction between the child and the school: what children *do* or *do not* do, what they *can* or *can not* do, what they *will* or *will not* do, and what they *should* or *should not* do. Although these ways of construing the interaction are logically separate, most analyses have failed to distinguish between them. It is easy to see why. In a culturally homogeneous population, what children actually do in an academic setting is based on what they can do and will do, and on what they understand that they should do. Similarly, what they don't do follows from what they should not, will not, and cannot do. Because White middle-class children participate in a relatively homogeneous cultural experience, they are likely to do what they can, will, and should do. Moreover, what the children themselves believe they should do is likely to be consistent with what their teachers believe: there is a congruence of value and belief. Separating questions of *will* and *should* from *can* is hardly necessary in such a context. In the case of Afro-American children, however, these distinctions become important.

What a child *does* or *does not* do is essentially the question of academic performance. It is what Black children do not do in school that created the need for the present volume. The issue of what a child *can* do, in contrast, is one of cognitive competence. In its strong form it implies maturational constraints or structural limitations on ability; in a weaker form it refers to what a child cannot do at present but could do in the future if conditions were favorable. *Will* refers to the child's motivation, reflecting issues of interest, preference, choice, persistence, and the effects of reward and punishment. The question of what a child *should* do reflects the values and beliefs that are brought to bear on his or her situation.

Given the bias toward cognitive interpretations in the Euro-American cultural ethos, *can* becomes the paramount question in analyzing the educational affairs of mainstream children. The mesh between competence and performance is the central concern (McClelland, 1971). When the typical Euro-American child does not perform, one tries to determine what he or she cannot do. It is usually taken for granted that the child wants to do well; issues of *will* and *should* are not seen as essential. These cultural blinders may explain why many analysts interpret the idea of a cultural mismatch as bearing only on competence, on what children *can not* do. Such assumptions are entirely inappropriate for children who begin with a different cultural style and encounter institutional contexts hostile to their well being.

Relations among the four planes of interaction are by no means straightforward for Afro-American children. When Black children don't do, there is no necessary implication that they cannot do (although this is possible). We must go beyond the can/cannot question to issues of will and should, i.e., to motives, beliefs, and values. It is more difficult to master three agendas simultaneously than it is to master one. Given the experiential complexity of the Black experience, there must be considerable confusion over the values and behaviors appropriate to academic settings. Then, too, it would be naive to expect value congruency between teachers and Black children. The academic dilemma of Afro-Americans must be understood in terms of the interrelations of cognitive, motivational, and value-belief considerations.

When they enter school, Black children naturally tend to apply the cultural and stylistic repertoire with which they are already familiar. This application is likely to have discouraging consequences. The child's "way of doing things" is often dishonored in the school setting, and a different set of styles is imposed — one that is different and unfamiliar and even "ungrammatical" from the child's point of view. It is reasonable to expect that children will be reluctant to give up the only way they know of interacting with the world and will resist having an alien set of styles imposed upon them. This situation can surely affect the child's *will* to learn. Black children are told to act in a certain way because it is consistent with certain values and beliefs, but those values, often contemptuously thrust upon the children, are not extrapolations from their accustomed cultural repertoire. The child often will resist the demands being made and may view the accompanying values with suspicion or contempt. These circumstances can work against the children's deciding that they *should* learn the material that is being presented.

Young children do not readily separate how people act from how they feel. Children who see that a teacher does not like what they do will quickly conclude that the teacher does not like them personally, does not honor them as individuals. If the teacher is simultaneously trying to impose an alternative set of values and beliefs that are incompatible with the child's own views, it will be especially hard for the child to put his or her own learning styles in the service of the school's requirements. There will probably be an adverse effect on interest, persistence, and attention to the academic activities promoted by the teacher. All of this is a tacit process. It goes on unreflectively, outside of awareness; even bringing it to the child's attention may be of little use.

From the Black child's standpoint, how might these inconsistencies be resolved? One method may be for the children to persist or increase their adherence to Black cultural behavior patterns, in spite of the teacher's efforts to get them to do otherwise. Such a tactic might act as a shield against attempts to undermine or dishonor them. Consider the work of Piestrup (1973). She found that greater incidence of Black dialect usage in the first grade was associated with the very teaching styles that attempted to minimize and undermine such usage. Yet, in settings where a "Black Artful" teaching style was used, i.e. where Black and mainstream dialect switching was not discouraged and at times was even encouraged, use of Black dialect was relatively lower.

Coping Strategies in School

Children who come to see the teacher as an oppressor may deliberately resist doing what the teacher thinks they should do. Such children may protect their own integrity by engaging in some of the coping styles discussed earlier. They may dissemble, for example, giving outer cues suggestive of cooperation while they are really trying to undermine the teacher's efforts whenever they can. They may also respond by "getting over," treating school as a big game of teacher against student. Because the teachers do not seem to have their real interests at heart, the children do not take the school's instructional agenda as their own. This subverts the learning process and replaces it with other goals that are to be attained through cunning or trickery. Children may even become contemptuous, cynical, and alienated from the school.

Children who come to view the educational context as hostile to their own interests and as undermining their integrity may (a) decide that what they *should* do is not what the teacher thinks should be done; (b) act in such a way that they *will not* do what the teacher wants, and (c) display what they *can* do in ways that are not in accordance with what the teacher prescribes. What such a child does in the academic setting is quite coherent and understandable, although perhaps not to the teacher. The child's actions may represent an internally consistent resolution of what can, will, and should be done in an oppressive setting.

The teacher's point of view is typically different. Teachers are likely to see the behavior of Black children as ungrammatical at best, inferior at worst. Because of the cultural blinders they often wear, teachers are usually oblivious to the possibility that other values may be competing with the ones they wish to inculcate. They tend to interpret the children's unsatisfactory performance in either of two ways. Some teachers conclude that the children fail primarily because they are unsocialized — that they just have wrong behaviors and bad attitudes. Such teachers concentrate on altering the inappropriate behaviors and trying to instill the correct ones. Other teachers retain their focus on the *can't do* problem and concentrate their efforts on trying to eradicate it, oblivious to cultural inconsistencies at the *will* and *should* levels. Such an attribute may contribute further to the cultural and negotiational impasse between teacher and students. In the end, both postures tend to exacerbate the problem, because they create situations in which behavioral control and discipline become elevated over all other pedagogical responsibilities.

As discipline and control come to occupy more classroom time, teaching time is proportionately reduced. Because it is axiomatic that amount of learning is directly proportional to time spent teaching, this means that the children now learn less than they did before. This intensifies the problem, so more social control is soon needed; teaching time is reduced still further as the cycle feeds on itself. Thus even actions that teachers undertake with the best of intentions may boomerang and end by solidifying negative attitudes toward students, creating an entrenched pessimism about their ability to learn. What keeps such teachers from becoming totally discouraged is the intermittent reinforcement they may receive from the occasional "successful" students, who likely abandon their cultural integrity and conform to the teacher's dictates. When the teacher holds such children up as ideals to the rest of the classroom, the impasse deepens.

Who are the children who "succeed" in this way? In many cases, they are those who have adopted a very different coping strategy. Schools can and do function as agents of hegemony in this society. Black children may succumb to that hegemony, and adopt passive coping strategies that are symptomatic of a mentally colonized state. They may deal with oppression by accepting the images presented to them by the institutions; they fall into line at the expense of retaining any esteem for the Black cultural ethos. They may deride the social time perspective as "CP time," or come to see an affective orientation as being "too emotional." They may view communalism as dependency, lack of commitment to academic material as laziness, and expressive individualism as "showing off". They may deride an orientation to rhythmic movement by saying that niggers just like to sing and dance. In this form of identification with the oppressor, the ways of Black folks are seen as inferior while the ways of White folks are actively embraced. These students, who often are among the most successful academically (Silverstein & Krate, 1975), try to shed their Black cultural background as fully as possible so they can conform to the Euro-American can-will-should solution.

Of course, the academically successful child is not always intellectually colonized. Similarly, it should not be asssumed that if academically unsuccessful children are alienated, they have escaped the influence of hegemony. It is conceivable that the educationally-at-risk Black child who becomes alienated in the academic setting may simultaneously be paying homage to the value system that undergirds American society and the school itself. Although those values may be viewed with suspicion, they so saturate the world to which the child is becoming attuned that they are almost inescapable. Indeed, there is considerable latitude for diversity of expression within the triple quandary.

Functions of Schooling

Our earlier discussions of hegemony implied that schools are multifunctional institutions. Not only do they operate to impart cognitive skills such as reading, writing, and arithmetic, they also serve a broader socialization function. As Parsons (1959) put it: "The school class can be treated as an agency of socialization. That is to say, it is an agency through which individual personalities are trained to be motivationally and technically adequate to the performance of adult roles. (pp. 297–298)

Indeed as far as Parsons was concerned, from kindergarten through the high school years, school is the "focal socialization agent" in shaping the lives and destinies of America's children. He goes on to say:

> The socialization function may be summed up as the development in individuals of the commitments and capacities which are essential prerequisites of their future role-performance. Commitments may be broken down in turn into two components: commitment to the implementation of the broad *values* of society and commitment to the performance of a specific type of role within the *struc-*

ture of society. . . . . Capacities can also be broken down into two components, the first being competence or the skill to perform the tasks involved in the individual roles and the second being "role responsibility" or the capacity to live up to other people's expectation of the interpersonal behavior appropriate to these roles. (p. 298)

From Parsons we glean four distinct functions that are served by the schools. The first is training in cognitive skills, as conventional wisdom suggests. But those skills are imparted within a particular social and ideological context, and the fabric of that context is apparent in the other three functions: training in an appropriate behavioral repertoire, training in an appropriate commitment to the existing social order, and training in the appropriate system of values.

The particular behavioral repertoire deemed appropriate for schools in America is difficult to reconcile with Black cultural styles. The school's expectation is close to what Sampson (1977) calls "self-contained individualism." One is supposed to be intrapsychically self-sufficient, to behave rationally rather than emotionally, to be field independent, to display impulse control and movement compression, to have high need for achievement and delay of gratification. These chateracteristics are just the familiar aspects of the Euro-American ethos, but the workings of hegemony make them appear to be inevitable characteristics of education.

The schools meet their commitment to train for the existing social order in a curious way: they simultaneously homogenize their students and differentiate among them. School socializes as it stratifies. Once the children have been properly standardized, they can be evaluated on a single continuum. This seems to create a "fair" process for discerning differential talent and ultimately for creating the different stamps of educational approval that are assigned to individuals to regulate their entry into the labor market. Such an approach cannot be entirely successful, because it works at cross purposes with the reality of cross-cultural pluralism in America. Its failure undermines claims of fairness in assessment and delegitimizes the credentials themselves. Differential assessment may result just as much from the failure of the socialization/homogenization process as from cognitive or motivational limitations in the children themselves.

This characterization is important for the issue of societal commitment. If children who wind up with a relatively low stamp of educational approval (and thus are earmarked for low status positions in society) believe that the assessment process is fair, they are apt to accept their lot and become good social citizens. If they judge the process to be unfair, however, they will not readily accept its outcome. They will become alienated from the social order rather than commited to it. Although such an outcome does not change the stratification function of schooling (indeed, it makes stratification easier to accomplish), those who emerge from the process near the bottom will be effectively disenfranchised. This scenario clearly describes the fate of all too many Black youth.

What about the school's function of creating a commitment to the prevailing value system? Consider this rather poignant quotation from Banks (1976):

> The knowledge which becomes institutionalized within a society is often designed to support the status quo and to legitimize the position of those in power. Thus [it] frequently reflects the norms, values, goals, and ideals of the powerful groups in society, it often validates and legitimizes those beliefs and ideologies which are useful for powerful groups and are detrimental to oppressed groups. (p. 394)

Implied in this quotation are two distinct types of value systems. A commitment to the prevailing cultural value system would be only to the norms and values that are extrapolated from the behavioral styles discussed earlier. But there is also what might be called a "psycho-ideological" value system, in which a commitment implies valuing the vantage point of those in power. It implies valuing existing power relationships, conditions for dominance and submission, and the political organization of the social order. When Afro-American children are presented with this value system, they are being taught to see the world through the eyes of those who enjoy majority status. As a result, they often come to see the existing order as legitimate even though they are not part of it themselves. They may even come to internalize the very position of inferiority that they appear to have when viewed from the vantage point of the dominant group.

To say that the schools create commitments to the existing social order and its values is to say that they serve a colonizing function (Carnoy, 1974). Middle-class children are taught to be middle class. White children are taught the value of whiteness. Lower-class children are taught the inevitability of their low social and economic standing. Minority children are taught to be minorities. Afro-American children are taught the ordained inferiority of their blackness and the value of emulating white people (see Bowles & Gintis, 1976; Carnoy, 1974; Ogbu, 1978; Persell, 1977). To the extent that Black children accept that schools should "civilize" them (teach them the proper way to talk and think and interact), to the extent that they embrace the ideals of the meritocracy (so that they accept individual responsibility for their own failures), and especially to the extent that they come to view the world from the vantage point of the ruling order — to that extent, the result will be successfully colonized minds.

In this way we come not to hold those in wealth and power responsible for our failure, indeed for succeeding on the very backs of our failure; we hold ourselves responsible instead. We don't get mad at those in power for possessing inordinate wealth. We envy them, want to be like them, desire the same wealth and power for ourselves. We even hold our own people in contempt for not striving to be like the privileged few. When this colonization process is successful, it makes the oppressed people partners with the ruling order in the perpetuation of their own oppression.

Even this depiction does not do full justice to the complexity of the triple quandary conjoined with the phenomenon of hegemony. For example, one can be alienated from the system at large even while coming to respect the values that it represents. It is possible to espouse those values in some form and at the same time view them with disdain, being unable to fathom any viable alternatives. One can become socialized to dishonor black cultural characteristics even while one is functioning, albeit unreflectively, in a Black cultural mode. Such paradoxes should not be unexpected. They pose a special challenge for those who are seriously intent on understanding the elaborations of Afro-American life.

Alternative Approaches to the Education of Black Children

How can schools meet the needs of Afro-American children more effectively? We address this question first at the level of training in cognitive skills, and then consider other, more fundamental aspects of socialization.

It often has been suggested that the academic problems of Afro-American children might be alleviated if Black culture were brought into the classroom in a meaningful way (Gay, 1975; Hale, 1980; Miller, 1973). Ogbu (1978) has characterized this position as follows:

> People in this [culturally based] position argue that the competence goals of the schools are probably different from the competence goals to which Black families have socialized their children. They suggest that to eliminate the conflict and increase Black motivation to perform in the classroom, the goals of education should be modified to make them more compatible with the values, goals, and learning styles of Black children. (p. 210)

However desirable this position may seem when it is stated in global terms, it has not been without its detractors. Ogbu points out that the advocates of the culturally based position:

> . . . do not say exactly what they consider these values, these goals, and these learning styles to be. Their main point is that since Black parents are not able to socialize their children to acquuire the White middle-class attributes that fit successful learning in school, the schools should modify their approach to fit the

qualities or skills possessed by Black children. One wonders how this modification would prepare Black children to participate competently as adults in a technological society requiring White middle-class qualities and competence. (p. 210)

This is a very cogent statement. Although this chapter has tried to describe Afro-American values and learning styles more precisely than the writers to whom Ogbu refers, it has not yet addressed his most significant criticism. Is it not true that success in America requires competence according to mainstream standards? Shouldn't Black children learn the academic skills that are required for gainful employment in our society? This is indeed a reasonable goal, but there is more than one way to approach it. At present, it is taken for granted that the process of teaching cognitive skills should be set in a particular cultural context, one that is informed by the dominant cultural ideals of the society. I suggest that we dis-embed the acquisition of skills from that context and place it in one that is more culturally congruent for Afro-Americans. If this is done, especially during the early years of school, the current negotiational impasse might be avoided. Teachers might not be so preoccupied with discipline and control at the expense of teaching; children might not become so alienated and cynical, or so mentally colonized. Once this had been acomplished, strategies for bicultural and bistylistic incorporation of cognitive skills might be implemented, enabling the children to adapt to a pluralistic society dominated by the Euro-American ethos.

The notion that schools teach cognitive skills in a particular context can be clarified further. For our present purposes, the context of schooling has three important manifestations. First, it refers to task *definition* itself: how a particular skill or competence is defined for students and how its purposes are presented to them. Second, it refers to task *format:* the manner in which the skills in question are acquired and performed. Finally, it refers to *ambience:* the environmental flux that envelops the task itself and forms the background for learning. All three of these manifestations have cultural implications and overtones; all three can be altered to provide greater cultural compatibility. The school's ambience can be made more conducive to task performance, task formats can be made less culturally stifling, and tasks themselves can be specified in a more culturally interpretable way. Boykin (1983) provides a fuller elaboration of curricular changes that would be consistent with the present analysis.

We must surely demand that the basic skills of reading, writing, and arithmetic be taught and taught well. But we must do more than find better ways to teach them; we must also unhook them from the cultural chauvinism and psychoideological hegemony that prevails in the schools. The acquisition of skills must be embedded in value constellations that promote human welfare and do not degrade the pluralistic society that is America. As we have seen, one of the functions of schooling is to support a particular social order. What social order should Afro-American children be committed to? Following Apple (1979), we can argue that it would be quite different from the order that prevails today: ". . . the progressive articulation of a commitment to a social order that has at its very foundation not the accumulation of goods, profits, and credentials but the maximization of economic and social equality" (p. 11).

Where might schooling fit in, in terms of helping to actualize such a commitment? A first step would be to abandon the present concern with the homogenization and differentiation of students and come to terms with the pluralistic reality of American society. An "equal-status pluralism" is required: not a ranking of individuals in terms of status and attainment, but a genuine acknowledgment of the meaningful social and cultural differences among American groups. White, Parham & Parham (1980) have suggested that we must give up our preoccupation with talent assessment and selection and concentrate instead on the development of the talents of people from culturally diverse backgrounds. This clearly implies a different function for schooling, one that accepts children for what they are and seeks to help them become competent adults by whatever pedagogical devices are appropriate.

What about values? The constellation of values offered by the schools should be a liberating one honestly assesses the reality of racism in America and promotes strategies for negotiating through the cultural environment that actually exists. Such a value system would emphasize collective responsibility while allowing for the vantage points of disparate groups. The Black community at large must come to see the limited utility in the current educational value system, which does not reflect the realities of racism and is not adaptive for people of minority group status. Such a system, although rewarding the individual efforts of a chosen few who conform to it, cannot be a beacon for generally, pervasively, and appreciably enhancing the life conditions of Black people. We need what Friere (1973) has called a "pedagogy of the oppressed": we must decolonize the schooling process and the knowledge that is imparted. The same skills should still be taught, but in a different context and from a Black social-cultural perspective. The kind of schooling that is required might appropriately be called "Afrographic" (Boykin, 1983) rather than Eurocentric.

Research Directions

It would be premature to delineate concrete proposals for changes in the schools at this time. Such proposals must be based on research on Afro-American culture and schooling. Such research is desperately needed to clarify issues and put problems into empirical perspective. Research of this kind will have to depart from traditional paradigms in many ways: in terms of the problems to be tackled, the way variables are conceptualized, the proper units of analysis, and the questions to be asked of the data and the functions that might be served. It seems appropriate to elaborate somewhat further on possible research directions.

First, more ethnographic research is needed to provide basic data on the texture of the Afro-American psychological experience itself. To understand the character of Black cultural styles and their manifestation in different contexts, we will have to go to street corners, basements, playgrounds, churches, and anywhere else that Afro-Americans congregate. Then, too, I advocate the study of "cultural contextual synergism" and initiated several projects to this end (Boykin, 1979; Boykin, 1982; Boykin & DeBritto, 1984). In this research the first step is to articulate a cultural style and the contexts that support it. The next is to adapt that style and those contexts to make them amenable to empirical testing. Then it becomes possible to create a microcosm of the teaching situation in which one can examine motivational factors and task performance, a "prescriptive pedagogy" (Boykin, 1977).

Our research has explored heuristic conditions that facilitate the task performance of Afro-American children. Those conditions are predicated squarely on the cultural integrity of Afro-Americans. In particular, our work has been based on the rhythmic-movement orientation and the concept of verve. It has produced encouraging results. There is no reason why a similar approach could not be taken to the study of certain adaptive or coping styles as well. Note that the aim of such research is not to discover particular "stimuli" that lead to given responses, but to explore the contextual variables that may affect or modify performance. One further word of caution is also in order. This method treats culture as an independent variable affecting task performance, but that is not the only or most crucial way in which culture affects education. When culture is properly understood as the very psychological texture in which schooling is situated, it can be "exploited" democratically to provide a more humane and effective education for all children in the pluralistic American order.

A second fertile area for research would be the study of ongoing personal interactions in classroom settings. What does the quality of the transactions between students and teachers, or among students themselves, portend for the learning process? Research of this kind has already been initiated. Piestrup's (1973) naturalistic study of teaching styles as they relate to read-reading proficiency and dialect usage is one noteworthy example. Another is McDermott's (1974) demonstration that students and their teachers can actively participate in "achieving" school failure. The work of Brown, Palincsar, and Purcell (this volume) should also be cited.

Because these studies were not conceived in terms of the present analytical scheme, they have not explored the implications of that scheme for classroom interaction. We need further research that takes cultural issues into consideration explicitly. How do the participants in a classroom interaction respond to a culturally divergent stylistic overture? More generally, how do questions of culture get played out in educational settings? What coping strategies do students use to deflect attacks on their integrity? What strategies can help to keep a student on task even when countervailing forces are present? Which teaching styles are most compatible with which cultural and coping styles? Research in this domain is difficult, but it is also essential. Perhaps it can be complemented by laboratory research that uses controlled tasks and conditions.

Another domain that deserves serious consideration is the socialization processes that go on in Afro-American families and communities. How do Black children learn the cultural and adaptive styles that they display? How are they prepared to function in the mainstream, minority, and Black cultural realms of negotiation? Who are the major role models for each realm? Do family structure and level of material affluence interact with the socialization processes? What are the relationships among the cultural and adaptive styles displayed at home, those displayed at school, and school performance? These concerns illustrate the wide range of research questions that are begging to be addressed.

Final Comments

Some fundamental assertions about the functioning of our society have been advanced here. American society is complex and culturally pluralistic. To treat its heterogeneity as if it simply reflected different degrees of compliance with one cultural standard is to misunderstand its true nature. We must begin by acknowledging the integrity of the diverse social-cultural frames of reference and understanding them on their own terms. Furthermore, we must find ways to incorporate that very diversity into the various social attainment processes. In particular, we must take account of the cultural diversity of the nation's children as it bears on their attainments in our schools.

Such a stance can generate new conceptual and empirical possibilities. It may help to lay the psychological foundation for different kinds of institutional practices and perhaps usher in a more humanistic complement of American values. Our focus would then shift from a premium on talent assessment and selection to one on talent development, as White et al. (1980) have already urged. This would be accomplished by discovering how to build on the various social-cultural frames of reference in the process of education itself. To the extent that this can be done, America will avoid the waste of human potential that we are witnessing today, and society as a whole will thrive.

None of this can be meaningfully accomplished without American society moving toward what has been called cultural democracy (Gordon, 1964; Kallen, 1924; Ramirez & Castaneda, 1974). Individuals should have the right to identify with the life styles and values of their homes and immediate communities, while also becoming conversant with those of mainstream Euro-American middle-class society. They should not have to choose the life style they will pursue until they are old enough to understand the consequences of that choice. It will not be easy to attain such a goal, in view of the prevailing hegemony and ideology. Only by altering institutions and values to make them consistent with cultural democratic principles can we make such choices realistically possible. Eventually we may be able to create a social order that truly maximizes economic, social, and educational equality.

REFERENCES

Akbar, N. (1976). Rhythmic patterns in African personality. In L. King, V. Dixon, & W. Nobles (Eds.), *African philosophy: Assumptions and paradigms for research on black persons.* Los Angeles: Fanon Center Publications.

Akbar, N. (1982). The evolution of human psychology for Afro-Americans. Unpublished manuscript, Florida State University.

Allen, W. (1978). The search for applicable theories of Black family life. *Journal of Marriage and Family, 40,* 117–129.

Apple, M. (1979). *Ideology and curriculum.* London: Routledge & Kegan Paul.

Baldwin, J. (1979). Theory & research concerning the notion of Black self-hatred: A review and reinterpretation. *Journal of Black Psychology, 5,* 51–77.

Banks, J. (1976). Crucial issues in the education of Afro-American children. *Journal of Afro-American Issues, 4,* 392–407.

Banks, W. C. (1976). White preference in Blacks: A paradigm in search of a phenomenon. *Psychological Bulletin, 83,,* 1179–86.

Baratz, S. & Baratz, J. (1970). Early childhood intervention: The social science base of institutional racism. *Harvard Educational Review, 40,* 29–50.

Billingsley, A. (1969). Family functioning in the low-income black community. *Social Casework, 50,* 563–72.

Blackwell, J. (1975). *The black community: Diversity and unity.* NY: Dodd Mead.

Blauner, R. (1970). Black culture: Myth or reality. In N. Whitten & J. Szwed (1970). *Afro-American anthropology.* NY: Free Press.

Bowles, S. & Gintis, H. (1976). *Schooling in capitalist America.* N.Y.: Basic Books.

Boykin, A. W. (1977). On the role of context in the standardized test performance of minority group children. *Cornell Journal of Social Relations, 12,* 109–124.

Boykin, A. W. (1979). Black psychology and the research process: Keeping the baby but throwing out the bathwater. In A. W. Boykin, A. J. Franklin, & J. F. Yates (Eds.), *Research directions of Black psychologists.* New York: Russell Sage Press.

Boykin, A. W. (1982). Population differences in the effect of format variability on task performance. *Journal of Black Studies, 12,* 469–485.

Boykin, A. W. (1983). The academic performance of Afro-American children. In J. Spence (Ed.), *Achievement and achievement motives.* San Francisco: W. Freeman.

Boykin, A. W., DeBritto, A., & Davis L. (1984). The influence of social process factors and contextual variability on schoolchildren's task performance. Unpublished manuscript, Howard University.

Bradley, L. & Bradley, G. (1977). The academic achievement of Black students in desegregated schools: A critical review. *Review of Educational Research, 47,* 399–449.

Caplan, N. & Nelson, S. (1973). On being useful: The nature and consequences of psychological research on social problems. *American Psychologist, 28,* 199–211.

Carnoy, M. (1974). *Education as cultural imperialism.* New York: D. McKay.

Carnoy, M. & Shearer, D. (1980). *Economic democracy.* White Plains, NY: Sharpe.

Caudill, W. (1952). Japanese-American personality and acculturation *Genetic Psychology Monographs, 45,* 3–102.

Center for the Study of Social Policy. (1982). A dream deferred: The economic status of Black Americans, a working paper. Washington, DC.

Cole, J. (1970). Black culture: Negro, Black and Nigger. *Black Scholar, 1,* 40–43.

Cole, M. & Scribner, S. (1974). *Culture and thought.* N.Y.: John Wiley.

Deutsch, M. (1963). The disadvantaged child and the learning process: Some social psychological and developmental considerations. In A. Passow (Ed.), *Education in depressed areas.* New York: Teachers College Press.

DeVos, G. (1982). Adaptive strategies in U.S. minorities. In E. Jones & S. Korchin (Eds.), *Minority mental health.* New York: Praeger.

Dixon, V. (1976). Worldviews and research methodology. In L. King, V. Dixon, & W. Nobles (Eds.), *African philosophy: Assumptions and paradigms for research on Black persons.* Los Angeles: Fanon Center Publications.

DuBois, C. (1972). The dominant value profile of American culture. In R. Shinn (Ed.), *Culture and school.* San Francisco: Intext Educational Publishers.

DuBois, W. E. B. (1903). *Souls of Black folk.* Chicago: McClurg.

Feshbach, S. & Adelman, H. (1974). Remediation of learning problems among the disadvantaged. *Journal of Educational Psychology, 66,* 16–28.

Friere, P. (1973). *Pedagogy of the oppressed.* New York: Seabury Press.

Furby, L. (1979). Individualistic bias in studies of locus of control. In A. Buss (Ed.), *Psychology in social context.* New York: Irvington.

Gay, G. (1975, October). Cultural differences important in education of Black children. *Momentum, 30*–33.

Gay, G. & Abraham, R. 1973). Does the pot melt, boil or brew? Black children and white assessment procedures. *Journal of School Psychology, 11,* 330–40.

Ginsburg, H. (1972). *The myth of the deprived child.* Englewood Cliffs, NJ: Prentice-Hall.

Gordon, M. (1964). *Assimilation in American life: The role of race, religion and national origins.* New York: Oxford University Press.

Gottlieb, D. (1967). Poor youth do want to be middle class but it's not easy. *The Personnel and Guidance Journal, 46,* 116–22.

Gutman, H. (1976). *The black family in slavery and freedom, 1750–1925.* New York: Pantheon Books.

Hale, J. (1980). Demythicizing the education of Black children. In R. Jones (Ed.), *Black Psychology* 2nd ed. New York: Harper & Row.

Hale, J. (1982). *Black children: Their roots, culture and learning styles.* Provo, UT: Brigham Young Press.

Hannertz, U. (1969). *Soulside: Inquiries into ghetto culture.* N.Y.: Columbia University Press.

Harrell, J. (1979). Analyzing black coping styles: A supplemental diagnostic system. *The Journal of Black Psychology, 5,* 99–108.

Harrell, J. (1981). Studies of stress and coping in blacks: Toward an understanding of individual differences in responses. In J. McAdoo, H. McAdoo & W. Cross (Eds.), *The Fifth Conference on Empirical Research in Black Psychology.* Washington, DC: NIMH.

Henderson, S. & Washington, A. (1975). Cultural differences and the education of Black children: An alternative model for program development. *Journal of Negro Education, 44,* 353–60.

Hill, R. (1972). *The strengths of black families.* New York: Emerson Hall.

Hofstadter, R. (1955). *Social darwinism in American thought*. Boston: Beacon.

Hoover, M. (1978). Community attitudes toward Black English. *Language in Society, 7,* 65–87.

Hunt, J. McV. (1973). Parent and child centers: Their basis in the behavioral and educational sciences. In J. Frost (Ed.), *Revisiting early childhood education*. New York: Holt, Rinehart & Winston.

Israel, J. (1979). From level of aspiration to dissonance. In A. Buss (Ed.), *Psychology in social context*. New York: Irvington.

Jackson, G. (1979). The origin and development of black psychology: Implications for black studies and human behavior. *Studia Africana, 1,* 270–293.

Jones, J. M. (1972). *Prejudice and racism*. Reading, MA: Addison-Wesley.

Jones, J. M. (1979). Conceptual and strategic issues in the relationship of black psychology to American social science. In A. W. Boykin, A. J. Franklin, & J. F. Yates (Eds.), *Research directions of black psychologists*. New York: Russell Sage Press.

Jones, J. M. (1983). The concept of race in social psychology: From color to culture. In L. Wheeler & P. Shaver (Eds.), *Review of Personality and Social Psychology*, Vol. 4. Beverly Hills, CA: Sage Publications.

Kallen, H. (1924). *Culture and democracy in the United States*. New York: Boni & Liveright.

Kamii, C. & Radin, N. (1967). Class differences in the socialization practices of Negro mothers. *Journal of Marriage and Family, 29,* 302–10.

Khan, V. (1982). The role of culture of dominance in structuring the experience of ethnic minorities: In C. Husband (Ed.), *Race in Britain: Continuity and change*. London: Huthinson.

Kitano, H. (1969). *Japanese-Americans: The evolution of a subculture*. Englewood Cliffs, NJ: Prentice-Hall.

Kluckhohn, F. & Strodtbeck, F. (1961). *Variations in value orientations*. Evanston, IL: Row, Peterson.

Labov, W. (1970). The logic of nonstandard English. In F. Williams (Ed.), *Language and poverty*. Chicago: Markham.

Levine, L. (1977). *Black culture and black consciousness*. New York: Oxford University Press.

Lewis, D. (1975). The Black family: Socialization and sex roles. *Phylon, 26,* 471–480.

Lewis, H. (1970). Child rearing practices among low income families in the District of Columbia. In M. Goldschmid (Ed.), *Black Americans and white racism*. NY: Holt, Rinehart & Winston.

Loye, D. (1971). *The healing of a nation*. New York: Dell.

Marans, A. & Lourie, R. (1967). Hypotheses regarding the effects of child-rearing patterns on the disadvantaged child. In J. Hellmuth (Ed.), *Disadvantaged child*. Vol. 1. New York: Brunner/Mazel.

Massey, G., Scott, M., & Dornbusch, C. (1975). Racism without racists: Institutional racism in urban schools. *Black Scholar, 7,* 10–19.

McClelland, D. (1971). Testing for competence rather than 'intelligence'. *American Psychologist, 28,* 1–4.

McDermott, R. (1974). Achieving school failure: An anthropological approach to illiteracy and social stratification. In G. Spindler (Ed.), *Education and cultural process*. New York: Holt, Rinehart & Winston.

Memmi, A. (1965). *The colonizer and the colonized*. New York: Orion Press.

Milgram, N., Shore, M., Riedel, W., & Malasky, C. (1970). Levels of aspiration and locus of control in disadvantaged children, *Psychological Reports, 27,* 343–50.

Miller, L. (1973, May). Strengths of the Black child. *The Instructor,* 210–211.

Moos, R. & Moos, B. (1976). A typology of family social environments. *Family Process, 15,* 357–71.

Nobles, W. (1976, December). *A formulative and empirical study of black families*. Final Report, DHEW, Office of Child Development, #90-C-255.

Ogbu, J. (1978). *Minority education and caste: The American system in cross-cultural perspective*. New York: Academic Press.

Parsons, T. (1959). The school class as a social system: Some of its functions in American society. *Harvard Educational Review, 29,* 297–318.

Persell, C. (1977). *Education and inequality: A theoretical and empirical synthesis.* New York: Free Press.

Piestrup, A. (1973). *Black dialect interference and accommodation of reading institutions in first grade.* Monograph #4, Language Behavior Research Laboratory, University of California, Berkeley.

Prager, J. (1982). America racial ideology as collective representation. *Ethnic and Racial Studies, 5,* 99–119.

Proshansky, H. & Newton, P. (1973). Color: The nature and meaning of Negro self-identity. In P. Watson (Ed.), *Psychology and race.* Chicago: Aldine.

Picou, J. (1973). Black-white variations in model of the occupational aspirational process. *Journal of Negro Education, 42,* 117–22.

Rainwater, L. (1966). Crucible of identity: The Negro lower-class family. *Daedalus, 95,* 172–217.

Ramirez, M. & Castaneda, A. (1974). *Cultural democracy, bicognitive development and education.* New York: Academic Press.

Rist, R. (1970). Student social class and teacher expectations: The self-fulfilling prophecy in ghetto education. *Harvard Educational Review, 40,* 411–451.

Rollins, H., McCandless, B., Thompson, M., & Brassell, W. (1974). Project success environment: An extended application of contingency management in inner-city schools. *Journal of Educational Psychology, 66,* 167–78.

Ryan, W. (1971). *Blaming the victim.* New York: Vintage Books.

Sampson, E. (1977). Psychology and the American ideal. *Journal of Personality and Social Psychology, 35,* 767–82.

Sampson, E. (1978). Scientific paradigms and social values: Wanted—a scientific revolution. *Journal of Personality and Social Psychology, 36,* 1332–43.

Schwebel, M. (1975). The inevitability of ideology in psychological theory. *International Journal of Mental Health, 3,* 4–26.

Shade, B. (1978). Social-psychological characteristics of achieving Black children. *Negro Educational Review, 29,* 80–86.

Silverstein, B. & Krate, R. (1975). *Children of the dark ghetto.* New York: Praeger.

Simmons, W. (1979). The relationship between academic status and future expectations among low-income blacks. *Journal of Black Psychology, 6,* 7–16.

Smitherman, G. (1977). Talking and testifying: *The language of black America.* Boston: Houghton-Mifflin.

Staples, R. (1976). *Introduction to black sociology.* New York: McGraw-Hill.

Stewart, W. (1970). Toward a history of American negro dialect. In F. Williams (Ed.), *Language and poverty.* Chicago: Markham.

Valentine, C. (1968). *Culture and poverty.* Chicago: University of Chicago Press.

Valentine, C. (1971). Deficit, difference and bi-cultural models of Afro-American behavior. *Harvard Educational Review, 41,* 137–57.

West, C. (1978). Philosophy and the Afro-American experience. *Philosophical Forum, 10,* 117–148.

White, J., Parham, W., & Parham, T. (1980). Black psychology: The Afro-American tradition as a unifying force for traditional psychology. In R. Jones (Ed.), *Black psychology.* 2nd Ed. Harper & Row.

Williams, R. (1974). Cognitive and survival learning of the Black child. In J. Chunn (Ed.), *The survival of black children and youth.* Washington, DC: Nuclassics and Science.

Williams, R. (1980, October). Invited talk. Howard University Medical School. Washington, DC.

Wilson, T. (1972). Notes toward a process of Afro-American education. *Harvard Educational*

Review, 42, 374–89.

Wirth, L. (1936). Preface to K. Mannheim, *Ideology and utopia.* New York: Harcourt, Brace & World.

Young, V. (1970). Family and childhood in a southern Negro community. *American Anthropologist, 72,* 269–288.

Young, V. (1974). A Black American socialization pattern. *American Ethnologist, 1,* 405–413.

Zigler, E. & Anderson, K. (1979). An idea whose time had come: The intellectual and political climate for Head Start. In E. Zigler & J. Valentine (Eds.), *Project Head Start.* New York: Free Press.

4 Characteristics of Effective Schools*

Ronald Edmonds

Although the other papers [in this volume] do have implications for the kind of work I do, I am not going to be able to attend very much to the issues they raise. If I were going to discuss them, John Ogbu's notion of the relationship between culture and education would drive me beyond a discussion of instructional effectiveness to a discussion of educational excellence. I would have to say, then, that a school that was excellent for black children would be substantially different from the kinds of schools I am going to consider. It would be different in the way it is governed: it would, for example, be governed by blacks. The school would be different in its curriculum because the curriculum would be derived from the needs of the community from which children come. It would even be different in the substance of what it teaches: for example, it would not fail to describe the intimate interaction between the American experience and the concept of racism. Nevertheless, these are not the issues I am going to talk about.

I am going to talk about an idea and its context. I begin with a couple of words about how I came to this work. I wasn't trained for it and didn't intend it. If somebody had asked ten years ago if I would be so preoccupied with it

*When Ronald Edmonds died on July 15, 1983, he had not yet completed a finished manuscript for this volume. The present chapter is based on a tape recording of his actual remarks at the Cornell Conference. I have lightly edited the transcript of that tape, but every effort has been made to preserve the exact original meaning as well as Edmonds' vigorous style. Although the bibliography is my own responsibility, I am grateful to Edmonds' colleague Professor Lawrence W. Lezotte of Michigan State University for assistance in identifying some of the works mentioned in the talk.

— Ulric Neisser

now, I would have said, "Absolutely not." Somebody else was going to do that! I joined the Harvard faculty in 1972 and moved to the Institute for Research on Teaching at Michigan State in 1981 because of the work that I describe here. The significance of my joining the Harvard faculty is that in 1972 my Harvard colleagues published the book *Inequality*. That book is more or less the piece de resistance of the familial effects interpretation of the origin of achievement. Beginning with Coleman's [Coleman, Campbell, & Mood, 1966] equal education opportunity survey in 1966, educational researchers had fixed on the idea that achievement is derived from variability in social class and family background, that poor children do poorly in school because there is something intrinsically disabling about being poor. That's why we got compensatory education. It was designed to compensate children for their intrinsic cognitive, linguistic, and intellectual disabilities. If the compensation worked, then these disadvantaged children would learn to learn in ways the schools were disposed to teach.

The 1972 Mosteller/Moynihan volume on equality of educational opportunity seemed to confirm the familial effects interpretation. Reading that book is an extraordinary experience. Its critique of the Coleman report must be the most devastating methodological critique to which anybody's work has ever been subjected, but its summary conveys just the opposite impression. Having taken the methodology apart (and you can't put it back together), the book went on to say that Coleman is essentially correct — achievement does derive from family background and characteristics that describe children. *Inequality* then added whatever reinforcement may still have been needed. It is now conventional wisdom among American social scientists, members of the Congress, policy makers, boards of education, most educators, and members of the general public that how well children do in school derives primarily from the nature of the families from which they come.

I didn't agree with that notion. I had my own reservations about the work of Coleman et al. (1966) and Jencks and Jensen (1972) and all the rest whom I categorized at the time as of the "familial effects" variety, i.e., as those who insisted on the causal interaction between achievement and family background. My essay in the *Harvard Educational Review* in 1973 was a substantial criticism of the book *Inequality* in particular and familial effects research in general. As a result of the essay, the Carnegie Corporation (which had funded most of the familial effects research) invited me to do what I was describing as an alternative interpretation of the interaction between pupil performance and family background. It was under those auspices that the work began.

I am not the only researcher in this area. I study what are called "school effects"; there are a number of other American educational researchers who have done complementary work. This work concludes that *variability in the distribution of achievement among school age children in the United States derives from variability in the nature of the schools to which they go.* Achievement is therefore relatively independent of family background, at least when achievement is defined as pupil acquisition of basic school skills (as I will define it). Other school effects researchers include Brookover and Lezotte (1977) of Michigan State; Weber (1971), who was probably one of the earliest to present this kind of alternative interpretation of the phenomenon; Madden, Lawson, and Sweet (1976) in California; more recently the book *15,000 Hours* (Rutter, 1978) which is a comparative analysis of instructionally effective and ineffective inner city London high schools. The argument is fairly straightforward. The familial effects people continue to argue that the key to improved achievement for low income minority children in the United States depends on getting those children to learn in the ways schools teach. The school effects alternative interpretation argues that the key to improved achievement among school-age children depends on our ability to compel schools — or persuade them — to profit from what we now know about how to be consistently effective for the full range of the pupil population, and epecially for low-income and minority students.

My own work began in 1973. Initially it was an attempt to determine whether schools existed anywhere in the United States that did not have a familial effect. Was it possible to find schools with a significant low-income pupil population (or a homogeneously low-income pupil population) in which those pupils were clearly demonstrating academic mastery? In this work, *mastery* is defined as performance on standardized measures of achievement that permits two reports: Report No. 1 is that this level meets the requirements for mastery in the local school district; Report No. 2 is that this level allows us to predict that the student would be academically successful next year anywhere in the United States, that is, even if they didn't go to the school district in which they performed on the achievement test. We also use a particular definition of an "effective school": it is one where the proportion of *low-income* children demonstrating academic mastery is virtually identical to the proportion of *middle-class* children who do so. If a school fails that test, nothing else will qualify it as effective. Suppose that a school is 50% middle class and 50% poor, and that 96% of the middle-class students anually demonstrate academic mastery: that school would be nominated as effective only if 96% of the poor children also demonstrate mastery. This does not mean that the schools necessarily get both groups of children to perform *identically*. Even in effective schools, the middle-class children as a group still outperform the poor children as a group. This does not violate our standard, because we require only that the proportion of those who *exceed the minimum* must be approximately the same. It turns out that the extent to which the minimum is exceeded is still highly associated with the social class character of the groups with which we are working.

One of the major methodological differences between our social effects work and the standard familial effects work is that we do not portray a school with any single description of achievement. For example, we would never say of an elementary or intermediate school, "Here is the mean level of performance on a standardized achievement test." We would first disaggregate the pupil population by social class and then ask what proportions of the children in the various social classes demonstrate academic mastery, preferably on a criterion basis. We would judge the school effective only if those proportions came very close to being identical. (Although five social classes were used in our work, we usually compared only mastery in the highest social class to mastery in the lowest.) In homogeneously low income schools, we would use data for the relevant social class in the school district as a whole. That is, in order to arrive at the normative basis for the effectiveness of a school that was 100% low income, we would ask, "What proportion of the fourth graders in this entire school district demonstrate mastery?"

We spent the years in the middle 1970's gathering data. First we gathered individualized social class data on all the children in grades 4, 5, 6, and 7 in the school districts we studied. There were 26 data bits on each child, including parents' occupations, parents' education, birth order, health history, assessed property value of the home, and so on. We used the 26 data bits to assign each child to a social class. We then recorded the children's performance on all the standardized achievement tests they'd taken during all the years they'd been in school, and used that data to decide whether or not mastery had occurred. Then we combined the two bodies of data to see if we could find schools that did not have the familial effect, in which probabilities of academic mastery would be independent of membership in social class. We did find such schools and by 1978 were working with a core group of 55 in the northeast quadrant of the United States. We never expected that the proportion of schools judged effective would be very high. For the point we were trying to make, the numbers matter more than the proportions. Indeed, the proportion of American public schools that even approach our standard of effectiveness is miniscule. Nevertheless, the numbers are more than sufficient to demonstrate the universal educability of school-age children. After all, if school-age children weren't universally educable, we oughtn't to be able to find even five effective schools, let alone 55. If 55 don't persuade you of the universal educability of school age children, I don't see why 555 would either. We have been content in our consistent ability to identify significant numbers of American schools that meet our standard of effectiveness.

The second phase of our work put the question, "What is the difference between effective schools and ineffective schools?" That is, how does one explain the fact that two schools in the same school district may be near neighbors and of approximately the same size, racial composition, social class distribution, per pupil expenditure, and pupil-teacher ratio, yet the proportion of children demonstrating academic mastery in one school is dramatically greater than the proportion in the other? To explore this question, we paired selected effective schools with ineffective schools, (controlling social class, size, location, etc.) and then did systematic long-term observations of the paired schools. From voluminous descriptors, we excluded those found to obtain in both effective and ineffective schools. If any descriptors remained, we may not have discovered the causal origin of the variability of achievement, but we would have discovered the correlates of that variability. In public policy terms, a good deal could be done with those kinds of findings.

We were successful. That is, we found a limited number of organizational institutional characteristics that consistently obtained in the effective schools and that were absent in whole or in part in the ineffective ones. Those characteristics, more than anything else, distinguish effective schools from ineffective schools. Before describing them, I must mention two limitations to what we know about them. One has already been mentioned: We don't know whether or not the correlates are causal. They may be, but we cannot be sure. The second limitation is that the characteristics cannot be put in a rank ordering of importance. That is, the fact that a correlate is listed as No. 1 does not imply that it's more important than No. 5.

The first correlate is that the principals of effective schools behave in ways that are observably, demonstrably, and sometimes dramatically different from the way principals behave in ineffective schools. The main difference is that principals of effective schools are the instructional leaders in their buildings, whereas those in ineffective schools are not. Considering this characteristic alone, it can be seen that the criteria of effective schools are not easy to meet. Principals are not trained for instructional leadership, they are not chosen for it, they are not evaluated on that basis, they are not rewarded for doing it, and they are not punished for not doing it. The typical career route to becoming a principal is first to teach in the social studies department and then become coach of the football team; by and by they make you a principal. It's therefore extraordinary in many respects that there are any principals at all who manifest instructional leadership. Fortunately, there are significant numbers of men and women presiding over public schools who do have this characteristic. I do not have space and time to describe all the behaviors that are associated with instructional leadership, but they can be inferred.

The second set of correlates has to do with school focus, instructional emphasis, and institutional mission. It is not the substantive content of the focus that concerns us: The key variable is the proportion of the adults in the school who *know what the focus is.*. We chose cross sections of adults in both the effective and the ineffective schools and asked them, "What does this school care most about?" In the ineffective schools, the answer depended on the person to whom we put the question. When we put it to a cross section of adults in effective schools, however, the answer was uniform. Almost everybody answered the question the same way. They didn't all say that they liked the answer, but they clearly knew what it was. The relationship of this correlate to instructional leadership is clear. It would be difficult for a principal to say to a teacher, "There is a discrepancy between your behavior and the institutional focus of this school" if there were no connection between the principal's and the teacher's definition of that focus. Collegial interaction is a good deal easier when there is widely understood articulation of the mission of the school.

The third set of correlates deals with *school climate.* These are almost tangible measures: effective schools are relatively safer, relatively cleaner, relatively more orderly, relatively quieter. We collected data about the incidence of broken windows in the effective and ineffective schools, the incidence of burnt out light bulbs, the content of the dirt in the corners and stairwells, patterns of interior decoration, and so on. (Make up your own favorite list of things you would like to know about schools: we probably recorded it somewhere.) The differences between effective and ineffective schools were "relative": the incidence of broken windows doesn't discriminate, but the time it takes to fix the windows does. Similarly, the quantity of dirt in the corners of the stairwells doesn't discriminate, but the turnover in the content of the dirt does. The substance of the pattern of interior decoration doesn't discriminate, but it is a notable characteristic of the effective schools that they tend to be physically dominated by student work. (I don't mean art work; I mean academic work). These findings bear on the question of whether the correlates are causal. It's pretty clear that broken windows don't cause either elevated or depressed achievement; the relevance of the window is that it's a stand-in for adult attention to the environment. A broken window that goes for a long time without being repaired sends a message to everybody that the people who are responsible for this place don't care very much about it. Display of student academic work clearly doesn't cause a rise or fall in academic achievement, but it's a stand-in for adult's attention to student work. The adults have to care about the work: they have to pick it, they have to choose it, they have to display it, they have to take it down and replace it. I think those are the kinds of analyses that are going to get us closer to a causal understanding of the correlates.

The fourth set of correlates is based on *classroom observation.* Our conclusions were vast. There were some dramatic variations in teacher behavior in the effective schools as contrasted to teacher behavior in the ineffective schools. For example, teachers in the ineffective schools tend to be highly selective in choosing students to recite; they are most likely to ask questions of students who they predict will know the answer. Teachers in ineffective schools often vary considerably in the imposition of discipline as a function of pupil sex, race, and social class. Some of them are more lenient with black children than with white children and others are the reverse; some are harsher with poor children than with middle-class children, or vice versa. The significance is in the variability. Teachers in the ineffective schools tend to vary their responses as a function of the characteristics of their students, whereas teacher behavior in the effective schools is much flatter. Our findings are related to those of the teacher effects research. For example, there is variability in the quality of teacher response to recitation. Teachers in the ineffective schools would hear a recitation from a middle-class child and they would evaluate it: they'd say, "The first part of the answer was right and the second part of the answer was wrong in the following ways, and you ought to think about this or that." There is much less variability in the behavior of teachers in the effective schools. The teachers in the effective schools make it clear that they expect some of their students to do better than others; they also make it clear that they are working with a minimum academic prerequisite and that they expect everybody to achieve it. They may expect variability in pupil performance, but they do not expect that any significant number of children of any race or social class will fail to demonstrate minimum mastery. They surround themselves with behaviors I have described as a way of reinforcing their commitment to this basic idea: that all their children are capable of acquiring basic school skills.

The final set of correlates, which may turn out to be the most powerful causally, concerns school use of performance on *standardized achievement tests* as a basis for program evaluation. People in the ineffective schools tend to be unmoved by pupil performance on standardized tests, especially when the data show that the middle-class students are doing well and the poor children are doing poorly. Such data have no effect on programs: people in ineffective schools explain them away. They say that the poor children have intrinsic disabilities — cognitive, linguistic, cultural, environmental, etc. — that explain their depressed achievement. The major characteristic of the ineffective schools is the extent to which they tend to perpetuate what they have been doing, even if it is to the distinct disadvantage of a significant proportion of their pupil population. The effective schools, in contrast, are driven by pupil performance on standardized tests. When they don't get what they want, they try something else. What they want, of course, is the continual demonstration of the universal educability of their pupil population. You might say that effective schools spend as much time avoiding things that don't work as they spend trying to gravitate toward things that do. That is probably the most powerful of the correlates, in the sense that it has the capacity to drive all the others.

This modest description of the characteristics of the effective schools in terms of the five correlates is the most widely disseminated and widely used part of our work. In the summer of 1978, while the work was still going on, I was invited to become chief instructional officer of the New York City schools. My invitation was based explicitly on this research. That is, I was invited to preside over the New York City schools to use our research as the basis for reforming them. I took the job, dividing my time between the University and New York City from the summer of 1978 until February 1981, when I returned full time to the University. I can tell you that it is a ticklish business for a researcher to translate what he purports to know into actual intervention in an institution. It does cause one or two moments of anxiety, I assure you. It's one thing for us to do learned portrayals of the schools while we are safely in an academic setting, and it's quite another to modify the behavior of 60,000 classroom teachers in New York City schools. What went on in New York City after the summer of 1978 and is still going on (although I have stopped presiding over it), was an attempt at systematic intervention that I will briefly describe. Although I will not be specific about which of the correlates prompted which of the interventions, I assure you that all of them were grounded in this discussion. I know the basis of every decision that was made, and the way in which it was derived from this portrayal of the characteristics that discriminate between effective and ineffective schools.

In the summer of 1978, New York City enrolled a million students in 1,300 schools in five boroughs. New York City is divided into 32 decentralized community school districts, which means that there are 32 locally elected boards of education in the city and 32 superintendents. Although the central board and the central administration do retain substantial authority, much of the discretionary authority resides in those local board and superintendents. About 100,000 adults work for the New York City schools. The first thing we did was to tell them to do their job, whatever it was, on the basis of three premises: (a) all the children who go to school in New York City are educable; (b) pupil educability derives from the nature of the school to which students are sent and is not associated with the character of the family from which they come; (c) if what you are about to do reinforces premises (a) and (b), do it — if it does not, don't. We said we would evaluate their work on the basis of whether it reinforced premises (a) and (b) and we would penalize them if we find out that they had undermined premises (a) and (b). And a good deal of undermining went on, as a matter of fact.

Our second change was to say that, after the 1978–79 school year, New York would operate on the basis of a standardized city-wide curriculum that described the bodies of knowledge and sets of skills that comprised the minimum instructional obligation in all 1,300 schools. Previously, the required level of curricular mastery had been consideraby different in Harlem than on Staten Island, and considerably different in some parts of Brooklyn than in the upper west side of Manhattan. After 1979, that variability ceased. The system began to operate with a uniform, standardized curricular set of requirements. We went on to say that students would be promoted from one grade to the next solely on the basis of their demonstrated mastery of the portion of the curriculum for which they were responsible. No evidence of any other kind could form the basis for student promotion. Students who failed as a result of these policies would not repeat the grade they failed, but would instead be enrolled in an alternative course of study. It was alternative in this sense: students who failed fourth grade were put the next year in fourth grade classes that were less than half the normal size and were taught by teachers whom we chose and trained to teach those classes, using instructional materials and programs that we selected for that purpose. Nevertheless, there was no variability in the curricular requirement.

The curricular requirements do not vary as a function of pupil eligibility either, or of bilingual education, or of special education. Some special provisions are made: students in bilingual education can, at their option, test for promotion a maximum of three times in their native language. But the fourth time the test is taken, it is compulsory in English. Thus, even students in a bilingual program are required to achieve an identical standard of mastery as a prerequisite to movement from one grade to another. The same is true of the children in special education. The variability in special education may be in instructional strategy or materials or the classroom setting — whatever the Individual Education Plan recommends — but there is no curricular variability. When I went to New York, I discovered that, as in most systems, significant numbers of students in the system didn't take the test at all. No special education students took it; nor did students in bilingual education. If a principal predicted that a certain student would do poorly, that student was often encouraged to stay home on the day of testing. So I wrote a memorandum that, as of the spring of 1978, when we scored the city-wide tests, we would record *all* students in *every* school as having taken them. If they hadn't actually taken it for any reason, we would simply score a zero. The proportion of students taking the standardized achievement test rose considerably.

Finally, there is a program in New York, the School Improvement Project, that gets a good deal of attention. It is designed to illustrate the premise that intervention can take place in any city school at any time: if the intervention succeeds in introducing the correlates of school effectiveness, there will be an early increase in the proportion of low-income children demonstrating academic mastery. (There will also be an increase in the level achieved by those students who are already doing well. Effective schools do not attempt to eliminate the achievement gap that separates poor children from middle-class children: they raise the floor below which nobody falls.) The program uses people that have been trained to do systematic evaluations — needs assessments — of individual schools. When a school has been selected for intervention, the first thing we do is a formal evaluation on the critical characteristics: administrative style, climate, and so on. We use those data to form a plan of intervention tailored to that school. If we find that some of the characteristics are there, we leave them alone. If other characteristics are either absent or weak, we try to intervene on those particular characteristics. The intervention consists of bringing in — on an ad hoc temporary basis — resources that teach the professional, organizational, and institutional behaviors associated with the particular characteristics on which we have fixed our attention. Our prediction is that as we succeed in introducing these characteristics, we will succeed in increasing achievement.

By spring 1982, just three years later, pupil performance in New York City on standardized achievement tests was well above national norms and rising. The most dramatic gains were in Bedford/Stuyvesant, Oceanhill, Brownsville, Central Harlem, South Bronx. Two things were happening in New York: (a) an annual and dramatic increase in proportion of low income children demonstrating academic mastery, and (b) an increase in the level of mastery to which those students who were already doing well rose. One result last year was something we had never seen before: when Edward Koch ran for reelection as Mayor, one of his platforms was his intimate association with the New York City schools! (I assure you that politicians running for any office in New York do not often mention anything other than an interest in burning down all the schools in the city.) This response, from a man who is as conservative and as modest in his enthusiasm as Edward Koch, is probably about as stirring an endorsement as we could possibly get. That is, the gains being made are so dramatic that it profits a public official to be associated with them.

The same story is being repeated around the country. Milwaukee, Wisconsin, used this research as a basis for a program of intervention in what the superintendent called the twenty worst schools in Milwaukee. Programs of intervention were instituted in school districts in New Jersey, Connecticut, and Pennsylvania. There are more programs in the State of Michigan because Larry Lezotte and I designed and administered a training program there. We trained school people to design and implement their own programs of school improvement. As far as we can tell, all school age children in the United States are educable. No group of children suffers from any intrinsic characteristics that would preclude educability, at least when it is defined as pupil acquisition of basic school skills.

The most powerful force in the kind of education that I'm discussing is the school itself. I have already argued that the school effect is more powerful than the familial effect, but it is also more powerful than the teacher effect. That is, the effectiveness of teachers is much more a function of the nature of the schools in which they work than of any set of characteristics that they possess as individuals. Similarly, the school effect is more powerful than the neighborhood effect, and more powerful than the cultural environment that describes the community.

In a sense, these schools succeed in what they do because they are coercive. I do not mean that they are coercive in the traditional sense; they don't spank children, and tend not even to punish them very much. They create their own environment, and it is so potent that for at least six hours a day it can override almost everything else in the lives of those children. These schools do not discuss what they plan to teach, because it tends not to be negotiable. They do not discuss whether or not they will use standardized achievement tests as the basis for evaluating instruction; they just do it. It is probably more difficult to discuss "bias in testing" in these schools than in any other schools in the country. These school people insist that their students be evaluated on the basis of the most middle-class, widely used, pedestrian, standardized achievement tests extant. Their students must not be evaluated on the basis of any relativist standard of academic mastery.

These schools have a rather modest sense of their obligation. It is modest because the only obligation they accept is to provide students with a body of knowledge and a set of skills that give them a choice of whether or not to go on to the next grade. That applies to almost every level of schooling that they offer. There is no attempt here to consider the relevance of instruction, no discussion of whether it is relevant to learn to read ordinary textual materials at all. Many of these schools have very low levels of community parental participation. Many of them also have high levels, but it is clear that there is no relationship between level of parent participation and school effectiveness. It is certainly desirable to have the highest level of parent participation possible, and we never design school improvement programs without including parent participation, but the lesson I learned from the data is that one can never depend on it. One of the great implications of this work is that programs of school intervention must fix their attention exclusively on those characteristics over which the school has control. Everything else is to be left to somebody else.

Perhaps these goals are too modest; they certainly exclude an extraordinary range of important relevant topics. That's why I started out by noting that this was not a discussion of educational excellence. I do not think it will be possible to move these children from academic competence to educational excellence unless we expand the agenda, but I don't press the point for now; I am prepared to take my chances on the uses to which these children may put the choices that they accumulate as a result of what they learn. Therefore, I am not apologetic about the circumscribed and modest character of the standard that I'm talking about. At least for now, I'm prepared to argue that it is a realistic approach to the problem of mass education in the urban environment, and that it is worth a good deal of attention.

REFERENCES

Brookover, W. B., & Lezotte, L. W. (1977). *Changes in school characteristics coincident with changes in school achievement.* East Lansing: Michigan State University College of Urban Development.

Coleman, J. S., Campbell, E., & Mood, A. (1966). *Equality of educational opportunity.* Washington, DC: U.S Office of Education, National Center for Educational statistics.

Edmonds, R. (1973). A black response to Christopher Jencks' *Inequality* and certain other issues. *Harvard Educational Review, 43,* 76–92.

Jencks, C. (1972). *Inequality: A reassessment of the effect of family and schooling in America.* New York: Basic Books.

Madden, J. V., Lawson, D. R., & Sweet, D. (1976). School effectiveness study: State of California. Paper presented to the American Educational Research Association, San Francisco.

Mosteller, F., & Moynihan, D. P. (1972) (Eds.). *On equality of educational opportunity.* New York: Random House.

Rutter, M. (1978). *Fifteen thousand hours: Secondary schools and their effects on children.* Cambridge, MA.: Harvard University Press.

Weber, G. (1971). *Inner city children can be taught to read: Four successful schools.* Washington, D.C.: Council for Basic Education.

5 Poor Readers: Teach, Don't Label

Ann L. Brown
Annemarie Sullivan Palincsar
Linda Purcell

INTRODUCTION

Learning to read is the major item on the agenda in grade school. Students who are not fortunate enough to come to school knowing how to read, and who do not acquire the necessary skills according to the locally agreed upon timetable, obviously get off to a bad start in school. And, because of the increasing importance of obtaining information from texts in the later grades, they run the risk of a cumulative decline in their academic status with a concomitant increase in stigmatization and labeling. In this chapter, we discuss some of the reasons why so many poor children experience problems learning to read, and we examine methods that are successful at overcoming some of the problems.

We begin with a thumbnail sketch (not to say stereotype) of the "high-risk" child in the latter part of grade school. Conventional wisdom holds that such children are emotionally warped in school settings. They are described as passive, resistant, other directed, extrinsically motivated, failure oriented — in short, learned helplessness is the dominant diagnosis (Covington, in press; Dweck & Elliott, 1983). They are described as lacking in a whole battery of necessary cognitive skills, and, perhaps more alarming is the currently popular diagnosis of deficient "metacognitive skills" (Brown & Palincsar, 1982; Meichenbaum, in press). The message received is that such children are especially lacking in the orchestration and direction of their own learning. They do not adequately plan, monitor, or oversee their own academic activities; they are not self-directed learners or "self-improving systems" (Clay,

1973). In short, they have not yet learned to learn effectively in school settings. If it were true, this would be a devastating indictment.

We are critical of much of the research that has reinforced these stereo-types (Brown & Palincsar, 1982; Campione, Brown, & Ferrara, 1982). Briefly, much of the traditional research favors a "one-shot," "horse-race" approach to comparative psychology, i.e., a labeled ("deficient") group is pitted against a "normal" group on some esoteric task that bears little relationship to real life or even school life. The less than surprising outcome is that the normal group does better than the labeled group. Assuming the stereotype to be true — there is at least an element of truth in it — if by the third or fourth grade we have on our hands batteries of helpless, failure-oriented, passive, turned-off, academic learners, can we pinpoint anything in their academic histories that might have contributed to this state of affairs?

In the first part of this paper, we argue that there is compelling evidence that passive-resistance is not an unrealistic reaction to academic learning situations by children who have experienced early school failure. For the sake of fueling an argument, we go further to make the strong claim that these children have been taught to behave according to the stereotype. In the second part of the paper, we argue that, with adequate diagnosis replacing labeling, what could become a cumulative academic deficit can be overcome. We claim that the basic skills of self-directed reading can be taught. And, along with the specific improvement in academic skills that follows adequate teaching comes important attitude change on the part of both child and teacher.

PRESCHOOL EXPERIENCES

Edmonds (1978, this volume) has lucidly pointed out the trap of blaming the family for the poor academic performance of minority students rather than placing responsibility with the schools, and we do not want to repeat the error. However, there is considerable evidence that majority culture children do experience a variety of preschool parent-child interactions that match very well with the type of teacher-child interactions that dominate classroom dialogue in the early grades. It is claimed that this match makes the transition to formal schooling easier for majority culture children. Although the preschool experience of minority students may be equally rich in linguistic and cognitive content, it is said to provide less of a match with school activities that are orchestrated by middle-class teachers and therefore, creates confusion for the child entering school. A common theme of this argument is that the child-rearing practices of the affluent favor a variety of mediated learning experiences directed to academic-like tasks, mediated learning being situations where the parent or caretaker models and guides the child through methods of elaborating and questioning knowledge. We illustrate this claim from two areas of research, preschool picture-book reading, and the development of questioning strategies in both majority and minority culture homes.

Story Reading

In middle-class homes, one arena for such interactions is the picturebook task, where parents and children engage in reading-like activities. For example, Ninio and Bruner (1978) observed one upper-middle class mother reading with her child, starting when the child, Richard, was only 8 months old and terminating (unfortuntely) when he was 18 months old. The mother initially did all the "reading," but at the same time she was engaged in seducing the child into the ritual dialogue for picture-book reading. At first she appeared to be content with any vocalization from the baby, but, as soon as he produced actual words, the mother increased her demands and asked for a label with the query, "What's that?" The mother seemed to increase her level of expectation, first coaxing the child to substitute a vocalization for a nonvocal sign and later a well-formed word for a babbled vocalization. Initially, the mother did all the labeling because she assumed that the child could not; later, the mother labeled only when she believed that the child would not or could not label for himself.

Responsibility for labeling was thereby transferred from the mother to the child in response to his increasing store of knowledge, finely monitored by the mother. During the course of the study the mother constantly updated her inventory of the words the child had previously understood, and repeatedly attempted to make contact with his growing knowledge base. For example:

1. You haven't seen one of those; that's a goose.
2. You don't really know what those are, do you? They are mittens; wrong time of year for those.
3. It's a dog; I know you know that one.
4. We'll find you something you know very well.
5. Come on, you've learned "bricks."

DeLoache (1984) has repeated many of these observations in a cross-sectional study of middle-class mothers reading to their children. The children ranged from 17 to 38 months. The mothers of the youngest children pointed to the objects and labeled them. In the middle age group, the mothers shifted more of the responsibility to the children. They asked the children to point to and label objects, and to provide other information about the pictures. These children often provided labels spontaneously ("There's a horsie"), or asked the mothers for information ("What's this?"). With the 3-year-olds, the mothers went far beyond labeling; they talked about the relation among the objects in the picture, related them to the children's experience, and questioned the children about their outside experience (e.g., "That's right, that's a bee hive. Do you know what bees make? They make honey. They get nectar from flowers and use it to make honey, and then they put the honey in the bee hive. "). The mothers use the situation and the material to provide the children with a great deal of background information. Mothers continually elaborate and question information, comprehension-fostering activities that must later be applied to "real reading" tasks.

In both the Ninio and Bruner and DeLoache dyads, the mother attempts to function in the child's "region of sensitivity to instruction" (Wood & Middleton, 1975) or "zone of proximal development" (Vygotsky, 1978). As the child advances, so does the level of collaboration demanded by the mother. The mother systematically shapes their joint experiences in such a way that the child will be drawn into taking more and more responsibility for the dyad's work. In so doing, she not only provides an optimal learning environment, she also models appropriate comprehension-fostering activities; these crucial regulatory activities are thereby made *overt* and *explicit*.

Disadvantaged children putatively lack experience in these activities (Feuerstein, 1979, 1980). This is a varient of the old "restricted-language code" argument (Bernstein, 1971), with all its attendant problems, which we will not discuss further. However, for our purposes here, it is claimed that for a variety of pragmatic and cultural reasons (such questioning rituals are inappropriate adult-child interactions in some cultures), poor children do not experience a great deal of the particular type of elaboration and questioning activities that they will encounter regularly in school.

Widespread as these assumptions are, they lack sufficient documentation. However, we would like to point out two confirmatory reports. First, Hall (work in progress) suggests that middle-class families, black or white, do engage in school-like prereading activities more than do black or white working-class parents. Second, in her study of poor black sixth graders who are above average readers, Durkin (work in progress) found that: (a) all had been early readers — they came to school reading; and (b) the majority had in their preschool lives a significant other (often a grandmother) who both valued reading and spent considerable time playing these reading games. These retrospective reports need to be subtstantiated, but they do provide preliminary support for the match-mismatch hypothesis.

Questioning

Another example of the lack of cultural congruence between black children and their white teachers is the role of questioning rituals and routines in home settings and classroom life. Many researchers have documented the pervasiveness of certain common classroom questioning rituals in the preschool home interactions of white but not black children. A particularly interesting study by Heath (1981) provides a comparison between the questioning behavior of the white teachers in their own homes and the home questioning behaviors of their black pupils.

Heath's white middle-class mothers begin the questioning game almost from birth and well before the child can manage an answer. For example, a mother questioned her 8-week-old infant, "You want your teddy bear?" and responded for the child, "Yes, you want your bear." These rituals set the stage for a general reliance on questioning and pseudo-questioning interactions that serve a variety of social control functions. It is important to note that the predominance of these questioning rituals systematically trains the children to act as reliable question answerers. Indeed, Heath argues that children exposed to these interaction patterns seem compelled to provide an answer and are quite happy to provide information that they know perfectly well the adult already possesses.

Such "known-answer" questions, where the interrogator has the information being requested, occur frequently in classroom dialogues (Mehan, 1979). Teachers routinely call on children to answer questions that serve to display their knowledge rather than to provide information that the teacher does not know. Similarly, in middle-class white homes, known-answer questions predominate. For example, in one 48 hour period, almost half the utterances (215) addressed to Missy (aged 2 years 3 months) were questions (48%). Of these questions almost half (46%) were known-answer questions (Heath, 1981).

One common form of known-answer question is to ask the child to comment on the physical characteristics of an object, its color, name or shape, thus training the children to act as "experts on knowledge about their world especially the names and attributes of items in their environment and those introduced to them through books" (Heath, 1981, p. 110). Another common known-answer ritual is to engage in conversations concerning information familiar to both interrogator and answerer. For example:

Mother: (Looking at a family photograph album with Missy, age 2;3) Who's that, Missy? (The mother has pointed to the family dog in one of the pictures)
Missy: That's Toby.
Mother: What does Toby say?
Missy: Woof woof, grrrrr, yip.
Mother: Where does Toby live?
Missy: My house.

In general, questions play a less central role in the social interaction patterns of the poor black children's homes and, in particular, there is a notable lack of known-answer rituals. On the other hand, as Heath explains, there are other rich verbal rituals played in these homes that serve the same function as the middle-class question games. These verbal interactions are not deficient, far from it, but they are certainly different. Heath did not claim that questions never occur. They occur frequently, but are of a different form, they serve a different function, and they are embedded within different communicative and interpersonal contexts. Common questioning forms are analogy, story-starting, and accusatory; the first two rarely occur in the white middle-class home.

Heath's black children were commonly asked to engage in the sophisticated use of metaphors by responding to questions that asked for analogical comparisons. The children were more likely to be posed with the query, "What's that like?" "Who's he acting like?" rather than the more typical attributional, "What's that?" of the white middle-class home. Such questions reflect the black adults' assumptions that preschool children are adept at noting likenesses between things, assumptions that are also revealed in speech forms other than questioning (frequent use of similes and metaphors). As one adult claimed, "We don't talk to our chil'un like you folks do; we don't ask them 'bout colors, names, 'n things." What they do ask about and value is metaphorical thinking and narrative exposition initiated by a storytelling question whereby one participant indicates willingness to tell a story by the question form (e.g., "Did you see Maggie's dog yesterday?"). The appropriate answer to such a query is another question (e.g., "No, what happened to Maggie's dog yesterday?"), which sets the stage for the initiator's narrative. Both adults and older preschool children are totally familiar with these questioning rituals and play them enthusiastically.

We cannot give full details of the excellent ethnographic work of Heath, but the above examples should serve to emphasize the systematic dfferences between the form and function of questioning behaviors in the black and white communities studied by Heath (1981). Neither community is "deficient," but the match between the activities that predominate in classrooms at the early grades and in white middle-class homes is greater. As white teachers continue to practice their familiar questioning practices with their pupils, it is not surprising that white pupils, sharing the teacher's background, succeed in filling the answerer role, whereas the black children are perplexed.

Heath gives delightful examples of this perplexity and the gradual realization of the difference between school questions and home questions. For example, the spontaneous questioning games of Lem, a precocious, talkative black 4-year-old, were observed before and after he began attending nursery school run by middle-class teachers. He had no lack of questioning behavior prior to the school experience, but the questions were information seeking, e.g.,

"Dere go a fire truck?
Where dat fire truck go?
What dat fire truck do?
What dat dog do at da fire?
Whose dog dat is?
How da fireman know where dey going?
How come dat dog know to stay on dat truck?" (Heath, 1981, p. 120)

During his first few weeks at nursery school, teachers repeated that Lem was unusually silent and had little interest in talk-centered tasks directed by adults. But, after 19 days of nursery school, his response to seeing the fire truck again was now:

"What color dat truck?
What dat truck?
What color dat truck?
What color dat coat?
What color dat car?" (Heath, 1981, p. 120)

Heath responded to this school-like ritual with, "What color is that truck? You know what color the truck is." Lem laughed and claimed he was playing teacher, a game he continued with Heath during their car rides — "What color dat? Dat a square? What's dat?"

Heath not only documented the difficulties caused by the mismatch of questioning practices at home and at school, she took steps to overcome them. At the beginning of the study, she found that the teachers were bewildered by what they regarded as the lack of responsible answering behavior on the part of their black pupils. For example:

They don't seem to be able to answer even the simplest questions."
"I would almost think some of them have a hearing problem; it is as though they don't hear me ask a question. I get blank stares to my questions. When I am making statements or telling stories which interest them, they always seem to hear me."
"The simplest questions are the ones they can't answer in the classroom; yet on the playground, they can explain a rule for a ballgame, etc. . . . they can't be as dumb as they seem in my class."
"I sometimes feel that when I look at them and ask a question I'm staring at a wall I can't break through."
(Heath, 1981, p. 108)

After sharing with the teachers her information about the types of preschool questioning the children were familiar with, Heath encouraged them to engage black children in metaphoric and narrative question sequences. Having established the children's competence in familiar questioning rituals, the teachers were able gradually to introduce the unfamiliar known-answer routines. This is an excellent example of the "two-way path, from school to the community and from the community to school" (Heath, 1981, p. 125), that is, a bidirectional communication necessary if the transition to formal schooling is to be made less traumatic for ethnically divergent groups. Not only can intervention be devised that would help minority-culture parents prepare children for school, but the schools themselves can be sensitive to the problems of a cultural mismatch without sacrificing what they regard to be good educational practice. The answer is not to concentrate exclusively on changing the child or changing the schools, but to encourage adaptive flexibility in both directions.

READING GROUPS IN THE EARLY GRADES

For a variety of reasons, children from divergent ethnic groups arrive at school differentially prepared to take part in reading group activities that loom so large in the early grades. In this section, we discuss the controversial differential-treatment effect, whereby it is claimed that children in low reading groups encounter a qualitatively different kind of learning environment than do children assigned to high reading groups, and that these differential learning experiences lead poor readers to evaluate the purposes of reading and their own competence as readers in quite a different light than do good readers.

Early descendants of the Pygmalion-in-the-schools research (Rosenthal & Jacobson, 1968) suggested that inner-city schools that serve the poor and suburban schools for the middle class provide different forms of teacher-pupil interactions, with inner-city schools favoring greater teacher control, discipline, and respect for authority. In contrast, middle-class schools were said to emphasize individual-initiative and self-directed learning (Leacock, 1969). These across-schools differences were later reported within schools but between academic tracks (Rist, 1970), specifically between good and poor readers in the same classes (Allington, 1980; Brophy & Good, 1969) and between dominant and nondominant dialect speakers (Piestrup, 1973).

Brophy and Good (1969) began the differential treatment controversy when they suggested that first-grade children in high reading groups were praised more and criticized less than those in the low reading groups. In addition, errors produced by the high achievers were more often tolerated than those of the low group members. Even when the teacher did note a good reader's error, she was more likely to provide the child with another opportunity for success, by rephrasing the question or giving more clues. In the low groups, the teacher was more likely to supply the answer when a child faltered or call on another child to complete the assignment.

Looking more closely at teachers' responses to errors, Allington (1980) confirmed the Brophy and Good finding that teachers interrupted reading more often when poor readers faltered (74%) than when good readers erred (31%). Furthermore, teachers were more likely to interrupt poor readers immediately they made an error, whereas with good readers teachers tended to wait until the end of a phrase or clause or other "meaning-chunk" before correcting the child. And, if a child needed help, the teacher provided a predominance of graphemic/phonemic cues to poor readers and semantic/syntactic aid to good readers.

Recent microethnographic analyses of reading groups tend to support the differential treatment effect (Au, 1980; Collins, 1980; McDermott, 1976). These studies show that good readers are questioned about the meaning behind what they are reading and frequently asked to evaluate and criticize material. A considerable amount of time in the good reading group is "on task," reading related activities are occurring, and a sizable number of the group's activities are of an optimal comprehension fostering type. In the good reading group, the teacher often adopts the procedure of asking every child to read in turn; but in the poorer reading group, turn-taking is at the teacher's request and, to save everyone embarrassment, often the really poor readers are not called upon to perform (McDermott, 1976). Also, in contrast to the good reading group, precious little time in the poor reading group is spent in comprehension-fostering activities; the lion's share of activities involves the establishment of such rituals as turn-taking and hand-raising. When required to read, poor readers receive primarily drill in pronunciation and decoding. Rarely are they given practice in qualifying and evaluating their comprehension.

These claims of differential treatment have not gone uncriticized. Weinstein (1976) reported that teachers provide more, not less, praise to those they perceive to be poor readers and this is especially true if the children have a special education label (Forness & Esveldt, 1975). Distribution of attention to successful or less successful students seems to be more a matter of individual teacher style than systematic bias (Brophy, 1979; Brophy & Good, 1974). There is no evidence of critical, nonsupportive teachers. There is also the perfectly reasonable defense that teachers' behavior seems to be a response to, not a cause of, children's behavior, i.e., poor readers make more and different types of errors and teachers correct accordingly (West & Anderson, 1976). However, although it can be shown that students' reading does play a major role in teachers' teaching, even with student behavior partialled out, the teacher is influenced by the child's sex, previously measured reading achievement, and preconceptions of the child's general reading proficiency (Pflaum, Pascarella, Boswick, & Auer, 1980).

Further, there is some evidence that children of identical tested reading level perform like poor readers if they are assigned to the low group and more like good readers if they are assigned to a relatively higher group (Cazden, 1981). This finding suggests that relative standing in the classroom (in terms of reading group assignment) rather than reading level per se is an important determinant of the behavior of both teachers and children.

In the most finely grained ethnographic study to date, Collins (1980) has provided a rich picture of what differential-treatment means. Only the highlights are reviewed here. Collins worked with first-grade, predominantly black, lower-class, poor readers and predominantly white middle-class good readers. Even though the reading tests were not available at the time of placement, and one of the observers determined that the children did not differ in letter identification, children were placed in reading groups, with more disadvantaged children assigned to the low groups, where they were given extensive letter recognition drill. The high groups began passage reading within the first month, but it was not until approximately the fifth month that the low groups actually read; they were too busy with pre-reading activities. Through out the year, 70% of the high group's time was spent on passage reading and comprehension questioning, compared with 37% for the low groups. To fill the time, low groups devoted 47% of their reading time to dictation and sound-word identification, compared with 17% of time spent in the high group on these activities. The general picture confirms the previous findings of differential treatment to high and low reading group children, not in terms of amount of attention but in terms of type of attention.

Collins' study does more than confirm previous findings. One particularly interesting comparison was between poor readers late in the year and good readers earlier in the year, i.e., the same teacher was observed working with "good" and "poor" readers on texts of equal complexity. Again, the general picture that emerges is the greater stress on reading as comprehension-seeking for the high group members. To this end, the teacher's repairs focused on meaning distortion for the high group students, ensuring that normal conversational flow was imparted to the reading aloud and that the message was understood. For the low group members, little attempt was made to ensure adequate prosody and meaning-seeking.

To illustrate this point, consider how a teacher corrected decoding errors in both groups. In the following example from the high group, the text is, "I'll paint the house and you can make the windows." The child reads up to "and you can make" and then pauses on window. The teacher responds with help for the difficult word "the . . . what's w-i-n . . . Put your finger over it — everything but w-i-n. Sound out w-i-n with a short i. Wind, what? Window!"

Having extracted the word, the teacher repeats the entire sentence with correct intonation and the child follows suit. Here the teacher not only provided "sound-out" help with the problem word, she made sure that the disruption was minimized by situating the problem word in a full sentence and modeling the correct expressive tone.

Consider another example: the high group child is reading, " 'I'll make you a doorway,' said mother." The child begins, "I'll make you . . ." and pauses, presumably over doorway. The teacher continues with the missing article "*a*" and then offers the following information, "*And here's another compound word, what?*" The child responds, "*doorway.*" The teacher then praises the response, "*Beautiful,*" and then models the full sentence with correct intonation, " 'I'll make you a doorway,' said mother." The child mimics the entire sentence.

In contrast, readers in the poor group tend to receive decoding correction that is focused on individual words, and little attempt is made to maintain intonation. For example, the text is, "The boy ran up to the girl. Do you want to come to the park?" The child reads "*The boy run*" — teacher "ran." Child, "ran up to the girl. Do you . . ." (teacher supplies missing word *want*). Child continues, "*want to come to the park?*" The teacher corrects words in isolation. During this process the reading flow is severely disrupted; there is no correction of the staccato broken intonation. In less finely grained analyses, all these interactions would be classified as decoding corrections, implying that highs and lows were receiving similar help.

Longer examples of these differences for high and low group students reading the same passage can be seen in Table 5.1.

In the high group, the passage length read is much longer, student-teacher exchanges are shorter, and teacher corrections concentrate on comprehension — "What did she mean by that?" and intonation, "Did he say come-in-Liza-come-in, or come-in-Liza — come in!" In the low group, there are many more interruptions, only one of which involves comprehension of a language unit larger than the single word. The main agenda seems to be to ensure the "correct" pronunciaation of the word "garbage."

In summary, there is considerable evidence that good readers spend more time reading for meaning and receive much more information concerning the principal purpose of reading — finding meaning. Errors are tolerated, especially if they are not meaning-distorting and care is taken to ensure reasonable prosody. Students are asked repeatedly to think about what they are reading. Poor readers receive much more attention on pronounciation and decoding, prosody is largely neglected, units of texts are read by fragments rather than larger meaning-chunks, and meaning is questioned much less frequently. Based on these observations, it would not be surprising if children in the low groups came to regard reading as a process of reading aloud to the

TABLE 5.1
Segments of High and Low Group Students Reading from the Same Story
(Collins, 1980)

A. High Group Texts:

"John, I have your boat," said Liza.
"And I have a fly for your frog too."
"But you can't have your boat or the fly if I can't come in."
John looked at the frog, and he looked at Liza.
Then he said, come in Liza. Come in.

1	C	John I have your boat/said Liza and| |
2	T	|and|
3	C	And I have a fly for your frog to //
4	T	What's she mean by that
5	C	For the frog to eat //
6	T	Okay //
7	L	but . . I . . but
8	T	wait a minute till she gets through//
9	L	but| |but|
10	T	|watch your books| |what your books
11	C	But you can't..have your boat/or the fly/if I can't come in//
12		John looked at his frog/ and he looked at Liza/..
13		Then he said come in Liza|
14	T	|what did he say//
15	C	Come in
16	T	How'd he say it //
17	C	Come in Li-|
18	T	|Did he say come in Liza come in// Or did he say . .
19	C	Come in| Liza/ come in//
20	T	|Come in/ Liza|

B. Low Group Text:

"He ran out of the house with his things.
And then he threw his boat into the garbage can.
Liza was there. And she saw what John did."

1	M	Here| |he/ . . ran/ . . out/ . . of/ . .
2	T	|he|
3	M	the house . . . wuh-| |with his things//
4	T	|with|

TABLE 5.1 *(continued)*

5	M	And then . . . he . . ⎢ ⎢threw his
6	T	⎢sound it out/ thr:ew⎢
7	M	bu- (boat) boat/ . . into the . ⎡ ⎡gahbage can//
8		⎢ guh-⎢
9	T	gar:bage// Say garbage//
10	M	gahbage
11	T	Don't say gahbage/ look at me//Say ga:r:bage/ gar:/ Say it//
12		Everbody say it//
13	CC	gar: bage
14	T	Celena/say it//
15	Ce	gar:bage⎢
16	T	⎢Right//Marlon/ Liza
17	M	Liza . . ⎢was . .⎤ there and she was
18	T	where are we Sherrie⎢ ⎢there
19	T	What⎢
20	M	⎢she was⎢ ⎢saw what . . .⎢
21	T	⎢no//ss...⎢ ⎢how does -j- sound //
22	M	juh//⎢
23	T	⎢What's the boys' name // . . John ᷉
24	M	John . . said⎢
25	T	⎢did// She saw what John did// Marlon/ what did he do//
26	T	She saw what he did//Now what did he do//
27	M	He threw his things in the gahbage⎢
28	T	⎢gar:bage// Right// Go on//

teacher with acceptable pronunciation and children in the high groups came away with the impression that reading is the process of extracting information from texts. We return to this point later.

DECODING VS. COMPREHENSION-BASED CURRICULA

In addition to the charge of differential treatment within a curriculum, the claim has been made that the selection of a reading curriculum is itself influenced by the economic status of the students. Bartlett (1979) claimed that disadvantaged children are likely to be exposed to early reading programs with a heavy emphasis on decoding, whereas middle-class children receive earlier exposure to programs that emphasize comprehension. Hence, a different type of instruction is aimed at children who already enter school differentially prepared for the experience.

Assignment to a heavily "decoding-based curriculum" has been defended on the grounds that children from deprived homes come to school unfamiliar with the basic skills of decoding and therefore need exposure to programs that are very successful at improving decoding skills. But minority children placed in heavily comprehension-based curricula can also succeed. One spectacular success is the Kamehameha Early Education Program (KEEP), a research and development program in Honolulu, Hawaii. The main aim of this program is to improve the educational achievement of native Hawaiian and part-Hawaiian (Polynesian) children who are at high risk for educational failure. The children who took part in the studies were of normal IQ, of low SES, and bi-dialectal (Hawaiian Creole English, pidgin, was their first language, and standard English was their second). During the course of the experiment, the reading program changed from a curriculum largely devoted to decoding to one with a main focus on comprehension. Comparisons in performance between cohorts in the decoding and in the comprehension programs are the main data base.

To give only the highlights of the comprehension program, reading instruction takes place in small groups for 25-minutes daily. The main focus is on comprehension, although, in the earlier stages of instruction, one-third of the time (approximately) is devoted to sight vocabulary and analytic phonics. Whenever possible, integrative instruction occurs, i.e., sight vocabulary and decoding instruction take place in the context of reading and understanding meaningful material.

Instruction in comprehension follows what is known as an E-T-R sequence (Au, 1979). The teacher introduces background knowledge from the child's own experience (experience, or E component). Lessons are introduced by the teacher by relating E to the topic of the story. For example, in the lesson entitled, "Freddy Finds a Frog," the teacher begins by asking the children what they would do with a frog. She then assigns the children a section of the story, which they are to read silently in order to answer questions. Following these periods of silent reading, of which there are usually several in a single lesson, the teacher asks questions that assess the children's understanding of the information in the text (i.e., the T component). Finally, the teacher attempts to draw relationships (i.e., the R component) between the material in the text and the children's own experiences. Throughout the session, the children are encouraged to ask questions of themselves and the teacher, the group mutually constituting a cohesive interpretation of the text. The questions the teacher asks encourage speculation; the teacher constantly makes relational statements that tie the text to personal experience.

Several cohorts have taken part in the comprehension program, together with control groups that experience a standard phonics reading program. The programs were alike in that they both employed stringent teacher-training and administrative control of instructional procedures, well-motivated teachers, a success-oriented classroom atmosphere with an abundance of positive reinforcement, conditions that produced between 80–90% "on-task" or "engaged-time" indices (Tharp, 1982). Both programs were highly structured with behavioral objectives, criterion-referenced testing, and direct instruction. The programs differed only in their prime focus, either on decoding or on comprehension.

Differences between cohorts in the comprehension and decoding program were marked; the comprehension program resulted in far greater gains in standardized scores in both comprehension and decoding. Comprehension-based reading curricula do appear to be successful at improving both decoding and comprehension scores of at risk children.

As an interesting aside, Au (work in progress) asked third graders who had taken part in the comprehension program to instruct first graders in a reading lesson. These experienced children had clearly internalized the ETR procedures they had been exposed to, for they asked their young tutees questions in the experience-text-relationship mode. Most of the questions queried why some activity occurred. In contrast, children from the decoding program rarely questioned their charges at all, concentrating on rereading, decoding, and pronunciation.

We do not claim that decoding-based programs should be replaced by comprehension-based curricula; indeed, as Resnick (1979) points out, there is considerable evidence to support the effectiveness of decoding training in the early grades. Indeed, the KEEP program devoted approximately a third of the lesson time to decoding skills; and Beck (1981) argues that improving the decoding aspect of the KEEP program could result in even greater gains. The main point about the KEEP program is that when decoding is practiced it is subordinated to the primary task of understanding the text. The main agenda is comprehension, and the children come away with an interpretation of the task of reading as one of meaning-making.

The ideal prescription for a reading curriculum is a comprehension-based approach, with practice provided in such supporting activities as decoding skills and vocabulary building. This prescription is particularly appropriate for disadvantaged children, who are less likely to receive it. The current state of affairs is that poor readers, particularly those labeled as learning disabled or mildly retarded, are unlikely in the present system to develop adequate reading comprehension skills. Decoding is mastered eventually, but reading comprehension scores tend to be permanently and severely depressed. There could be many reasons for this typical pattern, but one that is rarely addressed is the simple explanation of practice. Practice makes possible; if so, perhaps we should not be surprised to find a cumulative deficit in compre-

hension skills in those who do not receive adequate experience in comprehension-fostering activities at home, in reading group, or in their reading
curriculum.

THE IGNORANT AND THE HELPLESS

We began with a description of the disadvantaged child in the fourth or fifth
grade, a child who is characterized as lacking in fundamental knowledge concerning the purposes of literacy and in the ability to take control in academic
learning enterprises. More specifically, we have argued that the child is both
ignorant and helpless in the domain "reading." To support these claims, we
consider briefly the literature on metacognition and reading (for a complete
review see Baker & Brown, 1983, 1984, p b; Brown, Armbruster, & Baker, in
press; Paris & Myers, 1981) and the research on a particularly relevant form
of learned helplessness (see Covington, in press; Dweck & Elliott, 1983).

Metacognition

Generally accepted in the literature is the classification of two major forms
of metacognition: *knowledge about* cognition and *regulation of* cognition.
Knowledge about cognition refers to the theories one has about the domain
"thinking." It is a form of declarative knowledge like any other and, like any
other, it is the result of cumulative experience actually undergone by the child
or conveyed to the child via instruction. Regulation of cognition, often
referred to as executive control, incorporates planning, monitoring, and
evaluating activities that occur prior to, during, and after any thinking act.
Prime functions of regulation of cognition include *planning* activities prior
to undertaking a problem (e.g., predicting outcomes, scheduling strategies,
and using various forms of vicarious trial and error); *monitoring* activities
during learning (testing, revising, and rescheduling one's strategies for learning); and *checking* outcomes (evaluating the outcome of any strategic action
in terms of criteria of efficiency and effectiveness).

Both forms of metacognition can be readily applied to the domain reading.
The expert reader has a great deal of declarative knowledge concerning the
purposes of various forms of reading activities, together with a battery of
self-regulatory strategies that enable reading effectively for the purposes at
hand. Except in extremely specialized cases, expert readers appreciate that
reading is the process of winnowing meaning from texts. In order to do this,
they engage in a variety of comprehension-monitoring and comprehension-
fostering activities, i.e., activities engaged in by the reader to ensure that
comprehension is proceeding smoothly. In a variety of recent theoretical
treatments (cf. Baker & Brown, 1983, 1984; Brown, 1980; Collins & Smith,

1982; Dansereau, in press; Markman, 1981), several overlapping activities are repeatedly mentioned as prime comprehension-fostering skills.

These include: (1) clarifying the purposes of reading, i.e., understanding the tasks demands, both explicit and implicit; (2) activating relevant background knowledge; (3) allocating attention so that concentration can be focused on the major content at the expense of trivia; (4) critical evaluation of content for internal consistency, and compatibility with prior knowledge and common sense; (5) monitoring ongoing activities to see if comprehension is occurring, by engaging in such activities as periodic review and self-interrogation; and (6) drawing and testing inferences of many kinds, including interpretations, predictions and conclusions (Brown, Palincsar, & Armbruster, 1983).

Reading is one of the many areas in which the disadvantaged child can be said to experience problems both in understanding and in effective execution. In fact, it has been claimed that the child is not only ignorant but also secondarily ignorant (Seiber, 1968), i.e., the child not only does not know what there is to be known, but does not know that he or she does not know. Research supporting this point is legion, but we will restrict ourselves here to one finding of particular pertinence to our argument — that young and poor readers share a different conception of the purposes of reading than do older and better readers. Asked about the purposes of reading, the poor reader claims that reading is the process of decoding, i.e., pronouncing the words correctly for the teacher's approval, whereas the good reader believes that understanding the content is the prime aim of reading (Canney & Winograd, 1979; Clay, 1973; Denny & Weintraub, 1963, 1966; Johns & Ellis, 1976; Myers & Paris, 1978; Paris & Myers, 1981; Reid, 1966). We discuss two studies that have provided representative findings of this type of research.

Canney and Winograd (1979) studied children's conceptions of reading by using an experimental manipulation as well as an interview technique. Children in grades 2, 4, 6, and 8 were presented with passages that were either intact or disrupted at four levels of severity: (a) correct syntax, but some semantically inappropriate words; (b) semantic and syntactic violations, but some semblance to connected discourse; (c) strings of random words; and (d) strings of random letters. The children were asked if each type of passage could be read and why; they were also given a questionnaire probing their conceptions of reading. Children in second and fourth grades, and sixth graders identified as poor readers, focused on the decoding aspect of reading. In contrast, the better readers in sixth grade and all eighth graders knew that meaning-getting was the primary goal of reading. Older and better readers judged that the intact passages and those with a few semantic distortions could be read, but the remaining passages were rejected as unreadable. However, poorer readers often reported that all but the passage containing letter strings could be read. Since these children believed that reading is being able to say the words correctly, a passage of unrelated words seemed just as readable as an intact passage.

Younger and poorer readers seem to be unaware that they must expend additional cognitive effort to make sense of the words they have decoded. Myers and Paris (1978) examined another aspect of children's metacognitive knowledge about reading, their understanding of how different variables affect performance. Children in second and sixth grades were asked a series of interview questions assessing their knowledge about person, task, and strategy variables (Flavell & Wellman, 1977) involved in reading. Many differences were apparent in children's knowledge about comprehension monitoring. For example, older and better readers understood that the purpose of skimming was to pick out the informative words, whereas younger and poorer readers said they would skim by reading the easy words. These different skimming strategies reflect conceptions of reading as meaning-getting and as word-decoding, respectively. The older children in the Myers and Paris study also had more awareness of appropriate strategies for coping with words or sentences they didn't understand. They were more likely than younger children to say they would use a dictionary, ask someone for help, or reread a paragraph to try to figure out the meaning from context.

Poor readers in the early grades come to believe that reading is primarily a decoding activity whereas good readers assert that the primary goal is to understand. Poor readers rarely report using, or believing in the efficacy of, active strategies such as giving more weight to importance than to trivia, skimming for main points, strategic rereading, questioning, evaluating, predicting, etc. (Baker & Brown, 1983). In a fundamental sense, poor readers are ignorant of the purposes of reading. They are ignorant, not stupid; because they have not yet learned much about reading does not mean they cannot learn. And, at least part of the blame for this ignorance can be laid to the reading group activities experience by the poor reader. If by far most of the time is spent decoding and pronouncing, why should the child not believe that this is reading?

Turning to what children do rather than what they say, we see the same picture (see Armbruster, Echols, & Brown, 1982; Baker & Brown, 1983, 1984; Brown, Armbruster, & Baker, in press). Compared with good readers, poor readers show little evidence of using strategic activities such as skimming, look-backs, and other fix-up strategies. They fail to monitor their comprehension deeply enough to permit them to detect violations of internal consistency or even of just plain common sense. They rarely take remedial action even if an error is detected. In short, their comprehension monitoring is weak to nonexistent. And they fare little better in comprehension fostering, failing to question actively and evaluate the meaning of what they are reading. Again, at least in part, this dismal outcome is the result of lack of experience. It is difficult to perfect cognitive activities that are rarely modeled by the teacher or practiced by the student. Constructing meaning is not a dominant feature of the educational experience of the poor reader in the early grades of school. As a result, proficiency in meaning construction is at best delayed and perhaps permanently impaired.

MASTERY AND FAILURE ORIENTATIONS TO LEARNING

Habitual experiences in academic settings shape more than conceptions of cognitive strategies. Children develop theories of intelligence that include evaluation of their personal abilities; they acquire knowledge and strategies for coping with school work that are molded by feelings of competence, self-worth and personal efficacy (Bandura, 1977, 1980), as well as by their more strictly cognitive experiences. Children who view themselves as inadequate in school, as nonstarters in the academic race, often develop compensatory coping strategies for preserving their self-worth in the less than hospitable environment of, for example, reading groups and reading tests.

Merely being placed in the poor reading group must challenge the inchoate academic self-image of the entering school child. And the child has reason to be disturbed, given the evidence that such placement is not easily remedied. But the additional burden of repeated evaluation and labeling that accompanies continuing academic failure is even more damaging. Such children formulate a devastating diagnosis of their own capabilities. They readily describe themselves as "dumb," "not good at school things," "can't read," "too stupid to read." For example, consider a particularly sweeping self-diagnosis given by Daniel, a learning disabled 10-year-old, who worked with the first author. On encountering his first laboratory task, Daniel volunteered this telling comment: "Is this a memory thing?" (it wasn't) – "Didn't they tell you I can't do this stuff?" – "Didn't they tell you I don't have a memory?" Given this devastating estimate of his own ability, it is not surprising that Daniel is described as passive, even resistant, in situations that he classifies as tests of his nonexistent faculty. Daniel had spent four years being tested and evaluated, always with the result that he was officially classified as learning disabled due to memory problems. The system and Daniel concurred with the sweeping diagnosis; what was missing was a more fine-grained evaluation that would inform remediation. It would take many sessions of systematically mapping out the specific nature of his memory problem and providing feedback about just where the problem was acute and where there were no problems at all, before Daniel could evaluate his learning problem more realistically and consequently be willing to attempt active learning strategies in order to overcome his problem.

Negative conceptions of one's prognosis for school success at best lead to the development of defensive strategies of "passing" (Edgerton, 1979), coping (Covington, in press), or managing (Cole & Traupmann, 1980) that defend against exposure to evaluations that will further document one's inadequacies. Coping strategies include systematic devaluation of academic tasks, goals, and desired outcomes, and the justification of a lack of effort — "Who needs to read anyway?" Passing and managing tactics can be perfected, so that the wily child avoids occasions of challenge. Threatening tests of, for example, reading can often be avoided. Others will take responsibility for reading, teachers will avoid embarrassment by not calling on weaker children, etc. (Cole & Traupmann, 1980; McDermott, 1976). All these ploys serve to defend against damaging exposition and attribution of failure and the further erosion of the self-concept. Unfortunately, these defenses also are a formidable barrier to learning.

An extensive research program by Dweck (see Dweck & Elliott, 1983) has delineated many facets of the emergent theories of intelligence, both cognitive and motivational, that bedevil the child who experiences early school failure. Initially Dweck distinguished between children whose dominant motivation was failure-oriented and those who were mastery-oriented. Faced with a challenging task, failure-oriented children become incapable of performing effectively, whereas mastery-oriented children double their expenditure of effort and increase their concentration.

Failure-oriented children do not welcome a challenge. They display a typical pattern of learned helplessness in the face of obstacles or errors (Seligman, Maier, & Solomon, 1971). This pattern includes increased negative feelings, and the prognosis for further success is deflated. In addition to the negative feelings, there is a reduction in their learning efforts and strategies. Failure-oriented children attribute their errors to their lack of ability and often view temporary failure as an indication of a stable, generalized incompetence ("I'm dumb," "I don't have a memory," "I can't read"). In short, "helpless children rapidly question their ability in the face of obstacles, perceiving past successes to be few and irrelevant, and perceived future effort to be futile" (Dweck & Bempechat, 1984).

Mastery-oriented children, rather than attributing temporary setbacks to personal shortcomings, treat obstacles as a challenge to be overcome by perfecting their learning strategies. Their verbalizations following failure, unlike those of the failure-oriented children, who specialize in derogating their own capacity, consist of self-instruction typical of the self-regulatory routines described in the metacognitive section. These children spontaneously instruct themselves to slow down, try new tactics, evaluate the task more systematically, and so forth. They maintain their task involvement and their positive attitude toward the task, developing new strategies to meet the challenge (Dweck & Bempechat, 1984).

Dweck argues that these different reactions to academic difficulties reflect the child's conception of tasks as either performance situations in which competence is to be evaluated and perhaps found wanting, or learning situations, that offer an opportunity to acquire new competences. Children with performance goals are motivated to avoid negative judgments of their ability and, if possible, attract favorable judgments; whereas children with learning goals focus not on evaluation of outcomes but on learning opportunities. Performance-goal children feel that they have been successful when they "don't make mistakes," "get easy work," and so on, whereas learning-goal children feel successful when they have mastered a new skill. For example, one child reported feeling successful when faced with a task that "I don't know how to do, and it's pretty hard and I figure it out without anybody telling me" (Dweck & Bempechat, 1984).

Orienting attention and effort in school so that demonstrations of failure are minimized will lead to different cognitive consequences than actively seeking occasions for acquiring new knowledge; seeking a shield from failure may be a realistic reaction to repeated obstacles, but it is not an attitude that is conducive to new learning.

Failure per se is not the culprit. So-called errorless learning or mastery-learning programs that minimize errors also cause motivational problems. Because varients of basic-skills, errorless-learning reading programs are more often advocated for the poor than for the affluent, we examine a few pertinent features of such programs that might result in motivational problems.

Geared to standardized tests, which test skills one by one in a relatively random sequence, mastery learning programs tend to concentrate on skills, in isolation, and in a sequence that, if not random, is at least difficult to equate with any systematic body of knowledge, such as a subject matter. A mastery unit is constructed for a particular "skill," or, more precisely, for a particular standardized test item, and students work until it is mastered. Success is rewarded with entry to yet another unit, whose relation to the preceding or to the following unit is, at best, unclear. Worse, the child is not informed of the skill's place in the larger scheme of things, and increasingly, as the popularity of packaged materials grows, neither is the teacher — both student and teacher working in the dark. The relation of a skill to the child's out-of-school life is remote, and rarely discussed. The relation of the skill to those practiced by the successfully "schooled" is also obscure. The developmental linkage, the skill's history, is missing. The skill is presented in small steps that can be easily mastered (if too many fail, the item is revised). Failure is minimized, the aim being errorless learning. Goals are short term and concrete (master the unit), not long term and abstract (read, understand, etc.). Ambiguity is minimized; there is a correct method, a correct answer; and little is left open to questioning, judging, or evaluating. Finally, problem identification is in the hands of others; the child is not required to identify the kind of problem being mastered or to search among previously acquired skills in order to solve the new.

How do such prescriptions fit with current conceptions of learning? There are many who would argue that a key learning mechanism is analogy-seeking: the efficient learners seek relationships between what they know and what there is to be known; they reason through processes of analogy and shared metaphor. A key step to solving a problem is first to identify it (Getzels, 1976) or classify it as most like one or other previously encountered. If a problem is novel, the learner will not possess a neatly prepackaged skill or knowledge chunk to solve it; if he or she did, the problem would not be novel. Inexperienced problem solvers often react to the novel defensively, i.e., "I don't know how to do that, I haven't been taught." Children who are accustomed to having problem identification done for them are ill equipped to attempt problem detection and classification on their own. Few problems are entirely novel, however; correct classification of the problem often makes it possible to bring to bear relevant prior knowledge and in so doing refine and extend it. But, in the isolated-skills, mastery learning programs, problem identification is rarely the responsibility of the child (or even of the teacher) but of the program packager. The child is told what the problem is that must be mastered. There is a noticeable lack of practice in applying already acquired skills to novel domains, relationships among units are rarely stressed, and, there is a failure to capitalize on prior knowledge gained inside or outside of class.

Errorless learning presents another problem. A seductive feature of everyday thinking is the compelling tendency to seek confirmatory evidence for one's beliefs. But it is often more economical to seek invalidating evidence. Even three, four, or five confirming examples do not prove a theory, but a single piece of invalidating evidence requires that the theory at least be modified and perhaps improved. Failure can be more informative than success if it is regarded as a source of information rather than a threat. Successful learners not only tolerate failure, they invite it.

Consider in this light graduates from errorless learning programs who are not taught to deal with failure. As Dweck and Bempechat (1984) point out, "Regimes of programmed success have been shown to be ineffective in promoting persistence, . . . [they] foster, if anything, greater debilitation in the face of obstacles" (ms., p. 21). Children become dependent on easy success in order to feel smart and are more likely to interpret future setbacks as failures. A similar outcome follows the efforts of well-meaning teachers who praise less successful children for intellectually irrelevant aspects of their work or for outcomes that are not particularly noteworthy, or gloss over errors, or provide answers themselves to avoid embarrassment (Dweck & Bempechat, 1984).

Hutchinson (in press) describes the learning problems of students who have not learned to question their hypothesis or confront their errors. He was attempting to teach black inner-city junior college students to play Whimby and Lockhead (1982) reasoning games. A central feature of this procedure is that students work in dyads, one thinking aloud, the other criticizing. Hutchinson reported great difficulty getting this procedure off the ground, not because the students couldn't think or couldn't think aloud, but because the students were unwilling or unable to deal with problem difficulty or failure. They were intolerant of criticism from both themselves or others. Wertime (1979) has argued that we need to help students increase their "courage-spans" for academic problem solving, courage spans that would enable them to accept failures as temporary false starts and blind alleys that can be overcome, to regard errors as information to be evaluated and used. Students need to know that things are ambiguous; they must evaluate and judge information, seek invalidating evidence; they must become critics, and, most important, they must become self-critics (Brown, 1982, in press). But their criticism must be constructive, mastery-oriented self-guidance rather than destructive personal derogation.

In summary, children's theories of academic learning that are developed during the early school years have both cognitive and motivational components. When diagnosing a child's school difficulties, both factors must be taken into consideration. Further, attempts at intervention will succeed only to the extent that they improve the child's feelings of competence in academic milieux as well as in the specific cognitive skills in question.

DIAGNOSIS AND INSTRUCTION

So far we have dealt with the bad news, documenting everything that disadvantaged children may not know, feel or be able to do as well as their more successfully schooled peers. Although advances in both the theories and technologies of cognition, motivation and instruction enable us to draw a finer-grained portrait of the "cognitive deficit" in question—and this is undoubtedly an enormous advance on traditional testing procedures to label and classify children—these processes are still largely those of labeling. What is needed is instruction geared to the specific problems of the child. Although the function of schools and their agendas in our society has been called into question, at a practical level, it is the responsible course to prepare all children as far as is possible to meet the demands of schools as they exist now (Edmonds, this volume).

The kind of remedial reading instruction we advocate is one that is informed by the diagnoses. We have described these children as ignorant and helpless concerning the purposes and strategies of reading for meaning, and we have attempted to trace the roots of their problems to differential treatment in their early school careers, and perhaps even before. Repeated experience with experts (parents, caretakers, teachers, etc.) who situate, elaborate, evaluate, and extend the limits of their experience, provide many middle-class students with a battery of school-relevant skills that include comprehension-fostering activities ideally tailored for reading. Further, for a variety of easily defendable reasons, disadvantaged children experience extensive drill devoted to decontextualized skills of decoding, sometimes at the expense of comprehension. Given this argument, an appropriate training experience would be to attempt to mimic naturally occurring interactive learning settings as a context for instruction for the disadvantaged reader. In the next section we review a series of experiments from our laboratory that were successful at improving comprehension skills precisely because they attempted to help children adopt for themselves questioning and monitoring activities that they experience initially in interactive settings (see Brown & Palincsar, in press; Palincsar & Brown, 1984, for full details).

The previous section portrayed a thumbnail sketch of the types of knowledge, both cognitive and motivation, that poor readers need help in acquiring. In our studies we concentrated on four main cognitive activities that are central processes of critical reading. These are *summarizing* (self-review), *questioning, clarifying,* and *predicting.* These activities appear to be academic tasks in their own right. It is common practice to call on students to paraphrase, either orally or in writing, what they have heard or read in their own words. Similarly, students often are exhorted to question their assumptions and think critically about the content of what they are reading, or to answer questions on a passage. Critical evaluation of content for internal consistency, compatibility with prior knowledge, and common sense is an essential part of effective reading, as is the process of drawing and testing inferences of many kinds, including interpretations, predictions, and conclusions.

In addition to being recognizable school exercises, the four activities serve a double function: they can enhance comprehension, and they afford an opportunity for the student to check whether it is occurring. That is, they can be both comprehension-fostering and comprehension-monitoring activities if properly used. Summarizing as a process of self-review is an excellent example. Monitoring one's progress while reading, to test whether one can pinpoint and retain important material, provides a check that comprehension is progressing smoothly. If the reader cannot produce an adequate synopsis of what he or she is reading, this is a clear sign that comprehension is *not* proceeding smoothly and remedial action is called for. Self-directed questioning about the meaning of text content leads students to a more active monitoring of their own comprehension (André & Anderson, 1978–79). Asking questions of an *interpretive* and *predictive* nature (Collins & Smith, 1982) can improve comprehension and permit students to monitor their own understanding. These are also the kinds of active and aggressive interactions with texts that poor readers do not engage in readily. The need for explicit instruction in comprehension-enhancing activities is particularly acute for the slow-learning student (Brown & Palincsar, 1982).

In a series of studies, Palincsar and Brown (1984) combined the four activities of self-directed summarizing (review), questioning, clarifying, and predicting into a package of activities whose general aim was to increase understanding. Each activity, however, was used in response to a concrete problem of text comprehension. Clarifying occurred only if there was confusion either in the text (unclear referent, etc.) or in the student's interpretation of the text. Summarizing was modeled as an activity of self-review; it was engaged in to state to the group (or teacher) what had just happened in the text and as a test that the content had been understood. Inability to construct an adequate synopsis was regarded not as a failure to perform a particular decontextualized skill, but as an important source of information that comprehension was not proceeding as it should be and that remedial action (such as rereading or clarifying) was needed. Questioning, similarly, was not practiced as a teacher-directed isolated activity, but as a concrete task—what question could a teacher or test reasonably ask about that section of the text? Students reacted very positively to this concrete detective work.

In addition to these cognitive activities, we made every attempt to enhance the students' sense of competence and control. The adult teacher provided praise and feedback; the students kept their own graphed record of success, and the teachers paid considerable attention to the metacognitive setting. The students received explicit instruction, extensive modeling, and repeated practice in concrete versions of the trained activities; they were constantly reminded to engage in these activities while reading, indeed to read for the purpose of performing these activities for themselves. They were instructed not to proceed until they could summarize, clarify, and answer questions on each segment of text. Finally, the students were constantly reminded that the target activities were to help them improve and monitor their own comprehension, shown that their performance improved dramatically when they did so, and told that they should always engage in them while reading for academic purposes (Palincsar & Brown, 1982). With concrete examples of effective strategies, daily success experiences, a gradual progression in the demands placed on the student participants, and detailed practice in controlling their own strategies, the confidence of the students greatly increased during the course of the study.

We have argued that many students lack sufficient practice in interactive learning situations where comprehension-fostering activities such as the aforementioned are modeled and promoted. If this is true, then an obvious compensatory strategy would be to design instruction in which practice in the essential skills is embedded within an interactive learning situation that mimics the idealized mother-child, teacher-child dialogues also previously described. Therefore, we embedded the activities of summarizing, questioning, clarifying, and predicting within a training procedure that was very similar to the interactive mother-child, teacher-student dyads described in the previous section.

The students, both black and white from a low socio-economic background, had low "normal" IQ scores (mean IQ 84) and were participants in remedial reading classes. Despite their problems, they had achieved some success in that their decoding fluency was at grade level. But they were seriously delayed in their reading comprehension (2–3 year delays). In two replications of the procedure, instruction took place in small groups with one teacher and one or two students. In the third study, instruction took place in larger, naturally constructed, reading groups, where the teacher was the regular instructor.

Each day during reading, the teacher and the students engaged in an interactive learning game (referred to as reciprocal teaching) that involved taking turns in leading a dialogue concerning each segment of text. If the passage was new, the teacher called the students' attention to the title, asked for predictions based upon the title, and discussed the relationship of the passage to prior knowledge. For example, if the passage was from *Ship of the Desert,* the teacher and students would speculate about what the passage concerned and would review what they knew about the characteristics of the desert. If the passage was partially completed, the teacher would ask the students to recall and state the topic of the text and several important points already covered in the passage.

Following this general orientation, modeled after the ETR sequence of the successful KEEP program described earlier, the teacher assigned a segment of the passage to be read (usually a paragraph) and either indicated that it was her turn to be the teacher or assigned one of the students to teach that segment. The adult teacher and the students then read the assigned segment silently. After reading the text, the teacher (student or adult) for that segment summarized the content, discussed and clarified any difficulties, asked a question that a teacher or test might ask on the segment, and made a prediction about future content. All these activities were embedded in as natural a dialogue as possible, with the teacher and student giving feedback to each other.

Throughout the interventions, the students were explicitly told that these activities were general strategies to help them understand better as they read, and that they should try to do something like this when they read silently. It was pointed out that being able to say in one's own words what one has just read, and being able to guess what the questions will be on a test, are sure ways of testing oneself to see if one has understood.

At first the students had difficulty taking part in the dialogue, experiencing particular difficulties with summarizing and formulating questions. The adult teacher helped with a variety of prompting techniques such as, "What questions did you think a teacher might ask?" "Remember, a summary is a shortened version, it doesn't include detail." "If you're having a hard time summarizing, why don't you think of a question first?"

The adult teacher also provided praise and feedback specific to the student's participation: "You asked that question well; it was very clear what information you wanted"; "Excellent prediction, let's see if you're right"; "That was interesting information. It was information that I would call detail in the passage. Can you find the most important information?" After this type of feedback, the adult teacher modeled any activity that needed improvement: "A question I would haved asked would be . . ."; "I would summarize by saying . . ."; "Did you find this statement unclear?"

Initially, then, the experimenter modeled appropriate activities, but the students had great difficulty assuming the role of dialogue leader when their turn came. The experimenter was sometimes forced to resort to constructing paraphrases and questions for the students to mimic. In this initial phase, the experimenter was modeling effective comprehension-monitoring strategies, but the student was a relatively passive observer.

In the intermediate phase, the students became much more adept at playing their role as dialogue leader and by the end of ten sessions were providing paraphrases and questions of some sophistication. For example, in the initial sessions of the first study (Brown & Palincsar, 1982), 46% of questions produced by the students were judged to be nonquestions or to need clarification. By the end of the sessions, only 2% of responses were judged as either needing clarification or nonquestions. Unclear questions dropped out and were replaced over time with questions focusing on the main idea of each text segment. Examples of questions judged to need clarficiation, main idea, and detail are shown in Table 5.2.

A similar improvement was found for summary statements. At the beginning of the session, only 11% of summary statements captured main ideas, whereas at the end 60% of the statements were so classified. Examples of summary statements are shown in Table 5.3

A similar improvement in the quality of the dialogues over time was found in the two replication studies that took place in group settings (see Palincsar & Brown, 1984, for details). At the outset, students required more assistance with the dialogue, asked more unclear and detailed questions, and made more incomplete/incorrect or detailed summaries than they did on the last intervention day. Both main idea questions and paraphrases increased significantly over time, although students improved at different rates. Some caught on to the procedure immediately and needed only a few sessions before they could take their part as dialogue leader quite effectively. Others made much

TABLE 5.2
Examples of Student-Generated Questions During Reciprocal Teaching

Main Idea Questions

Why don't people live in the desert?
Where are the grasslands of Australia ideal for grazing?
What does the light on the fish do?
What did these people (the Chinese) invent?
Plans are being made to use nuclear power for what?
What are three main problems with all submarines?
Is there just one kind of explosive?
What are one of the things people used explosives for?
What are the Phillipine officials going to do for the people?

Questions Pertaining to Detail

Where were some of the nuclear bombs dropped?
How far south do the maple trees grow?
What color is the guards' uniforms?
How many years did it take to build the Great Wall?
What are chopsticks made out of?
Tell me where the cats hide?
What was the balloon material made of?
What (on the fish) overlaps like shingles on a roof?
How far can flying fish leap?
What is the temperature along the southern shores of Australia?

Questions Requiring Clarification (and Suggested Appropriate Questions Regarding the Same Material and Ideas)

What was uh, some kings were uh, about the kings? (Why is it that kings did not always make the best judges?)
What were some of the people? (What kinds of people can serve on a jury?)
What was the Manaus built for? Wait a minute. What was the Manaus built for, what certain kind of thing? Wait a minute. O.K. What was the Manaus tree built for? (Why was the city of Manaus built?)
What does it keep the ground? (What effect does snow have on the ground?)
What are the Chinese people doing today, like ... What are they doing? (Why are the Chinese people rewriting their alphabet today?)
There's you know, like a few answers in here and one of my questions is, uh, anything that burns and explodes can be fast enough to ... See, they got names in here. O.K.? (Name some explosives.)
In Africa, India, and the Southern Islands where the sun shines what happens to the people? You know, like ...? (Why do people who live in Africa, India and the Southern Islands have dark skin?)

slower progress. One black student (with the lowest IQ of the sample, IQ = 70) who began the study unable to formulate a question at all made slow but steady progress, as indicated by the dialogues shown in Table 5.4 The data are taken from Days 1 to 15, when he achieved a criterion of 75% on a daily comprehension test (discussed later). From a very slow start, this student did achieve an acceptable level of performance both on the dialogues and on his daily comprehension tests.

In all three studies, repeated interaction with an adult model performing appropriate questioning and paraphrasing activities enabled the students to perform these functions on their own. Over time, the students' questions became more like the tutor's, being classified as *inventions,* i.e., questions and summaries of gist in one's own words, rather than selections, repetitions of words actually occurring in the text (Brown & Day, 1983). An early occurring form of question might be to take verbatim from the text, "Plans are being made to use nuclear power," and append the question with the inflection, "For what?" Later forms of questioning were more likely to be paraphrases

TABLE 5.3
Examples of Student-Generated Summary Statements During Reciprocal Teaching

Statements Regarding the Main Idea

It says if a man does his job real good, then he will do better in his next life.
I learned that they have different kinds of Gods, not just Brahman, every family has their own.
It tells us about the two kinds of camels, what they are like and where they live.
My summary is that the part of the earth that we live on and see and know is the top layer, the crust.
This paragraph talks about what happens when people perspire or sweat. They lose a large amount of salt and they get weakness.

Statements Regarding Detail

It is a pair of fins which look like legs.
The sea horse always swims head up.
There were large lizards and four eyed fish and 30 foot dandelion.
What I learned is that a submarine went around the world in 84 days.
I learned that Cousteau's first artificial island was in the North Sea.
Professor Charles went 27 miles and rose 2,000 feet in his balloon.
They (the aborigines) don't wear much clothes on.
They (Egyptians) made bread a long time ago.

Statements That Are Incomplete

They talk about it was the richest island; but it didn't have something, o.k., it was the richest island but didn't have everything. They didn't have something. (Although this was a very rich land, no people lived there.)
If you pick a cherry branch in the winter you will have luck hoping they will bloom early. (If you pick a cherry branch in the winter, you will have no luck with it blooming.)
And uranium can be making explosion that equals a skyscraper. (A small amount of uranium can cause an explosion as great as a skyscraper full of dynamite.)

Examples of Student-Generated Critical/Evaluative Comments

"Boy, the paragraph sure is a mess. It is all over the place."
"I don't see how they can say 'heat lightning occurs on hot summer days.' How could you see it?"
"It says here 'cloud to cloud' then 'cloud to earth.' Wouldn't that be the same thing?"
"The word 'meter' throws me off in this sentence."
"What's the difference between soap and detergent anyway?"
"At first I didn't get this because I thought the word 'pumping' was 'bumping.' "
"I don't know what 'omitting' is."
"I have one, what do they mean by 'far away dreams?' "

TABLE 5.4

The Acquisition of Question-Asking by One Seventh Grade Student

---

Day 1:

S: What is found in the southeastern snakes, also the copperhead, rattlesnakes, vipers — they have. I'm not doing this right.

T: All right. Do you want to know about the pit vipers?

S: Yeah.

T: What would be a good question about the pit vipers that starts with the word "why?"

S: (No response)

T: How about, "Why are the snakes called pit vipers?"

S: Why do they want to know that they are called pit vipers?

T: Try it again.

S: Why do they, pit vipers in a pit?

T: How about, "Why do they call the snakes pit vipers?"

S: Why do they call the snakes pit vipers?

T: There you go! Good for you.

Day 4:

S: (No question)

T: What's this paragraph about?

S: Spinner's mate. How do spinner's mate ...

T: That's good. Keep going.

S: How do spinner's mate is smaller than ... How am I going to say that?

T: Take your time with it. You want to ask a question about spinner's mate and what he does, beginning with the word "how."

S: How do they spend most of his time sitting?

T: You're very close. The question would be, "How does spinner's mate spend most of his time?" Now you ask it.

S: How does spinner's mate spend most of his time?

Day 7:

S: How does the pressure from below push the mass of hot rock against the opening? Is that it?

T: Not quite. Start your question with "What happens when?"

S: What happens when the pressure from below pushes the mass of hot rock against the opening?

T: Good for you! Good job.

TABLE 5.4 *(continued)*

Day 11:	
S:	What is the most interesting of the insect eating plants, and where do the plants live at?
T:	Two excellent questions! They are both clear and important questions. Ask us one at a time now.
Day 15:	
S:	Why do scientists come to the south pole to study?
T:	Excellent question! That is what this paragraph is all about.

of the gist in the students' own words. For example, reading a passage about fossils, one student posed the following question: "When an animal dies, certain parts decay, but what parts are saved?" This question was constructed by integrating information presented across several sentences. Given the steady improvement on the daily comprehension tests (discussed later), it appears that students internalize these activities as part of their own repertoire of comprehension-fostering skills. In support of this statement are the data from peer tutoring sessions taken at the termination of the study. With naive peers, trained tutees did attempt to model main idea paraphrase and questions along with clarifying and predicting.

In addition to the qualitative changes in the students' dialogues, there was a gratifying improvement in the level of performance on daily comprehension tests. Each day, following the interactive learning sessions, the students read novel passages and independently answered ten comprehension questions on the passage. During pretesting prior to the introduction of the interactive sessions, students averaged 20% correct on such tests. After the experience of the reciprocal teaching sessions, students reach accuracy levels of 80–90% correct. The improvement on the daily comprehension tests was large and reliable. Of the ten students taking part in the first two studies, nine improved to the level set by good comprehenders. Of the 31 students in Study 3 (where volunteer teachers introduced the procedure in their reading group), all met this level. The effect endured; maintenance probes showed no drop in the level of performance for up to an 8-week period. Although there was a decline after 6 months (levels dropping from 80% to 60%), one session with the reciprocal teaching procedure was sufficient to raise performance back to the short-term maintenance level.

The effect also generalized to the classroom setting. During the course of the study, the students took comprehension tests as part of their regular science and social science instruction. They were not informed that these tests were related to the study. All seventh graders took the tests. The students began the study with scores below the 20 percentile rank; but, after the study, 90% of the students showed a clear pattern of improvement, averaging a 36 percentile rank increase, bringing them up to at least the average level for their age mates. Given the difficulty reported in obtaining generalization of trained skills across setting (Brown & Campione, 1978, 1981; Meichenbaum & Asarnow, 1978), this is an impressive finding.

Training also resulted in a reliable transfer to dissimilar laboratory tasks that demanded the same underlying processes. The tests of transfer were selected because we believed that they tapped the skills taught during the reciprocal teaching. Two of the four transfer tests were measures of the two most frequently engaged in activities during the reciprocal teaching sessions, summarizing (Brown & Day, in press) and predicting questions that might be asked concerning each segment of text. Two other tests were used as measures of general comprehension monitoring, error detection (Harris, Kruithof, Terwogt, & Visser, 1981; Markman, 1981) and rating importance of segments of narratives (Brown & Smiley, 1977).

The transfer tests were conducted on a pretest-posttest format. It would be impossible to go into all the details of the transfer probes here (for details see Palincsar & Brown, 1984). Briefly, significant improvement was shown on three of the four tests: writing summaries, designing questions to be asked on a test, and error detection. The students did not improve on the Brown and Smiley (1977) task of rating narratives for variations in importance, although they did improve in their ability to select important elements in their summary writing.

Thus, training resulted in reliable transfer to dissimilar tasks; summarizing, predicting questions, and detecting incongruities all improved. Again, this is an impressive finding given prior difficulty with obtaining transfer of cognitive skills training (Brown & Campione, 1978, 1981). In addition, sizable improvements in standardized comprehension scores were recorded for the majority of subjects. And, of prime importance, the intervention was no less successful in natural group settings conducted by regular classroom teachers than it was in the laboratory and conducted by an experimenter.

There are several possible reasons for the Palincsar and Brown studies' succeeding when so many other cognitive skills training attempts have failed to find durability, generalization, and transfer of the effects of training (Brown, 1978; Brown & Campione, 1978, 1981; Meichenbaum, in press). First, the training was extensive. Students received approximately 20 days of instruction. Second, the activities trained were well specified theoretically and well established empirically as particularly problematic for poor readers. Third, the training was specifically tailored to the needs of these particular students, good decoders but passive comprehenders. Fourth, the skills themselves could reasonably be expected to be transsituational. Such ubiquitous activities of self-review and self-interrogation are pertinent in a wide variety of knowledge acquisition tasks.

In addition, a great deal of attention was paid to metacognitive variables: The subjects were fully informed about the reasons why these activities were important; the subjects were given explicit information concerning the generality of the activities and their range of utility; the subjects were trained in self-regulatory activities, including checking and monitoring their own comprehension; and the skills were general comprehension-monitoring activities applicable in a wide variety of reading/studying tasks.

The reciprocal teaching mode itself could be responsible for the improvement. The interactive format permits extensive modeling of the target activities in a reasonably natural setting. It also forces the students to participate at whatever level they can so that the teacher can evaluate current states and provide appropriate feedback and assistance (see Table 5.4).

Finally, every attempt was made to increase the students' sense of personal efficacy. They plotted their success, they planned their strategies, they monitored their progress, they were shown to be competent and in control.

Whatever the reason for the improvement (see Brown & Palincsar, in press, for a discussion of this point), the intervention was a practical success. Disadvantaged students with severely depressed comprehension scores were able to function on a level set by their "normal" reading age peers. The effect was reliable, durable and transferred across tasks and settings.

Prior to beginning the study, teachers without exception expressed a degree of skepticism regarding their students' ability to participate in the reciprocal teaching procedure. At the conclusion of the study, the teachers were pleased not only with the progress demonstrated by the students in the reciprocal activities and with their improvement with the comprehension measures, but by other results as well. The teachers believed that general thinking skills seemed to improve. The students appeared better able to locate important information and organize their ideas — skills that the teachers regarded as important study skills. In confirmation of the teachers' observations, students reported that they were using the instructed activities (primarily summarizing and question predicting) in their content classes. As one student proudly reported to his reading teacher after a triumphant attempt to write a book report using the activities he had learned in the reciprocal teaching training, "Mrs. P, you'll be glad to hear this wasn't all for nothing." The students spoke positively of the procedure in general and particularly of the opportunity to assume the role of a teacher.

CONCLUSION

We have described pervasive reading problems experienced by many disadvantaged students in our schools. Some possible causes of these problems were traced to the educational histories of disadvantaged and minority culture children both at home and in school. We argued that advances in the observational, experimental, and instructional sciences have enabled us to describe the cognitive differences of poor readers. But beyond labeling is successful teaching. We cited examples of successful intervention motivated by ethnographic analyses (Au, 1980; Heath, 1981), curriculum development (Tharp, 1982), and experimental studies that progressed from the psychological laboratory to the classroom (Palincsar & Brown, 1984).

If we are to understand and eventually remediate, we need to consider the linguistic and cultural backgrounds of pupils and the (mis)match between their experience and classroom practices. In the case of reading, we have argued that regardless of their status as decoders, all students need practice in comprehension-fostering and monitoring activities that are the bases of effective reading. Equally important, all students should be helped to understand that the primary goal of reading is comprehension and that there are manageable and concrete activities that they can master that will improve their comprehension.

Finally, we have argued that the effects of inadequate early experiences with the types of interactive activities that clarify, elaborate, and extend knowledge can be overcome by providing the missing experience through explicit intervention. In the long history of intervention research, the essential element in traditional studies has been that the experimenter provides feedback and direction. It is the experimenter who undertakes the requisite task analyses, and, often, it is the experimenter who maintains all of the controlling and decision-making functions.

The current interest in dynamic learning situations has seen a move away from experimenter-controlled instruction of the traditional kind towards the interactive processes illustrated by the Palincsar and Brown (1984) study. Through the intervention of supportive, knowledgeable adults, the students are led to the limits of their own understanding. The teachers do not tell the students what to do and then leave them to work unaided; the teachers enter into an interaction where the children and the teachers are mutually responsible for getting the task done. As the children adopt more of the essential skills initially undertaken by the adults, the adults relinquish control.

Although the supportive other in the laboratory is usually an experimenter, these interactive learning experiences are intended to mimic real-life learning. Mothers (Deloache, 1984; Ninio & Bruner, 1978; Wertsch, 1978; Wood & Middleton, 1975), teachers (Collins & Stevens, 1982), and mastercraftsmen (Childs & Greenfield, 1980) all function as the supportive other, the agent of change responsible for structuring the child's environment in such a way that the child can first observe, then participate, and gradually increase the level of participation until the adult role is assumed.

Vygotsky (1978) has argued that many cognitive activities are initially experienced in social settings but, in time, the results of social experiences become internalized. Initially, the supportive other acts as the model and interrogator, leading the child to use more powerful strategies. The interrogative, regulatory role, however, becomes internalized by the child during the interactive process, and the child becomes able to fulfill some of these functions via self-regulation and self-interrogation. Mature readers (and thinkers in general) are those who practice thought experiments, question their own basic assumptions, provide counter-examples to their own rules, and so on. Through the process of internalization, mature readers and reasoners become capable of providing the supportive other role for themselves. Under these dynamic systems of tutelage, the child learns not only how to get a particular task done independently, but also how to set about learning new problems (Brown, Bransford, Ferrara, & Campione, 1983). In the domain reading, the student learns how to learn from reading.

In summary, there are theories and technology that enable us to diagnose a student's problem and perhaps trace its developmental history. We are also well on the way to being able to intervene and remediate effectively. Basic skills of self-directed reading can be taught. And along with the specific improvement in academic skills that follow effective intervention will come important changes in both the students' and teachers' theories of their competence. Success breeds success, because success breeds feelings of self-worth and personal "efficacy," i.e., the confidence to employ active learning strategies in the belief that they will work.

REFERENCES

Allington, R. (1980). Teacher interruption behavior during primary-grade oral reading. *Journal of Educational Psychology, 72* (3), 371–377.

André, M. D. A., & Anderson, T. H. (1978–1978). The development and evaluation of a self-questioning study technique. *Reading Research Quarterly, 14,* 605–623.

Armbruster, B. B., Echols, C. H., & Brown, A. L. (1982). The role of metacognition in reading to learn: A developmental perspective. *Volta Review, 84* (5), 45–56.

Au, K. (1980). *A test of the social organizational hypothesis: Relationships between participation structures and learning to read.* Unpublished doctoral dissertation, University of Illinois.

Au, K. H. (1979). Using the experience-text-relationship method with minority children. *The Reading Teacher, 32* (6), 677–679.

Baker, L., & Brown, A. L. (1983). Cognitive monitoring in reading. In J. Flood (Ed.), *Understanding reading comprehension.* Newark, Del.: International Reading Association.

Baker, L., & Brown, A. L. (1984). Metacognition and the reading process. In P. D. Pearson (Ed.), *A handbook of reading research.* New York: Longman.

Bandura, A. (1977). Self-efficacy: Toward a unifying theory of behavioral change. *Psychological Review, 84,* 191–215.

Bandura, A. (1980). Self-referent thought: The development of self-efficacy. In J. H. Flavell & L. D. Ross (Eds.), *Development of social cognition.* Hillsdale, NJ: Lawrence Erlbaum Associates.

Bartlett, E. J. (1979). Curriculum, concepts of literacy and social class. In L. B. Resnick & P. A.

Weaver (Eds.), *Theory and practice of early reading* (Vol. 2). Hillsdale, NJ: Lawrence Erlbaum Associates.

Beck, I. L. (1981). Comments on the reading program. *Educational Perspectives, 20* (1), 20–22.

Bernstein, B. (1971). *Class codes and control* (Vol. 1). London: Routledge & Kegan Paul.

Brophy, J. (1979). Teacher behavior and its effects. *Journal of Educational Psychology, 71,* 733–750.

Brophy, J. E., & Good, T. (1969). *Teacher-child dyadic interaction: A manual for coding classroom behavior.* Austin: The Research and Developmental Center for Teacher Education, University of Texas.

Brophy, J. E., & Good, T. (1974). *Teacher-student relationships: Causes and consequences.* New York: Holt, Rinehart, & Winston.

Brown, A. L. (1978). Knowing when, where and how to remember: A problem of metacognition. In R. Glaser (Ed.), *Advances in instructional psychology* (Vol. 1). Hillsdale, NJ: Lawrence Erlbaum Associates.

Brown, A. L. (1980). Metacognitive development and reading. In R. J. Spiro, B. C. Bruce, & W. Brewer (Eds.), *Theoretical issues in reading comprehension.* Hillsdale, NJ: Lawrence Erlbaum Associates.

Brown, A. L. (1982). Learning to learn how to read. In J. Langer & T. Smith-Burke (Eds.), *Reader meets author, bridging the gap: A psycholinguistic and social linguistic perspective.* Newark, DE: International Reading ASsociation, Dell.

Brown, A. L. (in press). Mental orthopedics: A conversation with Alfred Binet. In S. Chipman, J. Segal, & R. Glaser (Eds.), *Thinking and learning skills: Current research and open questions* (Vol. 2). Hillsdale, NJ: Lawrence Erlbaum Associates.

Brown, A. L., Armbruster, B. B., & Baker, L. (in press). The role of metacognition in reading and studying. In J. Orasanu (Ed.), *Reading comprehension: From research to practice.* Hillsdale, NJ: Lawrence Erlbaum Associates.

Brown, A. L., Bransford, J. D., Ferrara, R. A., & Campione, J. C. (1983). Learning, remembering, and understanding. In J. H. Flavell & E. M. Markman (Eds.), *Carmichael's manual of child psychology* (Vol. 1). New York: Wiley.

Brown, A. L., & Campione, J. C. (1978). Permissible inferences from cognitive training studies in developmental research. In W. S. Hall & M. Cole (Eds.), *Quarterly Newsletter of the Institute for Comparative Human Behavior, 2* (3), 46–53.

Brown, A. L., & Campione, J. C. (1981). Inducing flexible thinking: A problem of access. In M. Friedman, J. P. Das, & N. O'Connor (Eds.), *Intelligence and learning.* New York: Plenum.

Brown, A. L., & Day, J. D. (1983). Macrorules for summarizing texts: The development of expertise. *Journal of Verbal Learning and Verbal Behavior, 22* (1), 1–14.

Brown, A. L., & Palincsar, A. S. (1982). Inducing strategic learning from texts by means of informed, self-control training. *Topics in Learning and Learning Disabilities, 2* (1), 1–17.

Brown, A. L., Palincsar, A. S., & Armbruster, B. B. (1983). Instructing comprehension-fostering activities in interactive learning situations. In H. Mandl, N. Stein, & T. Trabasso (Eds.), *Learning from texts.* Hillsdale, NJ: Lawrence Erlbaum Associates.

Brown, A. L., & Palincsar, A. S. (in press). Reciprocal teaching of comprehension strategies: A natural history of one program for enhancing learning. To appear in J. Borkowski and J. D. Day (Eds.), *Intelligence and Cognition in Special Children: Comparative studies of Giftedness, Mental Retardation, and Learning Disabilities.* New York, Ablex.

Brown, A. L., & Smiley, S. S. (1977). Rating the importance of structural units of prose passages: A problem of metacognitive development. *Child Development, 48,* 1–8.

Campione, J. C., Brown, A. L., & Ferrara, R. A. (1982). Mental retardation and intelligence. In R. J. Sternberg (Ed.), *Handbook of human intelligence.* New York: Cambridge University Press.

Canney, G., & Winograd, P. (1979). *Schemata for reading and reading comprehension perform-*

ance (Tech. Rep. No. 120). Urbana: University of Illinois, Center for the Study of Reading.

Cazden, C. B. (1981). Social context of learning to read. In J. T. Guthrie (Ed.), *Comprehension and teaching: Research reviews.* Newark, DE: International Reading Association.

Childs, C. P., & Greenfield, P. M. (1973). Informal modes of learning and teaching: The case of Zinacanteco weaving. In N. Warren (Ed.), *Studies in cross-cultural psychology* (Vol. 2). London: Academic Press, 1980.

Clay, M. M. *Reading: The patterning of complex behavior.* Auckland, New Zealand: Heinemann Educational Books.

Cole, M., & Traupmann, K. (1980). Comparative cognitive research: Learning from a learning disabled child. In A. Collins (Ed.), *Minnesota symposium on child development.* Hillsdale, NJ: Lawrence Erlbaum Associates.

Collins, A., & Smith, E. E. (1982). Teaching the process of reading comprehension. In D. K. Detterman & R. J. Sternberg (Eds.), *How and how much can intelligence be increased.* Norwood, NJ: Ablex.

Collins, A., & Stevens, A. (1982). Goals and strategies of inquiry teachers. In R. Glaser (Ed.), *Advances in instructional psychology* (Vol. 2). Hillsdale, NJ: Lawrence Erlbaum Associates.

Collins, J. (1980). Differential treatment in reading groups. In J. Cook-Gumperz (Ed.), *Educational discourse.* London: Heinneman.

Covington, M. V. (in press). Strategic thinking and the feat of failure. In S. Chipman, J. Segal, & R. Glaser (Eds.), *Thinking and learning skills: Current research and open questions* (Vol. 2). Hillsdale, NJ: Lawrence Erlbaum Associates.

Dansereau, D. F. (in press). Learning strategy research. In S. Chipman, J. Segal, & R. Glaser (Eds.), *Cognitive skills and instruction.* Hillsdale, NJ: Lawrence Erlbaum Associates.

DeLoache, J. S. What's this? Maternal questions in joint picture book reading with toddlers. *The Quarterly Newsletter of the Laboratory of Comparative Human Cognition* 1984. *6,* 87–95.

Denney, T., & Weintraub, S. (1963). Exploring first graders' concepts of reading. *The Reading Teacher, 16,* 363–365.

Denney, T., & Weintraub, S. (1966). First graders' responses to three questions about reading. *Elementary School Journal, 66,* 441–448.

Dweck, C. S., & Bempechat, J. (1984). Children's theories of intelligence: Consequences for learning. In S. G. Paris, G. M. Olson, & H. W. Stevenson (Eds.), *Learning and motivation in the classroom.* Hillsdale, NJ: Lawrence Erlbaum Associates.

Dweck, C. S., & Elliott, E. S. (1983). Achievement motivation. In E. M. Heatherington (Ed.), *Carmichael's manual of child psychology.* New York: Wiley.

Edgerton, R. B. (1979). *Mental retardation.* Cambridge: Harvard University Press.

Edmonds, R. A. (1978, July). *A discussion of the literature and issues related to effective schooling.* Paper presented at the National Conference on Urban Education, St. Louis.

Feuerstein, R. (1979). *The dynamic assessment of retarded performers: The learning potential assessment device, theory, instruments, and techniques.* Baltimore: University Park Press.

Feuerstein, R. (1980). *Instrumental enrichment: An intervention program for cognitive modifiability.* Baltimore: University Park Press.

Flavell, J. H., & Wellman, H. M. Metamemory. (1977). In R. V. Kail, Jr., & J. W. Hagen (Eds.), *Perspectives on the development of memory and cognition.* Hillsdale, NJ: Lawrence Erlbaum Associates.

Forness, S. R., & Esveldt, K. C. (1975). Classroom observation of children with learning and behavior problems. *Journal of Learning Disabilities, 8,* 382–385.

Getzels, J. W. (1976). Problem-finding and the inventiveness of solutions. *Journal of Creative Behavior, 9,* 12–18.

Harris, P. L., Kruithof, A., Terwogt, M. M., & Visser, P. (1981). Children's detection and awareness of textual anomaly. *Journal of Experimental Child Psychology, 31,* 212–230.

Heath, S. B. (1981). Questioning at home and at school: A comparative study. In G. Spindler (Ed.), *Doing ethnography: Educational anthropology in action.* New York: Holt, Rinehart, & Winston.

Hutchinson, R. T. (in press). Teaching problem solving to developmental adults. In S. Chipman, J. Segal, & R. Glaser (Eds.), *Thinking and learning skills: Current research and open questions* (Vol. 2). Hillsdale, NJ: Lawrence Erlbaum Associates.

Johns, J., & Ellis, D. (1976). Reading: Children tell it like it is. *Reading World, 16,* 115–128.

Leacock, E. (1969). *Teaching and learning in city schools: A comparative study.* New York: Basic Books.

Markman, E. M. (1981). Comprehension monitoring. In W. P. Dickson (Ed.), *Children's oral communication skills.* New York: Academic Press.

McDermott, R. (1976). *Kids make sense: Ethnographic account of the interactional management of success and failure in one first grade classroom.* Unpublished doctoral dissertation, Stanford University.

Mehan, H. (1979). *Learning lessons: Social organization in the classroom.* Cambridge: Harvard University Press.

Meichenbaum, D. (in press). Cognitive behavior modification. In S. Chipman, J. Segal, & R. Glaser (Eds.), *Thinking and learning skills: Current research and open questions* (Vol. 2). Hillsdale, NJ: Lawrence Erlbaum Associates.

Meichenbaum, D., & Asarnow, J. (1978). Cognitive behavioral modification and metacognitive development: Implications for the classroom. In P. Kendall & S. Hollon (Eds.), *Cognitive behavioral interventions: Theory, research, and procedure.* New York: Academic Press.

Myers, M., & Paris, S. G. (1978). Children's metacognitive knowledge about reading. *Journal of Educational Psychology, 70,* 680–690.

Ninio, A., & Bruner, J. S. (1978). The achievement and antecedents of labelling. *Journal of Child Language, 5,* 1–15.

Palincsar, A. S., & Brown, A. L. (1984). Reciprocal teaching of comprehension — fostering and monitoring activities. *Cognition and Instruction 1,* 117–175.

Paris, S. G., & Myers, M. (1981). Comprehension monitoring, memory, and study strategies of good and poor readers. *Journal of Reading Behavior, 8,* 5–22.

Pflaum, S. W., Pascarella, E. T., Boswick, M., & Auer, C. (1980). The influence of pupil behaviors and pupil status factors on teacher behaviors during oral reading lessons. *Journal of Educational Research, 74* (2), 99–105.

Piestrup, A. (1973). *Black dialect interference and accommodation of reading instruction in first grade.* Monograph #4. Berkeley: Language-Behavior Research Laboratory.

Reid, J. F. (1966). Learning to think about reading. *Educational Research, 9,* 56–62.

Resnick, L. B. (1979). Theories and prescriptions for early reading instruction. In L. B. Resnick & P. A. Weaver (Eds.), *Theory and practice of early reading* (Vol. 2). Hillsdale, NJ: Lawrence Erlbaum Associates.

Rist, R. (1970). Student social class and teacher expectations: The self-fulfilling prophecy in ghetto education. *Harvard Educational Review, 39* (3), 411–451.

Rosenthal, R., & Jacobson, L. (1968). *Pygmalion in the classroom: Teacher expectation and pupils' intellectual development.* New York: Holt, Rinehart, & Winston.

Seligman, M. E. P., Maier, S. F., & Solomon, R. L. (1971). Unpredictable and uncontrollable aversive events. In F. R. Brush (Ed.), *Aversive conditioning and learning.* New York: Academic Press.

Sieber, J. (1968, August). *Secondary ignorance.* Paper presented at the NATO Conference on Learning and the Educational Process, Stockholm, Sweden.

Tharp, R. G. (1982). The effective instruction of comprehension: Results and description of the Kamehameha Early Education Program. *Reading Research Quarterly, 17* (4), 503–527.

Vygotsky, L. S. (1978). *Mind in society: The development of higher psychological processes* (M.

Cole, V. John-Steiner, S. Scribner, & E. Souberman, Eds. and trans.). Cambridge: Harvard University Press.

Weinstein, R. (1976). Reading group membership in first grade: Teacher behaviors and pupil experience over time. *Journal of Educational Psychology, 68,* 103–116.

Wertime, R. (1979). Students, problems, and courage spans. In J. Lockhead & J. Clement (Eds.), *Cognitive process instruction: Research on teaching thinking skills.* Philadelphia: Franklin Institute Press.

Wertsch, J. V. (1978). Adult-child interaction and the roots of metacognition. *Quarterly Newsletter of the Institute for Comparative Human Development, 1,* 15–18.

West, C. K., & Anderson, T. H. (1976). The question of preponderant causation in teacher expectancy research. *Review of Educational Research, 46,* 613–630.

Whimbey, A., & Lockhead, J. (1982). *Problem solving and comprehension.* Philadelphia: Franklin Institute Press.

Wood, D., & Middleton, D. (1975). A study of assisted problem-solving. *British Journal of Psychology, 66,* 181–191.

The Effects of Prejudice and Stress on the Academic Performance of Black-Americans

6

Reginald A. Gougis

Differences between black and white Americans in academic achievement have been intensively studied. The essential finding has been that the means for blacks as a group on various measures of academic achievement are significantly below the means for whites. These differences exist at every age, in every region of the country, and at every level of economic status. This chapter presents a new explanation of the origin of the differences and reports an experimental model to illustrate them. First, however, we review the significance of the facts themselves.

The Coleman Report released by the U.S. government in 1966 provided a detailed comparison of racial groups on achievement tests in various subjects. A national sample of students at varying levels of economic status was tested in grades 1, 3, 6, 9, and 12. Blacks averaged about one standard deviation below whites on measures of verbal ability, reading comprehension, mathematical ability, and general information. Assuming approximately normal score distributions, such a difference indicates that only about 16% of the blacks scored above the white means.

These differences persist. Data collected in 1971 and 1975 exhibited the same pattern (Galladay & Noell, 1980). In 1982, the College Entrance Examination Board reported that blacks scored below whites on every achievement test, including mathematics, literature, science, and foreign language. Averaged across all subjects, blacks scored 72 points (nearly one standard deviation) below whites on these tests. Aptitude test scores showed the same trend: the black mean was 100 points below the white on the verbal, and 121 points below on the math. Averaging verbal and math scores together, the difference was slightly more than one standard deviation (115 points). There is also a social class effect: in both races high-income students do better on the aptitude tests than low-income students. Although the black-white difference is smaller at higher incomes, there remains a substantial difference at all economic levels. In fact, even medium-income whites score higher than high-income blacks.

The adverse effects of the black-white achievement differences are tremendous. They contribute to the relatively lower occupational status, income, and overall quality of life among the black group. To illustrate how damaging a one standard deviation difference can be, consider this hypothetical case. A university receives 1,000 applications for positions in Ph.D. programs in social science. It plans to admit every applicant who ranks at or above the 75th percentile on the Graduate Record Examination (GRE). If different racial groups are represented in the application sample in the same proportions as in the U.S. population, there will be 83% white applicants, 12% black applicants, and 5% from other groups. If the mean GRE for blacks is one standard deviation below the white mean, only 3% or 4% of the 120 black applicants would be accepted, whereas 20% of the 830 white applicants would be. As a result, 97% of those selected would be white (166), whereas only about 2% would be black (4). If this process were persistent over time and consistent across most Ph.D. programs, these would be the black-white proportions of social scientists in the United States.

And this, in fact, is what happens. In 1980, about 22% of the whites tested and only about 4% of the blacks tested reached the 75th percentile on the SAT (College Entrance Examination Board, 1981). Similar percentile proportions can be expected on achievement tests for law, medicine, social science, and engineering (assuming the typical one standard deviation handicap for blacks). And, in 1980, 95% of all social scientists were white, whereas only about 4% were black. Blacks are underrepresented in similar proportions to whites in most high status occupations including engineering, law, medicine, and university teaching. The initial academic achievement deficit reduces the chances of blacks' entering high status professions, because access to these professions depends largely on entrance exam scores associated with professional education. No doubt this reduced representation contributes to the lower median income and annual salaries among blacks. The lower income, in turn, creates hardships that contribute to a poorer quality of life. In 1980, the median family income was about $20.5 thousand for whites, compared to $11.6 thousand for blacks. Blacks were also more likely to be below the poverty level, and less likely to have annual salaries of $20 thousand or more (U.S. Bureau of the Census, 1981). Moreover, statistics suggest that the quality of life is poorer among blacks. In 1980, blacks compared to whites were more likely to be unemployed (14% to 6%), divorced (20% to 9%), arrested, imprisoned, and killed by fellowmen (U.S. Bureau of the Census, 1981). If these conditions depend on income, then any gain in academic achievement might have broad consequences for the overall quality of life in the black population.

Although the black-white achievement difference has multiple causes, race prejudice appears to be the underlying root. Race prejudice can take many forms and its effects mediated in many ways. The relatively low economic status of the black group may be due partially to the institutionalized practices of job and wage discrimination favoring whites (e.g., Jones, 1979). The resulting economic hardships encourage social conditions and personal characteristics that contribute to lower achievement. The cultural learning style of many blacks, although having adaptive significance within the black community, may pose a handicap in an academic environment that is based on the learning styles of the white middle-class. Race prejudice in the form of ethnocentrism may act to institutionalize cultural bias. Prejudiced teachers can affect students in a more personal way; low expectations, hostility, and differential treatment can adversely affect blacks in the classroom. All of these factors are important. However, the focus of this chapter is on another, more direct consequence of race prejudice: the emotional stress it creates for blacks, and its effects on academic performance.

THE EFFECTS OF RACE PREJUDICE ON ACADEMIC ACHIEVEMENT

Race prejudice in American society is an "environmental stressor" that must increase emotional stress of blacks over and above that experienced by other groups in the U.S. That stress is likely to adversely affect students' daily academic performance by reducing their willingness to persist at academic tasks and interfering with the cognitive processes involved in learning. As this process continues over a long period, blacks do not develop the cognitive skills that are necessary for high academic achievement.

Race prejudice is pervasive, persistent, and particularly adverse for blacks in American society. In a systematic analysis of prejudiced attitudes, Pettigrew (1982) concluded that about 75% of white adults in the United States hold some degree of prejudice against blacks. This attitude has spanned the entire U.S. history. Prejudice has been expressed through institutionalized practices (such as slavery and job discrimination), cultural bias or ethnocentrism, and personal assaults. Personal assaults against blacks have varied in intensity from extreme terrorist attacks by organized hate groups such as the Ku Klux Klan, to nonverbal communication of hostility by teachers and other members of society. Although direct exposure to extreme incidents of prejudice (like lynchings and cross burnings) is now uncommon, indirect exposure to such incidents is frequently experienced through the media. Thus, race prejudice touches the lives of all blacks—rich and poor, young and old. No other group has been burdened with such a harsh atmosphere of prejudice.

Emotional stress may be caused by many different conditions, such as unemployment, divorce, or physical illness. Any event perceived by the individual as threatening is also stressful. Izard (1972, 1977) has shown that race prejudice is generally perceived by blacks as a personal threat, resulting in an elevation in emotional stress. Izard defines stress as a combination of emotions, such as distress, disgust, and anger. So, although all racial groups must encounter stressful conditions, blacks are exposed to an additional form of stress as well.

Some independent evidence suggests that stress is, in fact, greater in the black population than the white. Blacks are more likely to die from stress-related diseases such as hypertension, and overall they tend to die 5 years earlier than whites (National Center of Health Statistics, 1979; U.S. Bureau of the Census, 1981). Many of these stress-related reactions must be related to adverse social conditions such as poverty, unemployment, and crime, and exposure to race prejudice adds a further effect. Even high-income blacks are likely to experience more emotional stress than high-income whites; although free from the typical stressors associated with low income, they still encounter race prejudice.

Regardless of its cause, emotional stress can have adverse effects on academic performance. Stress can reduce any student's motivation to learn and can interfere with memory and other cognitive processes. Holmes (1974) reviewed and evaluated many studies on the effects of repression and anxiety. Although he concluded that there was little support for the repression hypothesis, the evidence for a direct adverse effect of anxiety (stress) on recall was clear. Stress-arousing information and information presented under stressful circumstances are not recalled nearly as well as neutral information that is presented under neutral conditions (e.g., Flavell, 1955; Zeller, 1950). Holmes attributed this reduced recall to the effects of distraction caused by anxiety and task-irrelevant thoughts. Stressed individuals tend to pay less attention to the material when it is first presented, and they do not rehearse it as much later. As a result, they recall less when the information is required.

Research on test anxiety further illustrates that stress has adverse effects on academic performance. A great deal of research shows that testing situations are often perceived as threatening and stress arousing. Many students in testing situations are preoccupied with doing poorly and other such worries. These thoughts interfere with effective use of their time, thereby contributing to poorer performance (see Sarason and Mandler, 1952, 1953; Speilberger, 1978; Wine, 1971).

The academic performance of both blacks and whites is affected by stress, but blacks are burdened with the added stress of race prejudice throughout their academic careers. Their academic performance is more impaired.

Recurring thoughts and feelings associated with race prejudice contribute to a reduction in their motivation to learn and to increased interference with the cognitive processes involved in learning. As this process continues over the years, its effects are cumulative. On the average, blacks will have spent less time trying to learn academic material and will have made less efficient use of their cognitive skills (attention, rehearsal, recall) in doing so. As a result, they will not have learned the necessary information or acquired the skills they need to perform well on achievement tests. Therefore, mean scores on standardized achievement tests will be lower for blacks than for whites. An achievement difference will remain even when comparing students of the same economic class, though it will be smaller at higher economic levels. The stress creates a learning deficit that worsens with each successive year. Whites learn a little more each year, blacks learn less.

AN EXPERIMENTAL MODEL OF THE BLACK ACADEMIC EXPERIENCE

Although many parts of the aforementioned process have been documented before, there has been no demonstration of it as a whole. Separate bodies of research suggest that race prejudice against blacks is widespread, that blacks are likely to experience emotional stress in response to that prejudice, and that stress can have adverse effects on cognitive performance. The present experiment is designed to show how all these factors interact, and thus serve as a model of the black academic experience. Although the experiment is based on only a single situation, it demonstrates the entire process under controlled conditions. The experience of prejudice encountered by the subjects was admittedly stronger than that in a typical academic situation, but this was necessary in order to demonstrate an effect in an hour's time.

Design

The experiment was designed to simulate an academic learning situation. Two groups of black college students were asked to study the lines of a character in a specially-written, three-character play. The lines to be learned consisted of a lecture on weather broadcasts and were the same for both groups. For the experimental group this material was embedded in a script that included many expressions of race prejudice and hostility by the other two characters (one black, one white); they were also shown pictures illustrating black oppression. For the control group, the weather material was embedded in a friendly, optimistic dialogue; they were shown pleasant pictures. Izard's (1972) Differential Emotion Scale was used to assess the emotional effects of these materials. The experimental group was expected to report greater emotional stress, to spend less time studying and taking notes on the weather material, and to recall less of the weather material after the learning session than the control group.

Subjects

Ninety black college students enrolled in introductory psychology courses at Howard University volunteered to participate. Each subject received academic credit for participation. Sixty-six were female and 24 were male. There were 45 subjects (33 female and 12 male) in each group. The subjects were tested in pairs, with the first subject entering the testing room assigned to the control group and the second to the experimental group. They were explicitly told they were free to discontinue their participation at any time without loss of academic credit.

Experimenters

There were two experimenters; a black male (R.G.) and a black female college student (A.M.). Both experimenters were aware of the hypotheses involved. R.G. tested 30 subjects in each condition (60 in all), while A.M. tested 15 in each condition. The role of the experimenter was to give out the written instructions and materials, to record study time, and to collect the subjects' written responses.

Scripts

The story was about a lecture being given on the topic of weather while two students sat in the back of the class having a private conversation. The weather material (lines to be learned) was identical in both scripts. It consisted of about 300 words extracted from a book providing facts concerning weather maps and weather broadcasting (Hedinger, 1979). This material had been used in a previous study by Boykin and Gougis (1982) and was rated as emotionally neutral. In this study the material was divided into 12 segments.

Dialogue lines of two additional characters accompanied each segment of weather material, along with appropriate narration. The total number of words was equal in both conditions. The experimental material focused on race prejudice and was intended to arouse emotional stress. It concerned the miseries of slavery and the contemporary sufferings facing blacks as a result of prejudice. The control material was intended to encourage pleasant feelings. It concerned the benefits of the ancient Chinese art of Tai Chi Chuan, a poem encouraging hopefulness, and inspiring words from the Bible. The script for each condition was prepared as a typed manuscript to be presented separately to subjects.

Pictures

Each group was given 22 pictures to look at. These were intended to reinforce the emotional mood of the corresponding scripts. The experimental pictures were depictions of assaults against blacks by whites. These ranged in intensity from sketchs of the slave trade to photographed lynchings of blacks by mobs of KKK members. The control pictures were photographs of a person executing the graceful and dancelike postures of Tai Chi Chuan. Each posture was set in a peaceful surrounding. The set of pictures for each condition was placed in a separate notebook to be presented individually to subjects.

The Differential Emotion Scale

Izard's (1972) Differential Emotional Scale (DES) was used to measure the subject's emotional state and the degree of emotional stress. The DES assumes that there are nine fundamental emotions: interest, joy, surprise, distress, disgust, anger, fear, contempt, and shame (guilt). Stress can be defined as some combination of these. The original DES included 67 adjectives representing the nine emotions, but the version used in this study included only 56 of those adjectives. They were presented on a single sheet of paper, each with a 5-point rating scale ranging from very slight or not at all to very strongly. Subjects were instructed to circle the response to each item that best indicated their present feelings.

Procedures

Subjects were initially told that we were interested in studying the psychological processes involved in play-acting. In the first part of the experiment, they were instructed to read the dialogue between the two student characters in the script appropriate to their group (i.e., the emotion-laden statements). They were given no more than 5 minutes to do so. They were then given the corresponding pictures to look at, to "help get in the proper mood for the script." They were given no more than 10 minutes to view the pictures, but were free to stop sooner. When they were finished with the pictures, they filled out the DES to describe their feelings.

After completing the DES, subjects were instructed to read the script a second time and learn the weather material (i.e., the lines of the lecturer character). They were warned that they would be given the lines of the student characters as cues and asked to recall the lines of the lecturer. They were encouraged to take written notes to help them learn the material. The instructions indicated that they could study as much or as little as they liked, but, in fact, no one was allowed more than 30 minutes. When the subjects had finished studying, they were given prepared test pages that provided the cue lines and were asked to write in the corresponding weather material as accurately as they could. They were given no more than 15 minutes for recall.

Dependent Measures

(1) *Emotional state and stress.* Scores from the DES were used to define the subjects' emotional states and the amount of stress they were experiencing as they tried to learn the academic material. Each subject received a score for each of the nine fundamental emotions (interest, disgust, etc.). In addition, a measure of emotional stress was computed by adding scores on distress, disgust, and anger, and dividing the sum by three. Mean scores on these measures were computed for each group. (2) *Study time.* The amount of time each subject spent trying to learn the weather material (during the second reading) was recorded in minutes and seconds. This study time was rounded to the nearest minute before computing group means. (3) *Written notes.* The number of words subjects wrote as notes during the study session was recorded for each subject, and means were computed for each group. (4) *Recall of learned material.* The amount of weather material recalled was measured by the number of words written by each subject in response to the 12 sets of cue lines. Means were computed for both groups. The recalled weather material was also rated for quality of recall. Six mutually exclusive quality types of recall were defined: verbatim, gist, misplaced gist, nonsensical error, and nothing. Each response was assigned to one of these types. Summing across the 12 cues, each subject received a score (0–12) on each type. Mean scores were computed for both groups for all six types.

RESULTS OF THE EXPERIMENT

The experiment was designed to illustrate the process by which race prejudice adversely affects the academic performance of black students. The major hypotheses were: (a) experimental subjects exposed to race prejudice would experience more emotional stress (or a more negative emotional state) than control subjects; (b) experimental subjects would spend less time studying; (c) subjects would take fewer written notes; and (d) those subjects would recall less of the lecturer's weather material than control subjects. The results that follow show that hypotheses (a), (b), and (d) were strongly confirmed but hypothesis (c) was not.

Emotional State

Scores on the 56-item DES allowed for a comparison between experimental and control groups on nine separate emotions. The results appear in Table

6.1. The highest mean score for both groups was on *interest*, with means of 3.47 for the experimental group and 3.53 for the control group. These means (which are not significantly different) represent a degree of interest between moderately and considerably. As expected, however, the groups differed substantially on *joy*. The mean for the control group was 2.96 (moderately) compared to 2.04 for the experimental group (slightly). This is a highly significant difference. Also as expected, the experimental group had higher mean scores than the control group on many of the negative emotions. The means for *anger, disgust,* and *distress* were all much higher for the experimental group than for the control group, and the differences were highly significant (see Table 6.1). There were no significant differences between groups on contempt, fear, surprise, or shame. In summary, the control group's emotional state was characterized by moderate to considerable levels of interest and joy. The experimental group was characterized by interest, anger, disgust, and distress.

Stress is defined here as a combination of distress, disgust, and anger (the sum of these divided by three). The stress mean for the experimental group was 2.47, and only 1.25 for the control—a highly significant difference. These means represent ratings between "slightly" and "moderately" for the experimental group, compared to ratings just above "very slightly or not at all" for the control.

TABLE 6.1
Mean DES Scores on Various Emotions for Experimental and Control Groups

Emotions	Experimental Group	Control Group	t	p
1. Interest	3.47	3.53	− .40	n.s.
2. Joy	2.04	2.96	− 5.48	.001
3. Surprise	1.49	1.56	− .45	n.s.
4. Shame	1.36	1.45	− .76	n.s.
5. Fear	1.66	1.62	.32	n.s.
6. Contempt	1.80	1.51	1.37	n.s.
7. Distress	2.20	1.32	7.57	.001
8. Disgust	2.52	1.21	8.48	.001
9. Anger	2.69	1.23	9.52	.001
* "Stress"	2.45	1.25	−	−

N = 90   df = 88

*"Stress" is the average of distress, disgust, and anger.

Study Time

As expected, the experimental group spent less time trying to learn the weather material than the control group: they averaged 15.36 minutes compared to 22.56 minutes for the controls. This 32% reduction is significant at the .001 level, t (88) = 4.78. When both groups are combined, the correlation between study time and emotional stress was also highly significant, -0.41. (The corresponding correlation was -0.23 in the experimental group taken separately and near zero in the control group, probably because of the restricted range of stress among the control subjects.)

Written Notes

The mean number of words written during the study session was 86.53 for the experimental group and 102.73 for the control. This is the expected trend, but the difference is not significant, t (88) = $-.93$. Although the correlation between notes and study time was a significant 0.43, there were no significant correlations between notes and stress, or between notes and amount of recall.

Amount of Recall

As expected, the experimental group recalled less weather material than the control group. The mean number of words recalled was 58.67 for the experimental group and 100.71 for the control. The difference is significant at the .001 level (t (88) = 3.94). The correlation between amount of recall and emotional stress was significant when both groups were combined; $r = -.24$, $p < .01$.

Amount of recall was also subjected to analysis of covariance with study time as the covariate. The analysis shows that the mean recall for the experimental group was significantly lower than for the control group, even after study time is controlled; F (1,87) = 5.40, $p = .022$.

Quality of Recall

The experimental group left an average of 6.82 segments blank (nothing), whereas the control group left only an average of 4.47 items; t (88) = 3.47, $p < .005$. In addition, there were differences at both major levels of recall quality. The control subjects recalled the gist or general idea correctly for an average of 1.27 segments, whereas the average for the experimental group was only .56 (t (88) = 2.91, $p < .0025$). The control subjects recalled the lecturer's lines verbatim for an average of 3.38 segments compared to 1.82 for experimental subjects (t (88) = 2.89, $p < .0025$). There were relatively few recall nonsensical errors or other errors made (i.e., incorrect material or re-calling material to inappropriate cue). There were no significant differences between the groups on these measures.

DISCUSSION

The results confirm that race prejudice can have adverse effects on the aca-demic performance of black students. Major findings are summarized in Fig. 6.1. Race prejudice increases emotional stress, and that stress then reduces the students' motivation to learn and interferes with the cognitive processes involved in learning.

The black students exposed to the race prejudice in this academic learning situation reported experiencing a moderate degree of emotional stress; an emotional state characterized by distress, disgust, and anger. This stress did reduce their motivation to learn. The experimental group spent 32% less time studying the weather material than the control group, and the correlation be-tween stress and study time was significantly negative. Moreover, the experi-mentally induced stress not only reduced motivation but interfered with the cognitive processes involved. The experimental group recalled less of the weather material than the control group, and this difference remained signif-icant even after the effects of study time were partialled out by an analysis of covariance.

Although this study has examined one stressful condition under somewhat artificial conditions, it does serve as an experimental model of the black aca-demic experience. The statements and pictures used may not be typical of the forms of prejudice encountered by most black students, but they illustrate the stressful effects of that prejudice. Typical encounters of prejudice may be equally or even more stressful. And though blacks may not encounter preju-dice or experience stress in all their academic learning situations, prejudice surely occurs many times during the years of education and has a cumula-tively stressful effect.

If this process recurs throughout the black academic experience, it must contribute to the substantially lower academic achievement scores observed for the black population. Figure 6.2 illustrates the entire cycle. Race preju-dice increases stress in the black population over that experienced by whites. The relatively greater stress among blacks decreases academic performance, resulting in a cumulative achievement deficit. This deficit then reduces em-ployment opportunity, income, and quality of life, which further increases stress. Thus, race prejudice is at the heart of a vicious cycle. Poor blacks are more affected by the added burden of poverty and related stress, but even high-income blacks are affected by race prejudice. Therefore, as long as the burden of race prejudice is upon the black population, they will continue to

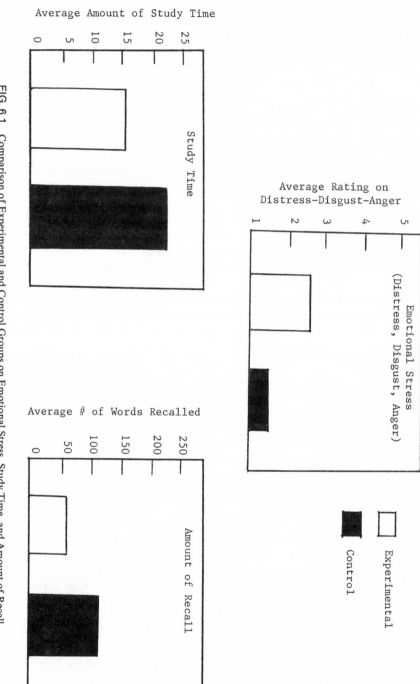

FIG. 6.1 Comparison of Experimental and Control Groups on Emotional Stress, Study Time, and Amount of Recall.

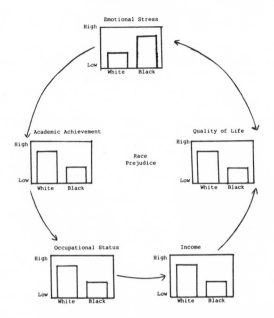

FIG. 6.2 Theoretical Illustration of the Relationship Between Emotional Stress, Academic Achievement, Occupational Status, and Income: by Race.

lag behind the white population in academic achievement, occupational status, income, and overall quality of life.

Given that race prejudice is an underlying cause of poorer conditions among blacks, improvement of those conditions may depend on our ability to eliminate prejudice or at least mitigate its stressful effects. It should be possible to develop and implement emotional support systems and therapeutic strategies to help students cope with stressful situations. For instance, schools and colleges could provide counseling services and cultural programs especially geared to helping black students cope with race prejudice and other stressors in the social environment. Future research should focus on strategies for coping with race prejudice and stress.

Efforts to reduce race prejudice itself must also be made, although they would require complex changes in institutional structure and attitudes. The elimination of prejudice would result in improved life conditions not only for blacks but for whites and the United States as a whole. It will not be an easy goal to reach. Nevertheless, seeing that race prejudice is a central factor in differences between blacks and whites in achievement, we have at least illuminated the root of the problem. Working together with this in mind, we can bring about a lasting solution.

ACKNOWLEDGMENT

This paper is based on a doctoral dissertation completed at Cornell University under the direction of Ulric Neisser. (Ulric Neisser made many useful comments in the development of this paper as well.) A. Wade Boykin and the psychology department of Howard University contributed significantly. Partial funding was received from the National Science Foundation.

Gougis, Reginald Anthony. The Impact of Race Prejudice on the Emotional State and Academic Performance of Black-American College Students. Ann Arbor, MI: University Microfilms International, 1983, #8328586.

REFERENCES

Boykin, A. W. & Gougis, R. A. (1982). *The effects of type of information and style of presentation on retention: Incorporating affect into the cognitive task.* Unpublished research paper, Cornell University.

Coleman, J. S., Campbell, E., & Mood, A. (1966). *Equality of educational opportunity.* Washington, DC: U.S. Office of Education.

College Entrance Examination Board. (1982). *Profiles, College-bound seniors, 1981.* New York: CEEB.

Flavell, J. (1955). Repressions and the "return of the repressed". *Journal of Consulting Psychology, 19,* 441–443.

Golladay, M. and Noell, J. (Eds.) (1980). *The condition of education 1978-80, statistical report.* Washington, DC: National Center for Education Statistics, U.S. Printing Office.

Hedinger, B. (1979). *Bud Hedinger's Weather Guide,* Syracuse, NY: WIXT Television, Inc.

Holmes, D. (1974). Investigations of repression: Differential recall of material experimentally or naturally associated with ego threats. *Psychological Bulletin, 81 (10),* 632–653.

Izard, C. E. (1972). Patterns of emotions: *A new analysis of anxiety and depression.* New York: Academic Press.

Izard, C. E. (1977). *Human emotions.* New York: Plenum Press.

Jones, J. (1979). Conceptual and strategic issues in the relationship of black psychology to American social science. In A. W. Boykin, A. Franklin, & J. Yates (Eds.), *Research Directions of Black Psychologists.* New York: Russell Sage Foundation.

Miller, N. E. (1983). Behavioral medicine: Symbiosis between laboratory and clinic. *Ann. Rev. Psychol., 34,* 1–31.

National Center of Health Statistics. (1979). *Advance data from vital and health statistics, No. 54.* Hyattsville, MA: National Center of Health Statistics.

Pettigrew, T. (1982). The mental health impact. In B. Bowser & R. Hunt (Eds.), *Impacts of Racism on White Americans.* Beverly Hills: Sage Publications.

Sarason, S. & Mandler, G. (1952). A study of anxiety and learning. *Journal of Abnormal and Social Psychology, 47,* 166–173.

Sarason, S. & Mandler, G. (1953). The effect of prior experience and subjective failure on the evocation of test anxiety. *Journal of Personality, 21,* 336–341.

Speilberger, C. & Sarason, I. (1978). *Stress and anxiety, Vol. 5.* New York: Wiley.

U.S. Bureau of the Census. (1981). *Statistical abstracts of the United States: 1981 (102 edition).* Washington, DC: U.S. Government Printing Office.

Wine, J. (1971). Test anxiety and direction of attention. *Psychological Bulletin, 76,* 92–104.

Zeller, A. (1950). An experimental analogue of repression: A historical summary. *Psychological Bulletin, 47,* 39–51.

7 Long-Term Effects of Preschool Programs

Richard B. Darlington

This chapter reports on the results of a collaborative project conducted by the Consortium for Longitudinal Studies on the long-term effects of preschool educational programs. More detailed descriptions are Lazar, Darlington, Royce, Murray and Snipper (1982) and Consortium for Longitudinal Studies (1983). The Consortium was founded and was chaired by Irving Lazar, of Cornell, and I was the member in charge of joint data analysis. The other members of the Consortium (in alphabetical order) are: E. Kuno Beller, of Temple University; Cynthia and Martin Deutsch, of New York University; Susan Gray, of George Peabody College and Vanderbilt University; Robert Jester, of the University of Florida, who replaced Ira Gordan when Ira died in 1978; Merle Karnes, of the University of Illinois; Phyllis Levenstein, of the Verbal Interaction Project on Long Island; Louise Miller, of the University of Louisville; Francis Palmer, of SUNY Stony Brook and later Merrill-Palmer Institute; David Weikart, of the High/Scope Foundation; Myron Woolman, of the Institute for Educational Research in Vineland NJ; and Edward Zigler, of Yale.

In 1975, when the Consortium was started, the best-known study on the effects of preschool programs was the 1969 Westinghouse Report on Project Head Start. This report reached negative conclusions about the value of the program, and the program was targeted for termination in th early 1970s. Perhaps the most prominent and eloquent person resisting this trend was Edward Zigler of Yale, who pointed out that the nation was wasting a data set potentially so valuable that he called it a national resource. In the 1960s and early 1970s a number of reasonably well-designed studies had been conducted on the effects of preschool programs. Several of these studies had large groups of children who had participated in such programs and reasonably well-matched groups of control children who had not. But only one of these studies, Weikart's, had funds to continue to follow the children after the end of the preschool program.

In late 1974, Irving Lazar decided to do something about this, the nation's failure to conduct a long-term followup study of these children. Working on a federal Administration for Children, Youth and Families (ACYF) grant of $5000, Lazar and a graduate student, Harry Murray, constructed a list of criteria to be met by studies included in the planned collaborative followup. To be included, a study should have a specific, replicable curriculum in its preschool program; should focus on children from low-income families; should have an original sample of at least 100 children between preschool and control groups; should have demographic data on the children and their families; and should have been completed by 1969.

Lazar and Murray identified about a dozen studies that met these criteria and contacted the investigators. All but one agreed to participate and thus the Consortium was formed. Our collaborative project includes virtually all the studies in the nation that meet certain identifiable criteria of quality and relevance.

The early education programs in the Consortium studies were located in urban and rural sites in the Northeast, Southeast, and Midwest. The programs were active from 1962 to 1972; only Levenstein's Verbal Interaction Project, Weikart's Perry Preschool Program, and Karnes' GOAL program continued to operate into the 1980s. Depending on the theoretical interest of the investigator, curricula included programs based on the Bank Street child development model, on Montessori methods, on Piagetian theory, on the Bereiter-Engelmann method, and others.

The Consortium studies can be categorized as center based, home based, or combination home visit/center programs. Center-based studies typically provided nursery school programs for 3- or 4-year-olds, with varying degrees of structure in the program curriculum. Instruction generally took place in small groups but in some cases was on a one-to-one basis.

Home-based studies directed their educational efforts primarily toward the parent, usually the mother, as the major instrument of change and influence in the child's life. Activities, toys, and games were brought to the family home by a parent educator or home visitor, who taught the mother to use the activities and to promote her child's development through parent-child interaction. These programs served infants and toddlers.

The third group of studies combined these approaches, providing a center-based nursery school program along with periodic home visits with both parent and child. In some programs, the emphasis during the home visit was closely related to the center programs; in others it had a more general content.

In addition to these differences, the projects differed in children's ages, the presence and degree of parental involvement in the project, in program duration, and in other ways. But the projects were also similar in many ways. All were carefully planned, well run, and carefully monitored programs. From the point of view of policy formation, I have always considered this scrupulousness to be perhaps the biggest limitation of our project. In an imperfect world, it is unreasonable to expect a typical preschool program to be run as carefully as these programs were. Thus the positive results I describe do not mean so much that Head Start *does* work as that Head Start *can* work, The work of Ronald Edmonds (this volume) has the same kind of implications. Where our project has shown that preschool programs can work, he has shown that programs in the public schools themselves can work under proper conditions. With diligence and good will, what has worked in a few cases can be made to work in many cases.

Working together, the Consortium members constructed a list of follow up measures that were undertaken in 1976. Early analyses of those results were unexpectedly positive, and Consortium teachers decided to conduct a second joint follow up in 1979-80, which for brevity I'll call 1980. The 1976 follow up included 2008 children from 11 projects. About 95% of these children were black. Boys and girls were represented about equally. The average child had a Stanford-Binet IQ score of about 92, had a mother with 10.4 years of education, and had 3.2 siblings. All these measures were taken at the time of the child's entry into the preschool program. Thus, the figure of 3.2 siblings or 4.2 children total considerably understates the ultimate family sizes of these children, inasmuch as it does not include the children born to these same mothers after the child in question had passed preschool age. In other words, these children are from large families. But the families were mostly intact: 62% of the children came from two-parent families.

In these followups, the Consortium members collected data from a larger percentage of their original samples than they had expected; the median recovery rate was 74% in 1976 and 79% in 1980. Attrition or loss of subjects was due almost entirely to simple inability to locate subjects or to budgetary constraints on data collection; fewer than 3% of the subjects contacted in either 1976 or 1980 refused to participate.

Recovered subjects were compared to those not recovered on four background variables — pretest IQ score, mother's education, Hollingshead SES (all measured at time of program entry), and IQ score at age 6 — to determine if any differences existed between the original samples and the follow-up samples or between the follow-up program and control samples. This resulted in over 300 significance tests for each follow-up. From these analyses, we concluded that attrition was random and that the follow-up program and control samples were equivalent. We are reasonably sure that our findings are not due to initial program/control differences, to nonequivalent attrition in program and control groups, or to selective attrition.

Even though I was the data analysis specialist on the project, I will describe the analytic methods here only very briefly. There were five major analytic techniques:

1. Regression to control for any preexisting differences between groups of preschool and control children.
2. The analytic methods developed by Jurs and Glass (1971) to check for nonrandom attrition. We invented these methods ourselves, but later found that the earlier Jurs and Glass paper recommended methods virtually identical to the ones we had used.
3. The Stauffer Summed-z formula for pooling the results of several different studies (Mosteller & Bush, 1954).
4. The Bonferroni method of correcting for multiple significance tests.
5. A method we originated, which we called a check for robustness.

If a result was significant when results were pooled across all Consortium projects, we then deleted the one project that had contributed most to the significance and repeated the analysis with that one project deleted. A pooled result was called "robust" only if the second analysis yielded a significant result at the .05 level two-tailed. We did this because otherwise it might have been easy to criticize our work in the following way: A critic could identify the one study that had contributed most to the overall pooled result, find some real or imagined flaw in that one study, and then say that our whole combined result depended on that one flawed study. Our robustness analyses go a long way toward eliminating that whole class of potential criticisms. Thus, where a typical statistical analysis yields results that are either significant or nonsignificant, we had three categories of results: nonsignificant, significant but not robust, and robust. As will be shown later, most of our important results were robust.

RESULTS

Our major results have been set forth in several dozen tables appearing in two other publications (Lazar, Darlington, Murray, Royce, Snipper, 1982; Consortium for Longitudinal Studies, 1983), and in other reports cited there. I will not repeat here the bulk of those presentations, but I will summarize the highlights and add some new interpretive comments.

After correcting for background differences between preschool and comparison groups, we found that differences in IQ scores between the two groups were significant and robust for 1 or 2 years after the end of the preschool programs, were significant but not robust 3 or 4 years after the programs had ended, but were not significant after that (Consortium, 1983). These results were consistent with the negative results of the earlier Westinghouse Report.

Most observers consider our results on school competence variables to be far more significant. Although IQ is often reified unjustifiably, we should remember that IQ began as basically a predictor of school performance. However, here we don't have to use substitutes for school performance — we can measure it directly. At the end of the 7th grade, on the average only 15% of the children in the preschool groups had been placed in special education classes for reasons other than speech or hearing difficulty, while the average placement rate for comparison groups was 35% (Consortium, 1983). Also, at the end of the 7th grade, on the average 32% of the children in the comparison groups had been held back a grade, but only 20% of the preschool groups (Consortium, 1983). Both these differences between preschool and comparison groups were robust and highly significant.

When we stopped collecting data in 1979-80 only four projects (Beller, Gray, Karnes, and Weikart) had students who had completed the 12th grade, so our 12th-grade results are based on far smaller samples. Nevertheless, the difference in special education placement rates was robust and highly significant; the average placement rate was 31% for comparison children and only 13% for preschool children (Consortium, 1983).

It could be argued that the dependent variables I have been emphasizing — special education placements and grade retentions — are biased toward positive findings by teacher expectancy effects. That is, a teacher might know that a child has attended a preschool program, expect the child to perform well, and overlook evidence that the child is performing poorly. I have never considered this teacher-expectancy hypothesis to explain our results. A reasonable teacher, seeing a child failing in school despite having attended a preschool program, would be *more* likely to conclude that the child needs special help. When the child's classroom performance is held constant, a reasonable teacher's knowledge that the child had attended a preschool program would increase, not decrease, the child's chances of being held back or placed in special education.

This response to the teacher-expectancy hypothesis is supported by our data. At the end of kindergarten, preschool children were retained more often and placed in special classes more often than comparison children (Consortium, 1983). Even at the end of grades 1 and 2, preschool children were retained more often than comparison children. None of these differences were statistically significant, but it is remarkable that they occurred at all, inasmuch as these were the very years in which the preschool children were significantly outperforming the comparison children on IQ tests, which presumably teachers use heavily in making these decisions. The difference at this time between average IQ scores of preschool and comparison groups was about 5 points (Consortium, 1983). The most plausible explanation for this finding is that, for a given level of classroom performance, teachers are more likely to retain a child in grade or place the child in a special class, on the theory that a child who performs poorly despite a preschool program must really need help. Thus the differences we observed at the 7th and 12th grades appear to be despite, not because of, teacher expectancies.

We might have avoided all uncertainties involving teacher expectancies by using more objective measures of school achievement, such as nationally standardized achievement tests. However, in our data set a substantial conservative bias is built into these test scores. First, most children in special education classes don't take these tests. Second, children who have been held back a year don't take the tests at the same age their classmates take them, so the results cannot be compared directly with those of their former classmates. Thus, these scores are best considered missing, along with scores of children in special education classes. So we have actual missing data or effectively missing data for a substantial fraction of the children. This data is not randomly missing — rather most of the missing scores are almost certainly the scores that would have been lowest. But, because more of the comparison children than preschool children were held back or placed in special classes, more of these low scores are missing from the comparison groups than from the preschool groups. This introduces a substantial conservative bias into any comparisons involving standardized achievement tests.

Nevertheless, we did look at differences between preschool and comparison groups on reading and mathematics achievement tests in grades 3, 4 and 5. We found significant gains on mathematics in all three grades, and significant effects on reading in grade 3.

We examined four principal measures of school success at the 12th grade: high school graduation, never retained in grade, never placed in special education, and "meeting school requirements," defined as never being held back or placed in special ed. Since the programs we studied had begun as independent projects, their children were of different ages, and in 1980 only four projects had children old enough to use in this analysis. Because only four projects are involved, the statistical power of these analyses is considerably less than in the previous analyses. In particular, our check for robustness becomes unduly severe when only four projects are in the analysis, so I shall omit this measure from the report of results, and discuss only ordinary statistical significance. I report the raw rates of events, but report the significance of differences between preschool and comparison groups after controlling by regression for differences between the groups on background variables. I report two-tailed p-values, differences in all four analyses were significant by one-tailed p's, although one of the two-tailed p's was .06.

We found that an average of 65% of the preschool groups and 53% of the comparison groups completed high school (p = .020). On the average, 13% of the preschool children and 31% of the comparison children had been placed in special ed classes sometime during their school career (p = .001). On the average, 32% of the children in preschool groups and 47% of those in comparison groups had been retained at some time (p = .060). On the average, 56% of the children in preschool groups and 38% of those in comparison groups "met school requirements" (p = .002). These results are from Tables 13.10 and 13.11 of the Consortium (1983) book. In summary, children from preschool programs performed substantially better in school than did the comparison children on all these measures.

We looked at two major variables measured after high school. One was employment; the other was a composite variable we called "adapting to mainstream society." This variable was formed in an admittedly subjective manner to measure whether a young person was conforming to the expectations of mainstream society. This variable was constructed and analyzed by Georgia Nigro. Young people were coded as adapting to mainstream society if they were in an educational program of any kind, were in the military, were employed with earnings of at least $50 per week (and did not list public assistance as their major source of income), were temporarily laid off from a job they had held, or were living with a working spouse or companion. All others were coded as not adapting to mainstream society. A great many of the latter were nonstudents listing public assistance as their major source of income. The "not adapting" group included both people looking for work but unable to find it and those not looking. It also included a few subjects in prison.

Only three projects had subjects old enough to include in these analyses. Perhaps for this reason, our standard methods of analysis, described and illustrated previously for other dependent variables, did not yield any significant differences between preschool and comparison groups. However, we did find small but statistically significant *indirect* effects of the preschool programs on both simple employment and adapting to mainstream society. An indirect effect is defined as follows: If a statistical and substantive analysis indicates that variable A affects variable B, and a separate analysis indicates that B affects C, then it is concluded that A affects C indirectly through B.

For instance, after correcting for differences in background factors, the median regression coefficient predicting "met school requirements" from preschool attendance was .190, and the median regression coefficient predicting employment from meeting of school requirements was .262. Both relationships were highly significant, with two-tailed pooled p's of .002 and .001 respectively. We assume these relationships are causal: preschool programs raise rates of meeting school requirements and meeting school requirements raises the likelihood of later employment. The simplest way to estimate the size of the effect of preschool programs on employment is to multiply the two regression coefficients, giving $.190 \times .262 = .050$. This calculation suggests that preschool programs raise employment rates by 5%, presumably an underestimate, inasmuch as this product is lowered by measurement error in the measurement of meeting school requirements, and also ignores effects operating directly or through other mediating variables. It is, therefore, difficult to estimate with any real accuracy the size of these long-term indirect effects in our data, beyond saying that they are probably small — as indeed we would expect from the great time lag between preschool and employment. Nevertheless, significant indirect effects of preschool were demonstrated for both employment and adapting to mainstream society.

In analysis of variance terminology, all the effects I have discussed so far — both direct and indirect — are main effects. Are there significant interactions? For instance, to say that preschool interacts with sex would be to say that preschool programs help boys more than girls or girls more than boys. We looked for a great many such interactions, but none were significant. The interactions we examined included the interactions of preschool program attendance with sex, SES, IQ scores before preschool, mother's education, and other variables. Thus the data do not support the contention that preschool programs are more valuable for one kind of child than for another.

We also asked whether one kind of preschool program is more successful than another. Our data were not well designed for testing this hypothesis, due in large part to differences in sample characteristics — the kind of children involved — from one location to another. But no effects of this type stuck out above the large amount of background noise. We thus can neither clearly confirm nor deny that some kinds of preschool programs are more helpful to children than others.

CONCLUSIONS

We believe we have shown that preschool programs help children. The Weikart project performed a cost-benefit analysis to assess whether the amount of help is great enough to justify the cost, and concluded that it was. It's not clear whether there is a greater return on the educational dollar by funding a preschool program than by upgrading the schools themselves (see Edmonds, this volume; Brown, Palincsar & Purcell, this volume), by providing remedial summer schools, or in other ways. But for now, we do have an educational program that seems to be successful, and it is worthy of development.

REFERENCES

Consortium for Longitudinal Studies. (1983). *As the twig is bent . . . lasting effects of preschool programs.* Hillsdale, NJ: Lawrence Erlbaum Associates.

Jurs, S. G. & Glass, G. V. (1971). The effect of experimental mortality on the internal and external validity of the randomized comparative experiment. *Journal of Experimental Education, 40,* 62–66.

Lazar, I., Darlington, R., Murray, H., Royce, J., & Snipper, A. (1982). Lasting effects of early education. *Monographs of the Society for Research in Child Development, 47,* (1–2, Serial No. 194).

Mosteller, F., & Bush, R. R. (1954). Selected quantitative techniques. In G. Lindzey (Ed.), *Handbook of social psychology, vol. 1.* Reading, MA: Addison-Wesley.

8 The Myth of the Deprived Child: New Thoughts on Poor Children

Herbert P. Ginsburg

The aims of this chapter are to evaluate the past 10 or 15 years' psychological research on the intellectual development and education of poor children's minds. Although much original work in this area was misguided, some insights have been gained into the intellectual functioning of the poor. In general, research suggests that poor children as a group do not suffer from massive intellectual deficiency. Their school failure — at least in the first several years of school — cannot be explained primarily in terms of cognitive developmental deficit. Hence, research on poor children and their education must take new directions. In the second part of the chapter, I offer speculations on the types of research we should undertake.

THE MYTH OF THE DEPRIVED CHILD

In evaluating previous research on poor children, it is useful to begin by describing the political and social climate of the late 1960s and early 1970s, a period of considerable ferment and conflict. One major force at the time was a kind of liberal environmentalism. In 1964, Lyndon Johnson proclaimed the war on poverty. On the assumption that education is the gateway to middle-class prosperity, one of the major campaigns of that war was to be the education of poor children, especially blacks. The task for the government, then, was to provide adequate education for those lacking it. Doing this required both legal and psychological remedies. Legal battles over desegregation were fought and sometimes won. But the liberals decided early on that desegregation was not sufficient. Poor children, especially blacks, did not perform adequately in the public schools, even when segregation was no longer in place. To remedy this situation, the Johnson administration leaned heavily on the advice of social scientists, who recommended, among other things, the creation of Head Start and the funding of psychological and educational research. The government offered considerable support for social science generally, including educationally oriented research (e.g., Project Literacy), and work on poor children in particular. The general aim of the research was to be the understanding of the problems of poor children, so that appropriate remedies could be developed. The results of this work were of two types: a body of research on poor children's cognitive functioning, and various attempts at "compensatory education," programs designed primarily to remedy intellectual deficiencies in preschoolers and prepare them for schooling.

Clearly, the liberal environmentalist approach was well intentioned. And in the political climate of the 1980s, that is no small compliment. Yet, several of us were dissatisfied on a number of grounds with the liberal environmentalist position. In the early 1970s, I wrote *The Myth of the Deprived Child* (Ginsburg, 1972), the aim of which was to offer a critique and analysis of existing work on poor children's intellect and education. The book made a number of points, and from them, I have selected a few major themes that are useful as stepping points for an analysis of the situation today.

The book began by stating the obvious, namely, that poor children as a group were doing badly in public schools and that the educational system required drastic improvement. The question then became: what do we know about poor children's intellectual capacities, and how can that knowledge be used to improve education? The bulk of the book focused on an analysis of psychological knowledge concerning poor children's intellect. The argument was roughly as follows: Liberal environmentalists (e.g., Hunt, 1969) believe that poor children develop in a deprived environment that stunts their intellectual growth. The environment fails to provide sufficient stimulation or provides the wrong kind of stimulation. As a result, poor children suffer from cognitive deficits. Nativist theory also postulates a cognitive deficit, but offers a different explanation of its origins. Jensen (1969) proposes that lower class children, and blacks in particular, suffer from a specific cognitive deficit, an inability to engage in "conceptual learning," and this inability is a result of genetic inheritance. According to both the environmentalists and the nativists, the cognitive deficit (whatever its origins) prevents poor children from learning the conceptual material taught in school.

I argued that both views, and a good deal of the research stemming from them, were misguided, and proposed an alternative view of "cognitive difference." The reasoning behind the argument was something like this.

1. Much of the empirical evidence supporting the deficit view could not be believed, largely on methodological grounds. As Labov (1972) pointed out at the time, many of these studies—like those of Bereiter and Englemann

(1966), and Deutsch (1967) — employed rigid methodologies and were not based on an understanding of children in general or poor children in particular. It is easy to get poor children to do badly on some standard test; it is much harder to employ methods sensitive to their true competence. Anyone who had real contact with poor children, I felt, would realize that much of the psychological research was insensitive, narrow minded, and wrong.

2. The cognitive deficit research seemed to ignore important cognitive universals. In the 1960s, cognitive theory was not well understood or accepted. I felt that, from a Piagetian perspective, the important point was not that poor children produced fewer Peabody correct responses than middle-class children, but that all children, poor and middle class alike, were probably capable of the concrete operations and even formal operations as well. The essence of the matter was commonalities in basic aspects of mental functioning, not individual differences. At the time, there was little empirical support for this position, aside from the work of Labov (1972) on black English. The main theoretical foundations were in Piaget's theory and Lenneberg's (1967).

3. A third argument stressed possible cultural differences. The general point was that poor children are not so much deficient as they are distinctive. Presumably, in response to the unique demands of their distinctive environments, they develop special kinds of adaptations — skills not possessed by middle-class children. Again, there was very little evidence to support this intuition. Labov's work on black English was again cited, as were anecdotes — perhaps apocryphal or even stereotypic — about black children's knowledge of arithmetic being expressed in numbers-running in Harlem.

4. Another theme was that poor children did not have to be instructed in basic intellectual skills; they were quite capable of learning on their own. A good deal of development takes place in a natural and spontaneous fashion. This position was partly a reaction against behaviorist theories of learning, some of which were still taken seriously at the time, and particularly work on cognitive socialization, like that of Hess and Shipman (1967). These researchers claimed essentially that (a) poor mothers did not know how to train their children in basic cognitive skills, and (b), by implication, if the cognitive skills were not trained, they would not develop. The counter argument was that many Piagetian-type skills develop independently, on their own, and that parents do not even know that the skills exist, let alone attempt to teach them. Hence, I stressed self-directed learning, and this position led to some recommendations concerning the implementation of "open schools," which were felt to provide a solution to the education of the poor.

5. Finally, I argued that it is necessary to examine what is meant by "success in school." Usually, school success is defined in terms of performance on standard achievement tests, which in turn conceptualize academic knowledge in limited, often trivial ways. Standard tests — and many educators and psy-

chologists who use them — conceive of academic knowledge in terms of correct responses, quantitative traits (e.g., "verbal ability"), and the regurgitation of prepackaged knowledge. Yet we know from cognitive theory that knowledge is complex: it involves construction; it must be conceptualized in terms of process and strategy; and the least interesting aspect is the surface response. Thus, the conventional conception of school success was superficial, missing the heart of the matter, namely, the cognitive analysis of children's concepts and strategies in particular areas of academic work. In the absence of such cognitive analyses, it was not possible to discuss intelligently what children, poor or otherwise, did or did not know or need to know in the school context.

I believe that my assessment of the situation in the early 1970s was not too far off the mark. The empirical research of both environmentalists and nativists was, indeed, insensitive and unconvincing. Both the environmentalist and the nativist theories were basically wrong. The "cognitive difference" view offered some useful insights. Let us see what events in the subsequent 10 or 15 years have to say about these matters.

First consider the social context. In the past 15 or 20 years, the political situation has changed drastically. Federal concern with problems of poverty has diminished steadily, so that the war on poverty seems light years away. Indeed, in the 1980's the Reagan administration seemed to be conducting a war on the poor, rather than on poverty, so that one positively yearns for the follies of the liberals. These comments on politics are not a digression; psychological research is heavily influenced by the political climate. The result of the political retreat from a concern with poverty is a correlated decrease in psychological research on the topic. With a few notable exceptions — including many authors of the present volume — the recent past has given us little research on poor children's intellect and education. An unanticipated benefit is that we do not have to contend with volumes of misguided research, but the general outcome is that psychological problems of poverty are being swept under the rug. With some notable exceptions — e.g., the work of Yando, Seitz, and Zigler, 1979; Ogbu, 1978; and Feagans and Farran, 1982 — research on poor children is no longer a popular topic in developmental psychology.

At the same time, some recent work does shed light on key aspects of the cognitive difference position and opens up important questions for future research and theory. Some of this work derives from the direct study of poor children; most of it stems from work in related areas.

1. *Methodology.* In the early 1970s, it seemed clear that much of the data purporting to demonstrate cognitive deficits in poor children were simply unbelievable. The research techniques employed were not sensitive enough to uncover the true extent of poor children's competence. Since that time, several developments have reinforced the basic point. Many cross-cultural re-

searchers have become dissatisfied with standard methods. Traditional cross-cultural research relied on standard Western techniques, like translated intelligence tests, to investigate cognition in "primitive" peoples. The general, and perhaps predictable, finding was that non-Westerners lack whatever cognitive skills were under investigation. Cole and Scribner (1974), providing a strong critique of this approach, showed that standard, traditional techniques often yield absurd results concerning traditional people's competence. Western tasks are not always interpreted in the way intended; they may be misunderstood, with the result that standardization often precludes validity. One alternative is to make every effort to discover tasks that are relevant for individuals in the context of the local culture. One task may be suitable for tapping competence in one culture, whereas an objectively distinct task may be suitable for measuring the same skill in another culture. Although the tasks are objectively different (dissimilar instructions, materials, etc.), they may be subjectively equivalent in tapping the same cognitive processes. Conversely, the identical task may be subjectively inequivalent between cultures. The key for measuring competence is not necessarily objective identity, but subjective equivalence.

The implications for methodology are enormous. Standardization often makes no sense and defeats the purposes for which it was intended. Extending the argument, we may think of children as analogous to cultures. Each child, or at least each developmental level, has its own perspective (culture). For subjective equivalence to be achieved, objective identity often needs to be abandoned and tasks adapted to each perspective.

If cross-cultural work suggests sensitivity to individual cultures or to the cultures of individuals, recent developments in cognitive research also point to flexibility of method. A good deal of the Newell and Simon (1972) research on complex problem solving in adults employs the talking aloud method, in which individuals say "everything that comes into their heads" as they are grappling with a difficult problem. The experimenter occasionally asks questions, but for the most part the data are essentially introspections. Several considerations lead these investigators to eschew simple quantifiable measures such as those usually obtained in the laboratory. One is that the investigators are interested in complex intellectual activities, which often cannot be expressed in simple ways. Another is that introspection can indeed be valuable at least for certain aspects of cognitive study. In any event, the use of the talking aloud procedure shows that serious psychologists are exploring flexible and nontraditional methods in the investigation of cognitive processes. (For further discussion of this point see Ginsburg, Kossan, Schwartz, & Swanson, 1983.)

A third example is even more directly pertinent to the question of poor children. Over the past 10 years, the clinical interview technique has played a very important role in research on mathematical thinking. Most investigators have come to make a common sensical distinction between competence and performance in intellectual functioning: it seems obvious that often children do not demonstrate in their performance the true extent of their knowledge. Young children in particular often know much more than they reveal. Often, too, standard tests fail to tap much more than the surface performance. Consequently, contemporary researchers often find it useful to employ the clinical interview method to assess competence. In this, they are indebted to Piaget, who recognized early on (1929) that the assessment of true competence often requires flexible questioning – questioning that is contingent on the child's response, that employs techniques like counter-suggestion, that deliberately manipulates phrasing, and that generally attempts to discover means for getting the child to perceive the problem in the manner intended. The clinical interview is deliberately nonstandardized; that is its strength for the purpose of assessing competence (Ginsburg, Kossan, Schwartz, & Swanson, 1983).

Following is an example showing how the clinical interview technique can be used to reveal unsuspected competence in a child who is performing poorly in arithmetic. Butch was in the third grade of an upstate New York elementary school. His teacher identified him as having severe problems in learning elementary school arithmetic. Both his grades and his achievement scores were low, in arithmetic as well as other school subjects, and he was a candidate for repeating third grade. He was not retarded or severely emotionally disturbed. Outside of the classroom, in the playground, he was lively and boisterous; his everyday behavior seemed to reveal at least average intelligence. Yet in the classroom he was quiet and obviously had considerable trouble learning arithmetic. Wanting to know why Butch was having problems in arithmetic, the teacher requested a diagnosis, which she hoped would produce an understanding of Butch and identify those factors responsible for his failure to learn.

In a clinical interview the following conversation took place. Asked what he was doing in school, Butch said he was working with fractions.

Interviewer: Fractions? Can you show me what you are doing with fractions?

Butch writes: 8 $\overline{)16}$
Interviewer: OK. So what does that say?
Butch: 8, 16.
Interviewer: What do you do with it?
Butch: You add it up and put the number up there.
Interviewer: OK. What is the number?

Butch writes: 8 $\overline{)16}^{23}$

Several features of the interview are notable. First, the interviewer allowed Butch to determine the topic for discussion, so that she could explore the issues that concerned him. The aim was to let Butch determine the agenda, not to impose on him a preconceived plan of interviewing. Second, the interviewer tried to get Butch to explain in his own words what he was doing. The questions were designed to be open ended, like "What do you do with it?", so that Butch could answer them in a way that would reveal his mental processes. In short, the interview aimed at discovering the child's approach: what are his concerns and how does he operate? These central features of clinical interviewing distinguish it sharply from normative, standardized testing.

To this point, the interview shows that Butch is doing something unusual. He confuses fractions with division and cannot calculate the simple division. He seems to lack an understanding of school arithmetic and engages in highly irregular procedures. What is going on? The next excerpt clarifies some of these matters and illustrates the power of clinical interviewing.

Interviewer: How did you do that?
Butch: I went, 16, 17, 18, 19, 20, 21, 22, 23. I added from 16.

It was clear that Butch got the answer 23 just as he earlier had said he did: "You add them up." The interview also revealed that Butch did this adding by counting on from the larger number. Thus, in this brief excerpt, the interviewer learned that Butch used the word "fractions" but wrote a division problem, solved a written division problem by addition, and did addition by counting! The clinical interview showed that Butch was not wrong simply because of stupidity, poor conceptual ability or the like. Instead, there were clear reasons for his mistakes, and he possessed surprising skill in mental calculation. Further, the information was provided by Butch himself, prodded by clinical interview techniques.

We all know intuitively that clinical interviewing is a sensible way to proceed. Even hard-nosed experimentalists use it. Before starting an experiment, investigators often use the clinical method (calling it pilot work) to find out what to do in the experiment. Then, if the experiment does not work, the experimentalist uses the clinical method to find out what went wrong. The actual experiment may be something of a formality. And, of course, college professors use the clinical method. Even though they may find it convenient to use standardized methods like multiple choice tests to assess the performance of large numbers of freshmen, they employ something like the clinical interview in examining Ph.D. candidates, when things are really serious. What professor would conduct a Ph.D. exam in a multiple choice format? In any event, the clinical interview is increasingly popular in research on mathematical thinking and often reveals surprising competencies in children who perform poorly in school arithmetic.

These recent methodological developments strengthen the earlier arguments concerning the irrelevance of much research on cognitive deficits in poor children because it was based on standard methods of limited sensitivity. Moreover, these developments have influenced at least two recent studies of poor children's intellectual functioning. Yando et al. (1979) made serious attempts to employ flexible methods in their research, and so did Russell and I in our studies of preschool and kindergarten children's mathematical thinking (Ginsburg and Russell, 1981). In our own research, we could not engage in extensive clinical interviewing, because the children were so young. Consequently, we spent many hours devising and revising experimental tasks so that children would understand them. Often, some minor change in wording or procedure made an immense difference, and it usually took many hours to discover these minor variations. For example, we began with what we thought was an easy task designed to measure the child's ability to determine the sum of two visible collections of objects. We presented a story in which the child was required to find the union of two static sets. For example: "Turtle has three nuts and owl has two nuts. That's three and two. How many do they have altogether?" When the task was presented in this manner, inner city children performed quite badly on the average. We revised the task, using problems that stressed the *active combining* of sets. Thus: "Puppet has two pennies. He's walking to the store and finds one more penny. How many pennies does he have altogether?" With this apparently minor change in the semantics of the problem, inner city children's performance levels improved, and class and race differences did not achieve statistical significance.

In brief, flexible methodology is at the heart of research on intellectual competence. Much cognitive deficit research has not used this kind of methodology and hence is irrelevant. Recent research, using flexible methods, uncovers important areas of cpompetence in poor children. It is to some of these competencies that we turn next.

2. *Universals.* Ten years ago, there was a bit of evidence suggesting that poor children are characterized by certain "cognitive universals," like the Piagetian concrete operations or basic syntactic processes. Recent research, most of it in the cross-cultural tradition, attests to the basic validity of this point of view. For example, a recent review of cross-cultural Piagetian research (Dasen and Heron, 1981) suggests that virtually all cultures examined seem to possess the capability for concrete operational thinking, although the evidence concerning formal operations is by no means clear. Similarly, the research of Cole and Scribner (1974) and their colleagues generally demonstrates that nonliterate West Africans show basic competencies in reasoning, memory, and the like, although these competencies may not be expressed in typically Western fashion. Thus, the Kalahari bushmen (Tulkin & Konnor, quoted by Flavell, 1977) demonstrate the capability for scientific thinking as they engage in the tracking of animals. At the same time, they would no doubt find it impossible to deal with such Piagetian formal operational tasks as the combining of chemicals.

Our own research (Ginsburg, Posner, and Russell, 1981a, 1981b, 1981c) examines the development of mathematical thinking in unschooled and schooled West Africans in two different cultures. One of these groups in the Ivory Coast, the Baoulé, is an animist, agricultural group, placing no particular emphasis on mathematics. Our research was conducted in areas where some Baoulé children attended schools, while others did not. The second group, the Dioula, are Muslims who have traditionally engaged in mercantile activities and are scattered throughout West Africa. The Dioula, although often illiterate, need to employ calculational processes in the course of commerce. Like the Baoulé, some Dioula subjects attended school and others did not. The two African groups provided a useful contrast in terms of hospitality to mathematical ideas and procedures. We used these groups to investigate the effects of schooling and culture on the development of informal mathematical skills.

One basic finding was that unschooled African children from both cultures possess fundamental informal concepts of mathematics, like more, equivalence, and adding. Posner (1982) found that Baoulé and Dioula children ranging from 4 or 5 years of age to 9 or 10 years of age perform about as well as Americans on the elementary concept of more. Young children in both African cultures ". . . possess the basic notion of inequality; by the age of 9- 10, regardless of schooling or ethnic background, they display a high level of accuracy. Moreover their methods for determining the greater set are similar to those of American children . . . suggesting . . . a universal capacity" (Posner, 1982). Although they may acquire this concept at a later age than Americans, the Africans do acquire it, without the benefit of schooling or middle-class American culture. Posner also investigated elementary addition and found that both schooled and unschooled Dioula are extremely skilled in this area, and that schooled Baoulé are also adept. Only unschooled Baoulé, members of the agricultural society, did relatively badly, perhaps because their culture places little emphasis on counting. In any event, the important finding is that unschooled Dioula children are competent in elementary addition using counting and other effective strategies, and that even the unschooled Baoulé achieve some success in this area.

Ginsburg, Posner, and Russell (1981a) investigated more complex forms of addition in schooled and unschooled Dioula children and adults, and in American children and adults. In general, unschooled Dioula children eventually exhibit a high degree of competence in the solution of verbally presented addition problems. The young Dioula begin with elementary counting procedures, but older Dioula switch to the extensive utilization of regrouping methods (e.g., $23 + 42 = 20 + 40 + 3 + 2$), which are more efficient, particularly in the case of larger numbers. At first, the Dioula do not employ the strategies with great accuracy but with age become increasingly proficient in their use, learning to discriminate among different types of problems and to apply different strategies where appropriate. Moreover, the strategies employed by the Dioula are essentially the same as those observed in American children. Schooling and American culture are not *necessary* for the development of mental addition strategies. Other cross-cultural researchers like Saxe (Saxe and Posner, 1983) find similar results. Apparently, illiterate children growing up in what we would consider the abject poverty of traditional cultures nevertheless manage to develop some fundamental cognitive concepts and skills.

Poor children in our own culture develop similar skills. That was the hypothesis of 10 years ago, and it is even more reasonable today. Basic cognitive skills should be no less prevalent in lower-class Americans than in unschooled Africans or middle-class Americans. Our research in the Washington, D.C. ghetto (Ginsburg and Russell, 1981) was designed to investigate the development of informal mathematical notions in lower- and middle-class children, both black and white, at the prekindergarten and kindergarten levels. Each child, seen individually, was given a large number of mathematical thinking tasks (17 in all), many derived from our work in Africa and from the work of investigators like Gelman. The tasks ranged from such informal skills as the perception of more, the understanding of addition operations, simple enumeration, and addition calculation, to such school-taught notions as the representation and writing of numbers.

In general, we found no social class differences and at most statistically insignificant trends favoring middle-class over lower-class children. In the vast majority of cases, children of both social classes demonstrated competence on the various tasks and used similar strategies for solving them. If these competencies and strategies were not evident at the preschool level, they emerged by kindergarten age in all groups. For example, middle- and lower-class children made effective use of counting strategies to solve addition calulation problems involving concrete objects. In general, the only large differences involved age: developmental changes from preschool to kindergarten far outweigh social class differences in this area. Furthermore, the research showed fewer racial than social class differences. Race has only trivial associations with early cognitive function. Jensen's (1969) notion that lower-class and black children exhibit weaknesses in abstract thought is wrong, at least with respect to early mathematical cognition. Many of the tasks employed in our study were prime examples of abstract thought (e.g., the understanding of addition operations) and yet were not associated with racial or social class differences. Our overall conclusion was that, at least at the age of 4 or 5, poor children, black or white, possess fundamental competencies in early mathematical thinking; there is little evidence of pervasive cognitive deficit.

3. *Cognitive difference.* Ten years ago, a number of us hypothesized that poor children were characterized by cognitive *differences,* not deficits (e.g., Cole & Bruner, 1971). The major evidence was Labov's work, showing that black English is different on the surface, but employs the same basic syntax as standard English. The basic argument was that cognitive differences were an expression of distinctive adaptations to unique environments.

While the argument was largely conjectural, there is some recent cross-cultural evidence shedding light on the question of cognitive differences. We know in a general way that cultures develop distinctive techniques for dealing with distinctive problems. Thus, the Puluwat islanders develop clever methods for navigating without special instruments (Gladwin, 1970). Our own research in the Ivory Coast examined the development of mathematical thinking within the contexts of two very different cultures, one Moslem and mercantile and the other animist and agricultural. The Dioula traditionally engage in commerce and have wide experience in dealing with the money economy. By contrast, the Baoulé practice agriculture and apparently are less hospitable than the Dioula to informal mathematical activities. We found that, although members of both groups possess fundamental mathematical concepts and skills, members of the Dioula group elaborate on them extensively, but the Baoulé often do not. We encountered Dioula adults who engaged in complex forms of mental arithmetic, and even understood basic mathematical principles in a practical fashion (Petitto and Ginsburg, 1982). Research makes it clear that cultural groups sometimes develop distinctive patterns of cognition in response to local environmental demands. Unfortunately, we know little more than this; we have virtually no solid information concerning the distinctive cognitive activities of sub-groups within our own culture. More about this below.

4. *Cognitive socialization.* My earlier critique stressed spontaneous development and downgraded the role of cognitive socialization. I argued that poor children can learn on their own, that cognitive socialization as carried on by the middle class is not necessary to instruct poor children in the basic intellectual skills that will later form the basis for school learning. In some ways the critique was accurate and in some ways a mistake. It was accurate in pointing out that children's learning — including that of poor children — is often spontaneous and does not always depend on adult instruction. Some aspects of cognition do indeed develop in a more or less self-directed fashion, without the necessity for parental involvement. Infants probably develop object permanence, action schemes, and perceptual skills on their own, without parental help or knowledge. Preschool children develop methods for addition and concepts of equivalence on their own, without explicit instruction (although parents or other agents of culture must of course directly or indirectly provide the basic counting numbers). We probably underestimate the

extent to which children spontaneously develop basic concepts, skills, and sensible views of the world.

The critique was also accurate in pointing out that much of the early cognitive socialization research was badly conceived and executed. For example, the influential studies of Hess and Shipman (1967) gave an oversimplified view of cognitive socialization and studied it poorly. These investigators conceived of cognitive socialization as a one-way process in which parents shape children's intellectual development. Such theorizing does not do justice to the self-directed aspects of human development and to the complex interactions between parents and children. Also, Hess and Shipman examined the parent-child interaction of lower-class families in a laboratory setting that required mothers to instruct children in an artificial task. This situation may have been comfortable for middle-class mothers and children, but for their lower-class peers it may have been uninteresting, and even threatening and condescending. For this group, the laboratory task appears to be culturally biased and lacking in ecological validity. Little can be learned from research of this type.

At the same time, even though my critique may have been reasonable, I probably underestimated the extent to which cognitive socialization is important and necessary for the development of basic intellectual skills. Perhaps I was too much of a Piagetian. Piaget never really understood the role of the social-cultural environment. But Vygotsky did. And recent research in the Vygotsky tradition (e.g., Greenfield, 1984; and Rogoff & Gardner, 1984), illustrates the subtle and important ways in which parent-child interaction shapes early cognitive development. Children do not learn everything on their own; parents seem to play a major role in shaping certain key elements of children's cognition.

What does this mean for the understanding of poor children? Probably it is still correct to maintain that they acquire certain intellectual skills on their own, in a self-directed fashion. In these cases, cognitive socialization may be beside the point. At the same time, cognitive socialization may be crucial for the development of some intellectual and other skills that may later play a major role in schooling. Hence, we need to use sensitive methods and sophisticated theories to learn more about cognitive socialization in general and in poor children in particular.

5. *Academic knowledge.* Ten or 15 years ago we seemed to know virtually nothing about academic knowledge and needed to know much more if we were going to say anything sensible about poor children's performance in school. Since then, we have made enormous strides in our understanding of schooled cognition. Now we can go far beyond our earlier intuition that achievement test scores do not tell the whole story. Now we have had more than a decade of serious research into such matters as reading (both decoding and comprehension), expository writing, and mathematical thinking. Having recently edited a book on the subject (Ginsburg, 1983), I am familiar with

the latest research on mathematical thinking. We now know a good deal about early counting activities and their role in early calculation (Fuson & Hall, 1983); the mental numberline and subsequent concepts of base ten (Resnick, 1983); the role of systematic strategies in the generation of calculational errors (VanLehn, 1983); the semantics and syntactics of word problem solving (Riley, Greeno, & Heller, 1983); and the basic strategies of algebraic problem solving (Davis, 1983). Children's knowledge of academic mathematics involves complex cognitive activities, whose nature and extent we are just beginning to understand.

One benefit of the work on academic knowledge is that we are now in a position to perform sensible and informative studies of school learning — on "excellence" (Edmonds, this volume). When we relied solely on achievement tests as the dependent measure, this was not possible. In the absence of a good theory of academic knowledge, it was impossible to come to a sound understanding of what children really learn in school. Now, however, we can begin to understand these issues, and this should be of great benefit in dealing with poor children's education.

In particular, the new contributions to the theory of academic knowledge allow us to come to at least a preliminary understanding of school failure. The desire to ameliorate school failure was the motivating force behind the early studies of poor children's intellect; now we have research that sheds light on the nature of school failure and hence on the school performance of many poor children. Russell and Ginsburg (1984) conducted a study of cognitive factors underlying low achievement in school mathematics. The study included both middle- and lower-class children at the third and fourth grade levels. (By implication, the study is especially relevant to understanding poor children, because they are disproportionately represented in the ranks of school failures). Our general aim was to determine whether fourth-grade children who scored at least one year below the norm on standard mathematics achievement tests displayed unusual patterns of thinking in several different areas of mathematical cognition. We wished to know whether the low achievers displayed weaknesses in the areas of: (a) informal mathematical thinking; (b) abstract thought; (c) calculational aspects of arithmetic; and (d) basic concepts (e.g. knowledge of base ten). We tested each child individually, again using clinical interview techniques and a large number of tasks developed over many years. Several findings are relevant for our concerns. First, the mathematics difficulty (MD) children possess fundamental informal concepts like the mental numberline and procedures like mental addition and estimation. They are capable of basic enumeration skills and even concepts of place value as applied to written numbers. They display insight into some structured tasks and can solve basic word problems. They make more errors, by definition, than do normal children, but the errors are the result of common "bugs" (Brown & Burton, 1978) or error strategies; MD children make errors for the same reasons as normally achieving children. Our general conclusion was that MD children are essentially normal with respect to basic mathematical thinking. They are capable of abstract thought and do not display cognitive processes of an unusual nature.

Of course, there are a number of cautions that must be raised in respect to this study. For one thing, we did not study all cognitive processes, so that our conclusions are necessarily limited to the particular measures employed. Second, we obtained some results that were incongruous and difficult to explain. For example, MD children have particular difficulty with elementary number facts. They had a harder time remembering that 2 and 2 is 4 than they did in performing some rather complicated mental addition strategies. This result is probably just the reverse of what Jensen would expect; in his view, poor children have special talent for rote memory and cannot handle conceptual tasks. The result contradicts Jensen's view, but I have no easy way of explaining it either.

Our results at present are inconclusive, and a good deal of research needs to be done. On the basis of clinical experience with children failing in school, I predict that research results would support the view that low achieving children as a group do not suffer from serious cognitive deficiencies like inability to understand abstractions. (See also Brown, Palincsar, and Purcell, this volume.) Furthermore, in at least the first several grades of school, low achieving children are not likely to display unusual patterns of academic cognition. They may get many wrong answers, but their basic understanding of school related work is not qualitatively different from that of normal achieving children. At the same time, there must eventually be a cumulative deficit that puts these children further and further behind. Thus, children who fail to learn simple addition and subtraction will be at a clear disadvantage in learning more complicated topics in arithmetic (like the long division algorithm). Thus, there must come a point where children who fail in school are really "out of it," and their academic cognition must eventually become deficient. But this does not reflect basic cognitive difficulties.

If the hypothesis is basically correct, that school failure does not originally derive from deficient cognition (but may eventually produce it), why do children exhibit school failure in the first place? The question leads us into areas like education, motivation, and style. With respect to education, it should be abundantly clear than many schools teach badly, and this is likely the major cause of children's academic failure. There is no evidence that under stimulating conditions poor children cannot learn quite well. Another factor is motivational: children prone to school failure may experience some form of distress that prevents them from exhibiting their capability or realizing their potential. And of course, once these children fall behind, the prophecy becomes self-fulfilling. Finally, there is the factor of style: some children's learning style or cognitive style may not mesh effectively with the teaching environment of the schools.

In brief, over recent years, we have made important advances in our understanding of appropriate methodology, in our understanding of basic and perhaps universal cognitive processes, in our knowledge of distinctive cognitive adaptations in response to unique environments, in our views of cognitive socialization, and in our conceptualization of academic knowledge. Most of these advances are indirectly relevant to the understanding of poor children, but importantly relevant nonetheless. In general, the findings support the hypothesis that poor children do not suffer from massive cognitive deficiencies. Poverty of intellect cannot explain their failure in school.

NEEDED RESEARCH

Cognitive developmental psychology is moving in new directions that can inform the study of poor children. Researchers are beginning to go "beyond the purely cognitive" (Schoenfeld, 1983) to propose new perspectives on issues of intellectual development. Some of these new ways of looking at mind may provide insights into poor children's intellectual growth and education.

1. *Learning Potential.* For the most part, cognitive psychologists have focused attention on a narrow aspect of mental life—the current cognitive structure of the individual. Traditional research has focused on such issues as the nature of concrete operations at ages X vs Y, or the counting strategies of young children. So-called developmental studies typically examine process A (e.g., egocentric communication) in different groups of children at ages X, Y, and Z. Even the few studies employing as subjects the same children at different age levels typically examine existing cognitive structures in a static fashion and do not focus on the developmental process itself. To be sure, there are exceptions to the situation I have described; some developmentalists have focused on development and learning. For example, after many years' exploring cognitive structures (concrete operations, formal operations, etc.) the school of Piaget turned in the 1970s to the examination of issues of equilibration (as in Inhelder, Sinclair, & Bovet, 1974). Yet most cognitive developmental psychology is not directly concerned with the process of development, but with the characterization of differences in current structures at various age levels.

For the purposes of education—whether of poor children or anyone else—the perspective of this kind of developmental psychology is valuable but at the same time has shortcomings. As I argued previously, it is important to understand the structure of academic knowledge—to analyze its concepts and processes. It is valuable to determine, for example, that at the pre-school

level poor children possess certain informal addition concepts and procedures (Ginsburg & Russell, 1981) or that mathematical errors are generated
by common error strategies (Ginsburg, 1983). Yet, for purposes of education, it is even more important to know how one can build on the informal
knowledge or eliminate the bugs; learning potential and development are the
crux of the matter, not current cognitive structure. The focus is on *becoming*
more than on *being*. Indeed, Papert (1980) even suggests that a focus on current cognitive structure may be counterproductive:

> The invention of the automobile and airplane did not come from a detailed
> study of how their predecessors, such as horse-drawn carriages, worked or did
> not work. Yet, this is the model for contemporary educational research. . . .
> There are many studies concerning the poor notions of math or science students
> acquire from today's schooling. There is even a very prevalent "humanistic" ar-
> gument that "good" pedagogy should take these poor ways of thinking as its
> starting point. . . . Nevertheless, I think that the strategy implies a commit-
> ment to preserving the traditional system. It is analogous to improving the axle
> of the horse-drawn cart. But the real question, one might say, is whether we can
> invent the "educational automobile." (p. 44)

Applying Papert's perspective to the case of poor children, we might argue
that it is less important to know what informal knowledge poor children possess at age 4 or why third graders in the current schools make addition errors
than it is to discover what poor children can do under more nearly ideal circumstances. Current cognitive structures, as they are shaped by the typical
school environment, may be almost irrelevant to the issue of learning in more
stimulating circumstances. Whether the poor child can or cannot count at age
4 or employs some error strategy may not be of great relevance for what he or
she can accomplish in the atypical classroom.

Much of the literature on radical educational reform supports this point.
Many years ago, educators like Kohl (1967), showed that unusual classrooms
could produce atypically fine learning in poor children. More recently,
Papert (1980) and his colleagues have shown that the LOGO computer environment can produce dramatic learning in physically handicapped children,
some of whom are even judged to be retarded in ordinary classrooms.
Edmonds (this volume) shows how even in New York City poor children can
learn effectively in certain types of public schools. Brown, Palincsar, and
Purcell (this volume) show that reading problems can be remedied even in
children who might be considered learning disabled. It is clear that the existence theorem has been clearly proven: poor children (and various handicapped children as well) *can learn* under unusual conditions. The potential
exists even if the effective educational environment is rare. Psychological
theories of learning disabilities should be treated with great skepticism — they
describe only what exists under current conditions, not what can occur.

Psychologists should focus more on the issue of learning potential and less on the description of cognitive structure conceived in static terms. For many years the psychological study of learning was dull and irrelevant; perhaps there were good reasons for abandoning it. But now it seems to be time, as Brown and French (1979) have suggested, to return to this ancient but still central topic.

2. *Noncognitive factors.* Motivation plays a fundamental role in education. We are all familiar with children who make great intellectual strides when they get "turned on," when there is interest in and passion for learning. The latest cultural phenomenon of this type is children who get hooked on computers and without the benefit of formal instruction—or despite it—become expert in their use. We are all familiar with other children who are frightened of learning—for example, fear of mathematics—or contemptuous of it, or afraid to exhibit to peers signs of intellectual interest. Ogbu's psychological analysis (this volume) focuses on the motivations, beliefs, and expectancies produced by the caste system in this country: some children do not learn in school because they perceive no social or economic benefits from doing so. Clinicians are familiar with children whose failure to learn is rooted in their neurotic character structure. For instance, the teacher's disapproval may be linked to the parent's, and subtraction in arithmetic may be seen as an instance of the "taking away" of love. Such aberrations may be more common than we think.

It is not enough to say, as Piaget seems to, that the cognitive structures are the source of their own motivation ("functional assimilation"). Certainly there is, can be, should be "intrinsic motivation," but many other forms of motivation are at the heart of education as well. Indeed, I would make two speculations. One is that most cases of learning problems or low achievement in the schools can be explained primarily on motivational grounds rather than in terms of fundamental cognitive deficit. Most children fail in school not because they are stupid (cognitively deficient, lacking in "formal operations", etc.) but because they are afraid, turned off, and the like. I think academic psychologists are out of touch with reality when they take so seriously the role of basic cognitive factors (i.e., intelligence, conceptual thought, Piagetian operations) in school failure. Of course, it's easier to measure cognitive variables than motivation and personality.

A second speculation is that understanding motivation may be at least as useful for educational practice—for remediation—as knowledge of cognitive structure or process. No doubt, as Brown, Palincsar, and Purcell (this volume) have shown, focused intervention based on cognitive analysis (diagnosis) of disruptions in process can provide successful remediation. But it may also be true that motivating poor achievers in new ways, without paying much attention to their cognitive processes, may also dramatically improve their learning. The evidence for this is largely anecdotal: these are cases of children who read poorly until for some reason they "decide" to read, where-upon they learn very rapidly, without the benefit of tutorial help based on profound cognitive analysis.

Motivation is central to learning, just as is cognition. It is foolish to argue about which is more important. Both are vital. But we developmental and educational researchers have tended to slight the motivational.

3. *Cognitive style.* As I tried to illustrate in the foregoing, poor children probably do not suffer from fundamental cognitive deficits. Instead, there is evidence for the existence of universal basic cognitive processes. At the same time, poor children — or any children — may develop distinctive intellectual adaptations to the special demands of their environments. This is the cognitive difference view, usually put in opposition to the deficit theory.

An important research question for the future has to do with the nature and extent of such cognitive differences and their role in education. One way of conceptualizing the differences may be in terms of cognitive style. This concept has a long and checkered history, originating in psychoanalytic theory but eventually becoming entombed in psychometric practice. The basic idea seems to be that intellect, like other aspects of psychological functioning, has a personality, a style. Intellect can be impulsive, or defensive, or vivacious, or dull, just as our social behavior can be. In an informal study of letters of recommendation, I found that professional psychologists relied heavily on style concepts in evaluating their students and colleagues. Hardly anyone spoke of *g;* many described "independence of mind."

One research issue concerns the extent to which poor children exhibit distinctive cognitive styles that interfere with school work. Boykin (1979) has suggested that blacks exhibit a "verve" of intellect that may clash with the expectations of the middle-class school. (For a recent review, see Shade, 1982). The personality of intellect seems basic to cognitive function; we need to know much more about the role of cognitive style in poor children's intellect and education.

4. *The individual in the social system.* Intellect and personality are embedded in social life; they cannot be fully understood in isolation. We need a genuine ecological psychology that interprets behavior and cognition in the context of the larger social-political system. Johnny fails in school not solely or primarily because he is dumb, but because of the motivation linked to his implicit beliefs concerning his place in the class and caste system, because of the way in which he is treated by teachers whose choice of profession is itself influenced by the class system and by social expectations concerning sex roles, and because of political-economic factors beyond his control that place him in a jobless family with few material resources. Education is a social-political phenomenon as much as a psychological issue. The espousal of a narrowly psychological perspective is naive.

Although over the past several years psychologists have become increasingly aware of the need for an ecological psychology (Bronfenbrenner, 1979; Neisser, 1976; Ogbu, this volume), a good deal of theoretical work needs to be done to make it a reality.

CONCLUSION

We have made progress in our understanding of poor children's intellect and education. The old myths of cognitive deficit are even less credible now than before. At the same time, we require more research and thinking about learning potential, motivation, cognitive style, and the role of social-political factors. To make progress, we need to supplement, or transform?, our cognitive notions with genuinely psychological and ecological considerations. This should lead to improved understanding of poor children, to reform of the educational system, and to the progress of psychology generally.

REFERENCES

Bereiter, C. & Englemann, S. (1966). *Teaching disadvantaged children in the preschool.* Englewood Cliffs, NJ: Prentice-Hall.

Boykin, A. W. (1979). Psychological/behavioral verve. In A. W. Boykin, A. J. Franklin, & I. F. Yates (Eds.), *Research directions of black psychologists.* New York: Russell Sage Foundatoon.

Bronfenbrenner, U. (1979). *The ecology of human development.* Cambridge, MA: Harvard University Press.

Brown, J. S. & Burton, R. B. (1978). Diagnostic models for procedural bugs in basic mathematical skills. *Cognitive Science, 2,* 155–192.

Brown, A. J. & French, L. A. (1979). The zone of potential development: implications for intelligence testing in the year 2000. In R. J. Sternberg & D. K. Detterman (Eds.), *Human intelligence: perspectives on theory and measurement.* Norwood, NJ: Ablex.

Cole, M. & Bruner, J. S. (1971). Cultural differences and inferences about psychological processes. *American Psychologist, 26,* 866–76.

Cole, M. & Scribner, S. (1974). *Culture and thought.* New York: Wiley.

Dasen, P. R. & Heron, A. (1981). Cross-cultural tests of Piaget's theory. In H. C. Triandis & H. Heron (Eds.), *Handbook of Cross-cultural Psychology.* Vol. 4. Boston: Allyn & Bacon.

Davis, R. B. (1983). Complex mathematical cognition. In H. P. Ginsburg, (Ed.), *The development of mathematical thinking.* New York: Academic Press.

Deutsch, M. (1967). (Ed.), *The disadvantaged child.* New York: Basic Books.

Feagans, L. & Farran, D. C. (1982). (Eds.), *The language of children reared in poverty.* New York: Academic Press.

Flavell, J. H. (1977). *Cognitive development.* Englewood Cliffs, NJ: Prentice-Hall.

Fuson, K. C. & Hall, J. W. (1983). The acquisition of early number word meanings: a conceptual analysis and review. In H. P. Ginsburg, (Ed.), *The development of mathematical thinking.* New York: Academic Press.

Ginsburg, H. P. (1983). (Ed.), *The development of mathematical thinking*. New York: Academic Press.

Ginsburg, H. (1972). *The myth of the deprived child: poor children's intellect and education*. Englewood Cliffs, NJ: Prentice-Hall.

Ginsburg, H. P., Kossan, N. E., Schwartz, R., & Swanson, D. (1983). Protocol methods in research on mathematical thinking. In H. P. Ginsburg (Ed.), *The development of mathematical thinking*. New York: Academic Press.

Ginsburg, H. P., Posner, J. K., & Russell, R. L. (1981a). The development of knowledge concerning written arithmetic: a cross-cultural study. *International Journal of Psychology, 16,* 13-34.

Ginsburg, H. P., Posner, J. K., & Russell, R. L. (1981b). The development of mental addition as a function of schooling and culture. *Journal of Cross-cultural Psychology, 12,* 163-178.

Ginsburg, H. P., Posner, J. K., & Russell, R. L. (1981c). Mathematics learning difficulties in African children: a clinical interview study. *The quarterly newsletter of the laboratory of comparative human development, 3,* 8-11.

Ginsburg, H. P. & Russell, R. L. (1981). Social class and racial influences on early mathematical thinking. *Monographs of the society for research in child development, 46,* serial no. 193.

Gladwin, T. (1970). *East is a big bird*. Cambridge, MA: Harvard University Press.

Greenfield, P. M. (1984). The role of scaffolded interaction in the development of everyday cognitive skills. In B. Rogoff & J. Lave (Eds.), *Everyday cognition: its development in social context*. Cambridge, MA: Harvard University Press.

Hess, R. D. & Shipman, V. (1967). Cognitive elements in maternal behavior. In J. P. Hill (Ed.), *Minnesota Symposia on Child Psychology,* Vol. 1. Minneapolis: University of Minnesota Press, 57-81.

Hunt, J. McV. (1969). *The challenge of incompetence and poverty*. Urbana, IL: University of Illinois Press.

Inhelder, B., Sinclair, H., & Bovet, M. (1974). *Learning and the development of cognition*. Cambridge, MA: Harvard University Press.

Jensen, A. R. (1969). How much can we boost I.Q. and scholastic achievement? *Harvard Educational Review, 39,* 1-123.

Kohl, H. (1967). *36 children*. New York: New American Library.

Labov, W. (1972). *Language in the inner city*. Philadelphia: University of Pennsylvania Press.

Lennenberg, E. H. (1967). *Biological foundations of language*. New York: Wiley.

Neisser, U. (1976). *Cognition and reality*. San Francisco: W. H. Freeman.

Newell, A. & Simon, H. (1972). *Human problem solving*. Englewood Cliffs, NJ: Prentice-Hall.

Ogbu, J. U. (1978). *Minority education and caste*. New York: Academic Press.

Papert, S. (1980). *Mindstorms: children, computers, and powerful ideas*. New York: Basic Books.

Petitto, A. L. & Ginsburg, H. P. (1982). Mental arithmetic in Africa and America: Strategies, principles, and explanations. *International Journal of Psychology, 17,* 81-102.

Piaget, J. (1929). *The child's conception of the world*. New York: Harcourt, Brace, and World.

Posner, J. K. (1982). The development of mathematical knowledge in two West African societies. *Child Development, 53,* 200-208.

Resnick, L. B. (1983). A developmental theory of number understanding. In Ginsburg, H. P. (Ed.), *The development of mathematical thinking*. New York: Academic Press.

Riley, M. S., Greeno, J. G., & Heller, J. I. (1983). Development of children's problem-solving ability in arithmetic. In Ginsburg, H. P. (Ed.), *The development of mathematical thinking*. New York: Academic Press.

Rogoff, B. & Gardner, W. (1984). Developing cognitive skills in social interactions. In B. Rogoff & J. Lave (Eds.), *Everyday cognition: its development in social context*. Cambridge, MA: Harvard University Press.

Russell, R. L. & Ginsburg, H. P. (1984). Cognitive analysis of children's mathematics difficulties. *Cognition and instruction, 1,* 217–244.

Saxe, G. & Posner, J. K. (1983). The development of numerical cognition: cross-cultural perspectives. In H. P. Ginsburg (Ed.), *The development of mathematical thinking.* New York: Academic Press.

Schoenfeld, A. H. (1983). Beyond the purely cognitive: metacognition and social cognition as driving forces in intellectual performance. *Cognitive Science, 7,* 329–363.

Shade, B. J. (1982). Afro-American cognitive style. A variable in school success? *Review of Educational Research, 52,* 219–244.

VanLehn, L. (1983). On the representation of procedures in repair theory. In Ginsburg, H. P. (Ed.), *The development of mathematical thinking.* New York: Academic Press.

Yando, R., Seitz, V., & Zigler, E. (1979). *Intellectual and personality characteristics of children: social class and ethnic group differences.* Hilldale, NJ: Lawrence Erlbaum Associates.

Author Index

191

Subject Index